# LIGHTER THAN AIR:
## Australian Ballooning History

**ALSO BY HELENE ROGERS**

*Brown, Dean and Coppin and Early Ballooning in Australia*
Chapter 1, History of Ballooning in *Hot Air Ballooning*

# LIGHTER THAN AIR:
## Australian Ballooning History

**Helene Rogers**

Printed in 2021
Text Copyright © Helene Rogers, 2021

Cover and internal design by Alex Nutman

Cover photo:
*Dawn over the Yarra Valley, Victoria*
© Filedimage, acquired through Dreamstime.com under licence

Helene Rogers
Printed and bound in China by RR Donnelley Asia Printing Solutions Ltd.

ISBN: 9780646820217

Author's Note

## Dedication

To my children, Rachel, Keiran and Daniel who lived with an oft-distracted mother during the long gestation of this book and whom I respect, admire and deeply love.

## About the Author

Helene Rogers has worked as a freelance journalist, as a communications officer, as a recruitment and media consultant and also in Women's and Children's Health for most of her life. Her love of history and words started at school and her love of ballooning much later.
After seeing Chris Dewhirst's film of his first attempt to overfly Mount Everest, and having interviewed him, she was inspired to write Australia's ballooning history.

Helene's favourite balloon flight in Victoria was in the Yarra Valley and, in Turkey, it was flying over the Fairy Chimneys of Cappadocia at dawn. Helene lives in Melbourne and spent decades researching, writing and editing this book.

She has also published a monograph, *Brown, Dean and Coppin and Early Ballooning in Australia* and was commissioned by Encyclopaedia Britannica to write the first chapter for their book, *Hot Air Ballooning* on the history of ballooning.

Other achievements include:
Consulting to Australian Geographic magazine and to Aerospace Laboratory, RMIT Melbourne.
Supplying two entries for The Australian Dictionary of Biography, on Charles Henry Brown and Joseph Dean.
Broadcasting on the BBC World Series Program UK.
Co editing The Singing Tree, an anthology of short stories and poetry.
Appearing as a guest speaker for Richmond Historical Society, Rotary International and Australian Balloon Federation.

# CONTENTS

# PART ONE


# AEROSTATION – A SCIENCE?

# Introduction

*"I have noticed hitherto that ballooning best
commends itself to general readers when
amusement is blended with instruction."*
Henry Coxwell.

From the beginning of time man, with his envious disposition and craving after the unknown, dreamed of imitating birds, of hovering in the air and defying gravity. He not only wanted to feel the sensation of being airborne, to explore space and to see his country from above, he also desired to master flight and to harness it for transportation in the atmosphere as well as for pleasure.

All over the ancient world people wondered at and experimented with the mysteries and principles of flight; sought to extend the boundaries of their natural territory on solid earth; to explore the sea and skies.

Once the first manned balloon flights were achieved many daring individuals ventured further with experiments, improvements and feats in the ongoing search for navigation of the skies. They made this new science and art of lighter-than-air flight their careers. Aerostation was born, but like any newborn animal it needed knowledge and nurturing to raise.

Their bold and adventurous spirits have inspired this book.

It is the courage of these brave men and women which excites as much as their balloons and the scientific facts they revealed. It is the drama, romance, misadventure, the humour and often tragedy these pioneers experienced which fascinate as much as dates and places and lists of achievements.

As aeronauts in England, Australia's pioneer balloonists were basically regarded as (and considered themselves to be) scientists. They were completely surprised on their arrival in the antipodes to be viewed as curiosities, as novelties to be displayed and exploited before crowds pursuing amusement and entertainment. These pioneers of Australian aerostation were not taken seriously. Rather they were virtually ignored, even ridiculed.

For their efforts in uprooting family and themselves across the world to share the new science of aerostation, the early balloonists were poorly recompensed and often left stranded in Australia, with no means of securing their passages back home. In return for their efforts, they were isolated from relatives, friends and from professional companionship and stimulation; they inadvertently abandoned any chance of advancement in their chosen careers as aeronauts.

This book is indebted to the first aeronauts brought out to Australia, and in particular to Charles Henry Brown, who methodically kept transcripts of letters to and from aeronauts in England and America and a mammoth scrapbook of newspaper clippings, handbills and calling cards from around the world: a history of world ballooning over eight decades, from 1783 to 1864. He also left a handwritten, chronological account - of 700 major ascents. It is from these records that personal details have been garnered of the historical figures in aeronautics who would otherwise be merely names; I have also found specific data on their flights and theories and inventions from this man's work, none of which was ever published.

2

Because he so meticulously pasted in his cuttings and copied correspondence, it is curious indeed that there is so little record of Brown's own personal life or balloon ascents. Perhaps he was too modest to record his own achievements: perhaps since Charles Brown's death, his own records and photograph have been destroyed or lost. What shines through clearly is that Brown had a vision for the future of flight.

To Charles Henry Brown I am indeed grateful; I quote freely from him in this book. His ballooning and writing achievements were largely overlooked and ignored in his lifetime; his tragic early death passed unnoticed and, once buried - in an unmarked weed-covered grave in Melbourne General Cemetery - he was completely forgotten by Australian aviation historians.

Now, over a century and a half after Brown's death, an attempt is made in this book to redress the imbalance and at last gain recognition for him and his fellow aeronauts, so that they can take their correct place in Australian history as the harbingers of aviation.

This book reveals the personal stories of aeronauts and parachutists; their travails and frustrations, from the early heady days of the science of aerostation, to their exploitation as showmen and to the sports balloonists of today's world.

# Early Attempts to Fly

*"There's something in a flying horse,*
*There's something in a huge balloon;*
*But through the clouds I'll never float*
*Until I have a little boat,*
*Shaped like the crescent moon."*
Wordsworth.

No book of Australia's ballooning history would be complete without mention of that which went before; of the endeavours of men and women in many countries to uncover the secret of flight and, once discovered, to harness it for the good of all.

It could be argued that the balloon was one of the world's greatest discoveries in terms of usefulness to mankind. Chronologically the balloon ranks third in significance after the discoveries of fire and the wheel. The balloon evolved from an exciting wave of scientific experimentation that took place from the seventeenth century on. The balloon cast its shadow before it: to the future, on which it was to have such an enormous influence.

For many centuries man had visualised himself in flight; the balloon dissipated his dreams and brought reality. The skies were no longer merely the province of gods, birds and fantasists; the world was at last open to all.

Little wonder then that the introduction of manned flight, pre-dating as it did the Industrial Revolution and the invention of the combustion engine, was to have such an impact on history. It led to a flurry of practical scientific experimentation which, in turn, linked it to the progress of technology. Although intended as a practical vehicle, the balloon with its beauty and grace, never lost its aura of romance and adventure; elements which remain today.

Although the Montgolfier Brothers of France are credited with the 'discovery' of the balloon (it was they who suggested the French word 'aerostat' be used to describe lighter-than-air craft), there were many before them who - except for fate - might have claimed that honour.

The longing to fly and to explore the heavens was woven into the oldest religions and very spirituality of man: gods in early art and literature are depicted as celestial beings with wings or flanked by angels. Those who dared explore the universe physically gave rise to superstition.

There emerged in mediaeval days winged dragons and beasts who dominated the air. Symbols of eagles became popular with warriors. The most intelligent, enquiring minds of the Greek, Roman, Chinese, Indian, Norse and American-Indians tried to invent a method of flying, concentrating their efforts usually on winged flight. In more recent times fairies with wings emerged in our literature; children magically flew after such figures as Peter Pan and Tinkerbell.

Among those interested in the theory of flight was Archimedes, who in the third century BC outlined the law of buoyancy: others were content with myths such as Pegasus the winged horse. One of western civilisation's enduring fables tells of the legendary Greek sculptor Daedalus who attached wings of wax and feathers to his shoulders and to those of his young son Icarus. They fled the wrath of King Minos by taking flight like birds, but Icarus soared too close to the sun, the wax melted and he plummeted into the sea - ever since called the Icarian Sea - and drowned.

The brilliant Leonardo da Vinci designed an ornithopter or bird machine with wings that flapped but there is no record of his putting his theory into actual practice.

For many more years, men continued to strap wings to their arms and to pit themselves against the laws of gravity and physics by jumping from heights; many to their deaths. Eventually man's attempts to flap through the air with feathers and wings ended - like the pterodactyl's - in extinction.

Those who looked at clouds for inspiration fared better with their designs, for the idea of lift was slowly dawning. The shape, design and construction of a balloon, and the principle of lift, is of such simplicity that aerostation could have been discovered and utilised thousands of years ago, when lightweight, closely woven textiles were available.

In the Yin dynasty (twelfth century BC) the Chinese harnessed heat from smoke to make paper lanterns fly; it is believed that they then made lanterns large enough to carry the weight of a man.

Researchers believe pre-Incan Nazca people of South America - whose symbol was the mighty condor - were capable of flight. In 1973 American Jim Woodman and British balloonist Julian Nott demonstrated that it was possible for the Nazca to have flown a balloon two thousand years ago, and to have understood the principles of hot air for lift. Woodman commissioned a reed gondola from the Indians at Lake Titicaca and made a tetrahedron balloon, the simplest of all shapes. On the morning of the experiment the two men sat astride the reed gondola and reputedly ascended to three hundred feet in the smoke filled *Condor1*. They used bags of desert sand as ballast on their short flight. When they descended and stepped off, the balloon flew solo to 1700 feet before returning to earth undamaged.

Yet other would-be inventors of flying machines looked at ships and machines for their aeronautical designs. In 1670, a Jesuit priest, Francesco de Lana designed an aerial boat with sails lifted aloft by four copper globes drained of air; however, his flying ship was scientifically unsound, for atmospheric pressure would instantly have crushed the sphere.

It was now the time for analytical chemists in Europe to strive to learn the physical properties of air. In 1766 English scientist Henry Cavendish identified a chemical substance he called 'flammable' air (hydrogen). Its propensity to lift heavier-than-air items, including man, was immediately realised.

On the other side of the world in Brazil, a Jesuit priest, Bartolomeu Lourenco de Gusmao was experimenting with balloons, decades before the Montgolfier Brothers' balloon made its first manned ascent.

Portugal's King John V commissioned Gusmao to construct a smoke-filled balloon, *La Passarola* (The Sparrow). From a contemporary account, it is clear that diplomats present at the palace witnessed a small balloon of paper and cotton ascend twelve feet to the ceiling of a drawing room. According to this account, a reed basket was attached within which a fire was lit. Gusmao made three attempts to fly his craft, succeeding in October 1709 when he flew over Lisbon for a distance of a kilometre. Vatican archives record this as man's first ascent.

History recorded Gusmao as aviation's true pioneer, then forgot him and his achievement. In Europe his invention was overlooked but in Brazil, in the Rui Barbosa Santos, his countrymen erected a bronze statue to the priest and encircled it with paving stones inlaid with designs of early balloons and dirigibles. A nearby monument depicts a balloon in flight above the rooftops of old Lisbon. Its inscription reads,

"The Empire of the Skies was Reserved for the Gods Until It
Was Conquered by Man on 8 August, 1709.
From the city of Santos to its glorious son,

Father Bartolomeu Lourenco de Gusmao, the precursor
of aerial navigation - 1685 - 1724.
Presented with gratitude from the municipality
of Santos and the Aeronautical Academy of
Bartolomeu de Gusmao, Paris." (1)


It seems extraordinary that the French - in 1783 the recognised proponents of successful aerostation - contributed to this memorial to a South American balloonist who flew 74 years before their own countrymen. There are other commemorative plaques to him in Lisbon and on Gusmao's grave in Toledo, Spain.

In 1909, a medal was struck in Paris to honour the bicentennial of flight; it shows the flight of Gusmao's balloon and boat-shaped gondola. Brazil issued two airmail postage stamps in the inventor's honour: one depicted Gusmao's portrait, the other his statue.

However conclusive the evidence that Gusmao constructed the first successful hot air balloon, history credits Joseph and Etienne Montgolfier with this achievement. Over two centuries later, it is difficult to determine if this honour has been inaccurately bestowed or otherwise.

The late eighteenth century saw the marriage of science, technology and craft. It was a time of intense excitement, stimulus and striving which spawned the great age of aeronautics.


1)   J Cornu, La Navigation Aérienne.

# Manned Flight Achieved, Early Fatalities

*"To attract influential patronage, those bubbles of air
gained attention by colourful decorations - painted
patterns, or gods and goddesses, stars, the sun,
signs of the zodiac, mottoes and coats of arms
and bedecked with patriotic flags."*
Unknown.

The Montgolfier Brothers did not so much invent the balloon, rather they were the ones who used the materials, laws and principles that had been known for centuries, to build an aerial balloon.

Joseph Montgolfier, the twelfth child of Pierre Montgolfier - a paper manufacturer in Annonay - was an absent-minded dreamer, whereas his reliable younger brother Etienne, the fifteenth and youngest child, took over the management of the paper mills on their father's retirement and led them to prosperity.

Legend has it that the two brothers were throwing rubbish on a fire and observed how the debris rose with the smoke. Joseph the dreamer was astute enough to realise that this vapour could be a source of lift; he persuaded Etienne to help him with further experiments, by holding balloon models over fires of wet straw and rags, using the resulting thick smoke as fuel. Success came at their first public demonstration with a linen model that flew unmanned a distance of 1½ miles at Annonay on 5 June 1783. They decided to move to Paris to further their experiments.

French physicist Professor Jacques Alexandre Cesar Charles was soon a rival. Charles assumed hydrogen was the lifting element for the June flight. He and the Robert Brothers, Jean and Nicholas, constructed a balloon and filled it with hydrogen, made from pouring sulphuric acid over iron filings.

The thus-named Charlière model, or hydrogen balloon, was launched by the trio from the Champs de Mars on 27 August that year. Among the spectators was seventy seven year old Benjamin Franklin, the American philosopher, in Paris as diplomat and envoy to the rebellious American colonies.

Inspired by the possibilities of the balloon, Franklin wrote to President George Washington stressing its military potential and sent an account of these first unmanned flights to his friend in England, Sir Joseph Banks, President of the Royal Society. Banks, as botanist and scientist on the *Endeavour*, had sailed with Captain James Cook on his first voyage of discovery to Australia, thirteen years earlier.

The race for manned flight was now on between Professor Charles and the Robert and Montgolfier Brothers, and so it was that Etienne Montgolfier appeared at the Palace at Versailles on 19 September 1783 and sent aloft a sheep, a duck and a cock; the first aerial voyagers in history.

A young physician, Pilâtre de Rozier, taking no risks, went up to the limit of a tethering rope in a Montgolfière balloon, thus preventing unexpected lift. Although seemingly tame by today's standards, man's first tethered balloon ascents took the courage of any first tentative step into the unknown. (The word pilot is said to derive from the name Pilâtre).

On 21 November 1783, before forty thousand spectators - surely Paris' total population then - watched Rozier and army major, the Marquis d'Arlandes, mount the open gallery of the large platform the Montgolfiers had made, suspended beneath their balloon. The highly decorative paper and linen balloon rose skywards from the Chateau de la Muette and slowly flew five miles over the rooftops of Paris and the towers of Notre Dame Cathedral.

King Louis XVI and Marie Antoinette (who is credited with dubbing ballooning the 'Sport of the Gods') celebrated the historic manned flight with champagne, thereby establishing a tradition to which balloonists adhere today.

The aeronauts' first manned hot-air balloon flight was not without incident. The Marquis, as passenger, was so enthralled with his flight that he failed to notice the balloon fabric smouldering: the envelope had caught alight from the brazier they carried beneath the canopy. Pilot Rozier calmly smothered the fire with a wet sponge carried for that express purpose, while chastising the Marquis for his lack of attention.

Only a week after man's inaugural flight in a hot air Montgolfière balloon, Professor JAC Charles and one of the Robert Brothers, on 1 December flew his hydrogen balloon, *The Globe*, from the Tuileries Gardens and flew 27 miles, landing in the village of Nesle, where it was attacked and destroyed by a mob of terrified peasants with pitchforks and scythes.

The era of flight was born, and the new science of aerostation was enthusiastically embraced in Europe and England, despite early mishaps and fatalities.

A craze for anything ballooning swept over many countries where the balloon shape inspired fashions, appearing on plates, vases, ornaments, wallpaper, jewellery, clocks, chandeliers and in furniture, engravings and lithographs.

The respected men who first braved the air now had to change from being men of science to mere showmen, who satisfied crowds with daring feats, thrilling and amusing the spectators. Balloons were gaudily embellished and became part of spectacular displays that included fireworks, ascents on horseback and falls by parachutes.

More important perhaps than the science versus exploitation aspect of aerostation, was the familiarity with the previously unknown realm of the air. Fear of the skies and superstitions were broken down and gradually dissipated. Nevertheless, it was to be many more decades before man could truly declare his superiority in the air.

# Emergence of Professional Aeronauts

*"Lo! on the shoreless air the intrepid Gaul*
*Launched the vast concave of his buoyant ball."*
Dr Charles Darwin
*The Illustrated Journal of Australasia* March 1858.

In the ensuing years, many 'firsts' were notched up and many valuable discoveries made that facilitated aerial voyages. Madam Thible became the first woman to ascend, in France in February 1774, just three months after the inaugural flights by her compatriots.

That same year Scots scientific writer (and editor of the second edition of the Encyclopaedia Britannica), James Tytler took up the challenge in Great Britain. Disreputable and poor, Tytler sought funds by public subscription and built *The Grand Edinburgh Fire Balloon*. On 27 August 1784, he reached an altitude of 350 feet and a distance of half a mile, thus having achieved the honour of flying first from British soil. Four days later he was again successful. James Tytler, "dingy, untidy (of) clothes and (with) a hole in his hat, thriftless, improvident and disreputable," found himself taken seriously, hailed as a courageous pioneer and congratulated on his persistence Despite best efforts, Tytler was unable to gain funding for further aerial voyages, due to his caustic writings and appearance. (1)

A few weeks after Tytler's flight, James Sadler became the first Englishman to man a balloon, when he ascended from Oxford on 15 September 1784. Sir Joseph Banks, as President of the Royal Society, had lent his name to the subscription to raise money for this first English ascent.

On the same day, a minor Italian diplomat, Vincent Lunardi, ascended in London. He introduced beautiful actress Mrs Sage to ballooning, who became the first woman to ascend in England in 1785 and was said to never be out of work again.

The dubious honour of being the first balloon fatality went to the first man to fly, Pilâtre de Rozier and his companion Pierre Ange Romaine, during a futile attempt to cross the English Channel, from France to England on 15 June 1785.

The Romaine Brothers had fabricated a unique balloon for de Rozier, by combining both hot air and hydrogen: the idea of this invention being to ascend with a higher flame and to descend without the need to vent the more expensive agent, hydrogen.

Twenty minutes after launching, a thick cloud of smoke issued from the upper part of the balloon; it burst into flames instantly, the whole falling to earth with incredible velocity. The fire was deemed to have started by static electricity, caused by the outside valve line rubbing against the envelope.

The death of de Rozier and Romaine just nineteen months after de Rozier's historic inaugural flight hastened the demise of the hot air balloon. It rapidly lost favour and all but disappeared between 1800 and 1960 whilst, for the next 160 years, the gas balloon was to reign supreme.

Ironically, a successful crossing of the Channel had already been achieved five months earlier, by Frenchman Jean-Pierre Blanchard. He was the first aeronaut to embrace aerostation as a profession, becoming the first person to fly the English Channel and the first to carry airmail. At Dover Castle the eventful journey began on 7 January 1785. The envelope kept losing hydrogen and much of their provisions had to be jettisoned to gain lift. The pair threw overboard every unnecessary item; out went books, the netting, the ballast. Monsieur Blanchard cast off his great coat then his trousers, but they landed at Calais with the mail bags intact if not their dignity.

Blanchard travelled widely and made a fortune from public exhibitions but eventually died destitute, leaving a young widow and nothing but debts. His widow, Marie Madeleine Blanchard had made her first solo flight in 1805 but determined now to embrace her late husband's profession. She became the darling of royalty and flew often at their request, celebrating Emperor Napoleon's marriage with a balloon ascent in 1810. Madeleine Blanchard was a skilful and daring balloon pilot but took increasing risks. Her 67th and last flight took place on 6 July 1819 on a night ascent in Paris.

Suspended beneath the wicker basket was a wooden hoop fixed with fireworks to illuminate her progress in the air. On this occasion, sparks fell from the balloon and ignited the hydrogen envelope. The flaming balloon emptied its gas and crashed on to a roof, precipitating Madame Blanchard head-first on to the street below. Madeleine Blanchard, 41 thus became the first woman aeronautic fatality. She was interred in the Père Lachaise cemetery, her tomb surrounded by a globe in flames.

There were to be many more accidents, fatalities and scrapes with death. Undoubtedly, part of ballooning's appeal to the public was its romance and the reverse, its danger, but wise aeronauts soon learnt that a mistake could lead to a terrible death.


(1)    Sir James Fergusson, *Balloon Tytler*.

# Aeronautic Families

*"Bound on a dangerous voyage in quest of fame...*
*like ancient Barons future bards shall fare,*
*in their own castles built up in the air."*
Mr Wilson
*Universal Magazine*, November 1784.

By the end of the eighteenth century science had advanced sufficiently to allow mankind to float across the countryside, but at the mercy of the winds. Balloons lacked the steering ability that rudders gave boats; they specifically lacked propulsion. Man now looked to the boat for inspiration to overcome these obstacles. A progression of rudders, oars, paddles, sails, pedals, parachutes and revolving fans were introduced, but all failed.

The nineteenth century saw ballooning spread around the world. France retained its dominance over the skies, but efforts doubled in England and America to provide aerostation with navigation.

Like his compatriots, John Felix Tournachon (known as Nadar) flew hundreds of miles during the four-month long Franco-Prussian siege in 1870/71, but his fame was as a photographer. In 1858 he became the first person to take an aerial photograph, from a tethered balloon, thus combining his twin passions of aeronautics and photography.

Entire families and generations of professional balloonists were spawned: those of Garnerin, Godard, Green and Graham, but it is the Green family that was relevant to Australia.

Possibly the greatest of all English balloonists - certainly the most famous and popular of his time - was Charles Green. Regarded as the father of ballooning in England he always attracted a huge gathering of spectators. He made several major contributions to aerostation and is acknowledged as introducing in 1821, the use of coal gas, instead of hydrogen, for lift. In 1784, a Monsieur Thisbaert had used coal gas to inflate a balloon and it was again proposed for usage in 1816 by Dr William Bland (who played several important roles in Australia).

Not only was coal gas cheaper, it also made inflation easier and speedier; it was claimed to be less damaging to silk fabric and it did not penetrate the fabric as readily as hydrogen. Such a balloon could fly longer and further as the gas expanded and contracted more slowly. The use of coal gas as a filling agent became widespread and led to the construction of larger balloons which could carry more passengers.

Green was also the first to make practical use of the guide or trail rope. Trailing on the ground below the balloonist, the guide rope let the basket drift low over the countryside at a constant height, thus conserving ballast. In 1836, when Green was in Paris, he had bestowed on him a medal for his 'invention' of the guide rope. This so incensed Charles Brown that he wrote in a letter to renowned American aeronaut John Wise, "it does not appear to be generally known that the guide-rope was the invention of Thomas Baldwin, of Chester, being described in a work entitled *Airopaedia*, and pulled by that gentleman in 1786." (1)

The trail rope, when attached to a 42 pound grapnel, could have undesirable effects; it could injure or blind someone; demolish haystacks and interrupt unsuspecting lovers. Consequently, the drag rope eventually disappeared from use.

Two hundred and five ascents and fourteen years after his first ascent, Charles Green had an attempt at the record books. He piloted one of the first really successful balloon voyages. Robert Holland, an MP, provided the finance and Monck Mason, an Irish theatre producer, suggested an international flight and went along to witness this ballooning achievement.

Monck Mason wrote a book on the 18 hour journey from London to Germany, made on 7 - 8 November, 1836. They drifted night and day over sea and countryside and even convinced two farmers not to shoot them as they landed in the Duchy of Nassau. The balloon was re-named the *Great Nassau Balloon*, carried up to thirteen passengers and was used for over thirty years.

That 480 mile journey remained an unbroken record for an incredible 71 years, until 1907. Thomas Monck Mason's first balloon ascent with Charles Green had not been as successful, for it was on this flight - Green's 223rd - that parachutist Robert Cocking was killed, in September 1836, another unfortunate first.

A further contribution made by Charles Green was the first balloon ascent for scientific purposes, made in September 1852. Green and his passenger ascended to 19 200 feet in temperatures below -25 degrees Fahrenheit, resulting in oxygen deprivation and frostbite. Green made other high altitude ascents: with Edward Spencer he reached 27 146 feet, before making his last ascent on 12 September 1852.

Brothers of Charles Green made many ascents: William flew thirty times; Henry ascended one hundred times as did James (George) Green. Charles' wife and other females in the family made aerial trips, but it was his son Charles Green junior, who became a professional aeronaut and who had a fifteen-year career, making over 375 ascents; however, he never attained his father's reputation. He died in February 1864, six years before his father. His death closed the active record of the Green family of aeronauts in England, although William Green junior (nephew and cousin of the Charles Greens) was later employed in Australia as a balloonist.

In America it was Monsieur Blanchard's demonstrations in 1783 that introduced ballooning there. Ironically, in the same month and year of Blanchard's death was born the baby who was destined to become one of the most celebrated American aeronauts of his time, John Wise, who also wrote 2 valuable books on his favourite subject: *Through the Air* and *A System of Aeronautica*.

Aged 27, Professor John Wise made his first public ascent on 2 May 1835, in Philadelphia and invented the rip panel, a safety device in the upper balloon envelope which allows rapid elimination of gas, and rapid deflation just prior to landing; it is still used in modern balloons. In later experiments, John Wise realised clouds were good reflectors of heat and light and was convinced that "the science of electricity and meteorology would be much improved by the aid of balloons." He wrote, prophetically in the year 1847, that "our children will travel to any part of the globe without the inconvenience of smoke, sparks and seasickness, and at the rate of 100 MPH." (2)

One theory Wise put forward has since proved correct: that there existed 'jet streams' or currents of air - constant, predictable winds at high altitude. Convinced that the atmospheric air currents always blew in a west to east direction, Wise announced to friends further east his intention of visiting them by balloon. In May 1843 he did just that: he had 'directed' his balloon; he could foresee the balloon's usefulness for long distance and transoceanic journeys, thus proving to the public the practicality of aeronautics.

Between two Atlantic crossing attempts, the Unionists engaged Wise as an army aeronaut in their balloon corps when the Civil War broke out in 1861. Quite the entrepreneur, he ran a School of Aeronautics to teach beginners; he was also a prolific letter writer and corresponded with Charles Brown over many years, both in England and Australia. After a career spanning 44 years and 443 flights, John Wise, aged 71, drowned on 29 September 1879 when his balloon suddenly dipped into Lake Michigan.

From 1844 onwards many 'Madames' or 'Professors' - the traditionally adopted show business names - travelled all over, exhibiting their skills, performing oft-dangerous feats for money. They became the first American generation of aeronautical showmen and women.

(1)    Charles Henry Brown, Notebook.
(2)    John Wise, *Through the Air* 1873.

# Showmanship Versus Science

*"To Montgolfier the Invention's due*
*Unfinished as it lies*
*But his will be the glory who*
*Direction's art supplies."*
Anon, 1786.

In England at this time was Charles Henry Brown, later to settle in Australia as a pioneer balloonist. Brown was a chronicler of anything aeronautical; he kept a scrapbook of newspaper cuttings dating back to the first manned flight in 1783. A second book recorded, in his own handwriting, contemporary ballooning events; a third, copies of letters sent to, and received from, ballooning identities in England and America. From his collections, I have gleaned much of the personalities of his fellow aeronauts, as well as their place in history.

Charles Brown was aligned with the scientists in aerostation and spurned the showman balloonist. Although the showmen undoubtedly became wealthier than their scientific counterparts, it is the names of those who pushed atmospheric science further that live on.

While reading the highly principled Mr. Brown's scathing comments and criticisms of those who exploited aerostation for its remunerative and amusement abilities, it is necessary to realise that very few balloonists could have afforded to ascend had it not been for the paying spectator. At that time - the mid-nineteenth century - ballooning was at a peak of popularity, not to be matched for another 130 years, until the 1980s.

Frenchman Monsieur Margat was the first to thrill crowds with strange aerial spectacles when, in Lyons, he ascended on a stag. Others followed Margat with more daring, outlandish feats. Jules Poitevin, also French, and his wife became famous for their aerial antics. The following is an account of some of their ascents taken from Charles Brown's scrapbook,

"AUGUST 23, 1850 Ascent from the Hippodrome, Paris standing erect on his horse's back.
SEPTEMBER 1, 1850 Seated on an ass. The "animal bled from the mouth and nostrils".
SEPTEMBER 27, 1850 Madame Poitevin up on her husband's pony in a riding habit.
AUGUST 18, 1851 3 horses and riders taken up.
OCTOBER 3, 1850 Jules Poitevin astride an ostrich suspended beneath the balloon. It tried to fly.
AUGUST 30, 1852 Madame Poitevin from Royal Cremorne Gardens, London performed "perilous movements on the back of the bull" which had to be destroyed on landing." (1)

Charles Brown, in a letter to American aeronaut John Wise, wrote with sarcasm, "ballooning has come to something, at last, what with the exploits of a rope-dancer and of equestrian aeronauts." (2)

George Gale, an Englishman, made ascents in 1846 and 1847, with lions. Lieutenant Gale became a professional aeronaut with 114 ascents in England and France. He often ascended with 'serious' aeronauts Charles Green, Henry Coxwell and Richard Gypson. Gale may even have been a catalyst for Charles Brown's own career, as in 1848, he ascended from Brown's hometown of Leeds. In his career, George Gale - whose wife also made many ascents - only ever had one accident; in the September 1849 flight, he and "his assistant Joseph Dean" (who became Australia's first balloonist) both injured fingers. (3)

Stuntmen Edouard and Jean Bouthellier, as the 'Italian Brothers', wowed the English crowds in the summers of 1852, 1853 and 1854 with their daring feats on the trapeze, yet another novelty introduced as a crowd-pleaser. William Green - only a few years before he left for Australia - took the brothers up, suspended on the trapeze by feet or legs.

During the 1850's there was still a core of balloonists who took their profession seriously and who attempted to advance the balloon as a utility, not an amusement. Richard Gypson ballooned from 1836-1856, even accompanying the renowned Coxwell on night ascents in 1856. Charles Brown records over 100 ascents and reports that his own father, opposed to ballooning, read him a newspaper account of Gypson's harrowing experience when he came down in the Irish Sea in June 1843.

One of the first 'special shape' balloons constructed was that of Hugh Bell, a London medico and inventor who patented his balloon and ascended in it several times in May 1850. The egg-shaped conveyance "was in the form of a vegetable marrow" and must have presented a strange sight, steered as it was "with propellers and a rudder." (4)

Bell's invention was yet another attempt to solve the problem of aerial navigation. We learn no more of Bell's special shape until 1853 when Lieutenant Stephen Chambers RN, ascended in Charles Brown's town, Leeds, in a pear-shaped balloon, The *Victory*, "formed out of the silk of Mr Bell's Locomotive Balloon." (5)

Another of Royal Cremorne's stable of professional aeronauts was John Hampton, who corresponded for years with Charles Brown. In a letter to John Wise in America, Brown spoke disparagingly of him,

> "Hampton is noted for his parachute descents, and for the many accidents he has had. In his first ascent he broke his arm, in the second...and fourth he fell in the sea; four days after, he ascended with his arm in a sling. On his first parachute descent he was insensible for some time - this he told me himself - and he received a cut over his eye. The second descent he was dashed violently against the side of a house; the third descent he fell among trees and was nearly killed. In an ascent from Dublin his balloon came in contact with a chimney on fire; the balloon exploded; he leaped from the car, rolled off the roof of the house, and would have been spiked through by some iron palings, had he not been pushed off in his descent by a man...Since that time he has twice fallen in the Irish Channel." (6)

Charles Brown went on to castigate Hampton as not willing to descend in a parachute "unless tempted by an offer of a large sum of money. In my opinion he has not the confidence in a balloon that you appear to have, and he says that the conduct of Mr Graham and Lieutenant Gale, two of our professional aeronauts, is shameful in allowing their wives to go up with a balloon." He confides to John Wise that, the "public (are) under the impression that aerial navigation is an impossibility." Blame for the slow progress of aeronautical science he placed on the head of people like Hampton, for the "ridiculous feats" of the professional aeronauts who "are doing great injury to the infant science." (7)

John Hampton had left the Royal Navy and began his career as a professional aeronaut in June 1838. He travelled all over England and Ireland with the Royal Irish balloon *Erin go Bragh*, making 120 ascents in all. Certainly, he was motivated more by the rewards of showmanship than the pursuit of science.

Hampton himself wrote a letter responding to taunts of being dangerous. *The Morning Advertiser* of 18 September 1851 published it,

"I will agree that a balloon is sometimes uncontrollable - so is a ship at sea, and a spirited horse also. It does not follow that we are to give up the use of the ship or horse, nor does it follow that we are to give up railway travelling because numbers of people are annually crushed to pieces by the negligence or carelessness of the parties having the control of the trains. Again, let us go hunting, horse racing, steeplechasing, and yachting - all these are for the gratification and amusement of the masses. Are they all to be put to a stop because accidentally a huntsman breaks his neck, or a man in the boat may fall overboard and be drowned?"

Charles Brown's collection of letters fascinate, revealing some of the jealousies and pettiness which existed between the professional aeronauts at this most competitive of times, the 1850's. The letters detail intrigues within relationships and highlight the ongoing divisiveness between those who ballooned to further science and those who were showmen. From his writings, Charles Brown could be seen as a troublemaker who pandered to different aeronauts at various times, with a single purpose in mind: to fly balloons. For at this stage, the chronicler, collector of aeronautical books and expert on aerostation, dedicated and enthusiastic as he was, still had not yet flown.

Brown, raised and working in Leeds, tried to ingratiate himself with the balloonists, hoping they would adopt him into their fraternity; many had promised him a flight over the years, but nothing had eventuated.

Brown's correspondence with Hampton begun in 1849 when he wrote to advise him of the best place in Yorkshire to ascend. In that letter he introduced himself: "I am enthusiastically fond of ballooning - it has been my constant study for a period of 18 years." Brown had half made a balloon but gave up due to lack of finances. He wrote to John Hampton with a proposal to construct a balloon for him, apologising that he had no money to make it as he was "but a clerk in the Post Office here, at a low salary." He offered Hampton accommodation. (8)

Hampton replied, "I see by your letter that you are still determined to become an aeronaut" and hoped that Brown had his wife's consent to do so. He expressed a wish to meet and talk it over, stating he wanted no fuss when staying with the Browns, as "I am a homely and plain man." He promised "next summer you shall ascend with me". (9)

Hampton stayed with the Browns in Yorkshire that Christmas and in the New Year of 1850, Brown submitted a book of aeronautical facts to Hampton for publishing, but he considered it too dear to publish and advised Brown not to risk the sum himself to self-publish.

There developed a friendship between the historian and aspiring author and the established balloonist. They spoke of starting up an aeronautical magazine and exchanged helpful hints. In April 1850, Charles Brown wrote his friend, "I have let off a great number of balloons filled with linseed oil alone, but it would be better with a little spirit of wine." They were trying to find a fireproof material for the balloon Hampton was constructing and discovered oil spat and smoked too much and spoilt balloons. Brown mentioned John Wise's newly released book, *A System of Aeronautics* and the engravings of fourteen books he owned, "I wish to collect everything I can relating to aerostation" to preserve it for posterity. (10).

At the same time, Brown corresponded with a friend of Henry Coxwell, Irishman James MacSweeney. In one letter he poured out his soul, "I have an irresistible desire to become an aeronaut, and indeed it has been my desire ever since I was five or six years old; and if Hampton acts according to promise it shall not be long before I rise in the world." (11)

Hampton never fulfilled his promise to Brown but continued to let him think he would. In his eagerness to please Hampton, Brown sent him ideas and improvements for a fire balloon; Hampton, in Dublin, copied the drawings to make a balloon and passed it off as his own. Brown rightly protested that, "you are not doing justice to me, for all the plans you have adopted are my own." (12)

Hampton was quick to reply and disclaim he had taken credit for any discovery or new principle, "I only claim the merit of the practical application and improvement of principle already known and sometimes acted upon. You, like many more, have read much about balloons, and you flatter yourself you know more than the practical aeronauts." He also expressed surprise at Brown's lack of humility, "I think you have taken too much upon yourself, to tell a practical aeronaut of ten years practice, that you have a right to the credit of his experiences, because you have given a few suggestions!" Hampton then added fuel to his cruelty,

"My advice to you is, that you never think of Balloons, only to read and write of them, which I think you are capable of doing. Do not think I am jealous of your becoming an aeronaut; if I thought you had the capabilities, I would have done my best to have forwarded your views - but you yourself must be well aware you could never manage a balloon - even could you do so, you would be a better friend to your wife and family to have nothing to do with ballooning". (13)

Charles Brown, stung by the acrimonious tone of this letter and in particular, to the reference that his crippled arms rendered him incapable of flying a balloon, promised to expose Hampton for not crediting him with the fireproofing plans.

A month later Brown, from Leeds, turned his attention across the Atlantic, and began writing to John Wise, introducing himself, "I am a Chronicler of historical matters, and although not an aeronaut I live in hopes of becoming one: poverty has alone prevented me thus far." (14)

Wise had replied, with friendly advice and sympathy. "When I began I had no guide - no practical instruction, and had never seen an ascension - but I strove until I got a tolerable knowledge of its true philosophy, and now I want the world to realise some of its uses; because the human family is entitled to the grand and glorious prerogative of Aerial locomotion." (15)

Brown must have been delighted to receive such a letter, for here was a man who shared his own sentiments regarding aeronautics and who promised to visit, saying "when I come to England, I will endeavour to spend a few hours with you". (16)

Curiously, Hampton and Charles Brown continued to exchange letters, albeit cool in tone and full of recriminations. Trials in Ireland with John Hampton's balloon were a failure; he had not followed Brown's advice on inflation and placed the fire too high. The weather too was poor, then winter closed in and ascents ceased.

Late that year, Charles Henry Brown began signing 'aeronaut' after his name, although he still had not flown in a balloon. (17)

He had added yet another correspondent to his list, Monsieur Dupuis Delcourt, to explain his idea of a double parachute and to make his favourite lament, "our English aeronauts appear to care nothing about improving aerostation - they are all simply showmen, and only exhibit their balloons for the purpose of putting money into their pockets. I am fairly disgusted with them." He was especially critical of Charles Green, for he perceived him as having plenty of money and rich friends, while other showmen aeronauts were at least poor. (18)

Delcourt replied that French compatriots were also showmen. "In their hands the aerostation art is become a trade." Delcourt - who wished to circumnavigate the earth by balloon - obviously thought little of Charles Green either, writing of "the cupidity and narrowness of mind of that little man." (19)

From Bradford, Brown sent a curt note to Hampton, now in London, asking to buy his balloon or "let it out for one experiment." He enclosed postage stamps for a reply. (20)

Notwithstanding this insult, Hampton wrote inviting Brown to London. Perhaps, in view of his failures in Ireland, Hampton was prepared to listen to Brown's ideas, for he was apologetic. "As for what I stated in one of my letters to you, respecting your incapability to manage a Balloon, was only in friendship to you, knowing that you are crippled in you (sic) arms." He made no reference to Brown's request. (21)

That same month John Wise wrote to Brown, expressing an idea for an aerostatic convention in London or Paris, "likely to induce and produce much to the improvement and development of this great and unexplored field of science and art. We are working too scattered. A concentration of thought would most certainly bring out genius faster." (22)

Brown liked the idea but doubted England would do much, for "Green is too selfish - he will not part with a shilling to do the science good: he ought to be ashamed of the little he has done." (23)

The convention never eventuated, for on Wise's side of the Atlantic they were also "ignorant and selfish." Wise's vague promise of "a trip with me to the clouds this summer" did not eventuate either. Despite his disappointment, Wise was enthusiastic about Brown's decision to make and fly balloons. "I am really rejoiced to hear from you that you have determined to go into the business of Ballooning practically." He wanted success for Brown "for the sake of your London aeronauts, who would fain make you believe that none, but heroes can and ought to balloon". He further inspired Brown with the words, "be not dismayed nor discouraged" and "ask, and it will be given to the best of my ability." (24)

Overcome with emotion Brown replied, "You have opened my eyes considerably by means of your book and your correspondence, and I shall ever feel grateful for the same. Amongst heroes I could only reckon yourself and Lieutenant Gale as true friends. Gale was not a selfish man: he would give information on aeronauts freely." (25)

Brown was now constructing a fireproof, hot-air balloon of cotton lined with paper. He intended making his first ascent on Easter Monday in Bradford. "If I am successful with this balloon, I intend making five or six ascents with it, then build a gas one." He told Hampton of the commotion the plans were causing, for it had been 23 years since a balloon rose above the Yorkshire town. Brown could not refrain from accusing John Hampton of feeling fear at his venturing into the aeronautic field. He mentioned his friendship with Russum, a Leeds aeronaut who had made about nine ascents. (26)

William Russum, whose first flight with Charles Green junior, had taken place in Leeds on 3 September 1830, had been requested by Brown's father to talk sense into his adventurous son. He "spoke to me of the dangers of ballooning and told me that in consequence of my being crippled in the arms I could never be able to open the valve." (27)

Easter Monday dawned and found Charles Brown excited and optimistic for his first attempt at ballooning. With a "brisk wind blowing" the fire was kindled, while his wife Eliza, the Mayor and the police looked on. Then Russum appeared and told the Mayor "I should not ascend. This spread like wild-fire through the crowd" who began to taunt Brown and large bets were taken against his going up. Disaster struck when his inflated balloon fell, covering and almost suffocating the helpers, due to a large rent made by a lad with a knife. While the balloon was hastily repaired, "someone set fire to the basket and the balloon." Others slit the balloon completely and spread the fire "in all directions." A man grabbed Brown and "threatened to send a bullet through me." He was rescued from the threat, and from the dense black smoke billowing from the burning envelope, put in a cab and sent home, shocked and dismayed at these events. (28)

A riot ensued on the launching ground, causing the Mayor to sentence seven or eight rioters to 14 and 21 days imprisonment and to press Charles Brown for an explanation of his failure. Although Brown explained the principles of flying a Montgolfier balloon, "no one would believe it was practicable for a man to rise with a fire balloon". (29)

Needless to say, John Hampton lost no time in contacting Brown and upbraided him for attempting to ascend with a fire balloon. Determined still, Brown and a friend made a gas balloon of muslin. The tiny *Celeste* was to be launched at Wakefield on 14 July 1851. The inflation failed for the balloon was "torn by the violence of the wind" (30).

Four days later a further attempt was made in a new balloon, but when half-filled, "a further supply of gas was refused" so Brown let the balloon rise itself. "It soon disappeared in a cloud" and landed in a field eleven miles away, "where it was destroyed by a number of hay makers". (31)

For the next two years Brown recorded no further attempts, either being too humiliated or too impoverished, with an ever-increasing family to provide for on a clerk's wage. His fortune appeared to change in the 1853 season, when Thomas Clapham, lessee of the Leeds Royal Gardens, sent a telegram to Charles Brown, requesting he fill in urgently for Stephen Chambers, who was refusing to ascend at a charity benefit. Brown was assured "the gas manager and police will assist you" so made his way there with (one can imagine) haste and excitement. Chambers unfortunately saw him and "guessed the object of my being there" so filled the balloon and took off into the skies." (32)

Clapham wanted an aeronaut to ascend in the 1854 summer at the gardens. He had been disgusted with Chambers who had only made ten out of twenty contracted ascents. Never one to bear a grudge and without a balloon, Brown recommended Hampton (who refused as his balloon had been burnt). He then recommended Henry Coxwell, who wrote to Charles Brown from his aptly-named home at Aerial Cottage Middlesex, expressing his interest and saying he was keen to shake Brown's hand and to renew "personally an acquaintance already formed by the pen." Coxwell reiterated that they were "kindred spirits who love the science and wish to advance it respectably and genteelly." Coxwell could not refrain from criticising Wise's book, with a terrible pun: "I cannot boast of having become wiser thereby" and, more caustically, that it was "not a record of the doings of a professed scientific man - they are better adapted for the lover of horrors than the student of aerostatics". (33)

However, Coxwell and Brown were not yet destined to meet: Coxwell wanted £40 per ascent at Leeds, so Clapham engaged aeronauts from the Royal Cremorne stable for £30.

Throughout his let downs and disappointments, Brown diligently continued his missives to numerous aeronauts; letters boosted his morale and determination. John Wise wrote that they shared the same ideals: "we want practical principles of the art to promote its usefulness." This was late in 1857, just as Brown's life was poised to change forever. (34)

The petty jealousies, criticisms, accusations and manoeuvring between aeronauts continued over the years and were duly recorded in Charles Brown's notebooks. Former friends turned against each other; with oceans and national borders no barrier to disloyalty and slander.

Hampton's letters claimed Coxwell as "dishonourable", for he passed off the *Sylph* balloon as his own, when in fact it belonged to the Cremorne Gardens. He complained of him to Brown, "I have been badly treated, and much deceived, and shamefully so by that fellow Coxwell, that it makes me doubt all men." Hampton, whilst in the mood for venting his opinions, gave his views on women balloonists saying, "Lady aeronauts... are as much fit to command a line of battle ships, a steam engine on the railway, or a steam-boat, as to manage a balloon." (35)

It is on record that Brown agreed with Hampton that it was "shameful" to allow "wives to go up with balloons." In fact, Brown's own wife Eliza went aloft as a passenger on several occasions in England and later, in Australia. (36)

Despite criticism and hurtful comments; despite poverty, misfortune, early failures and his physical disability, Charles Brown never allowed obstacles to prevent him becoming an aeronaut. Whether we regard him as fanatical, obsessed, selfish, stubborn, foolish, or as honourable, strong and far-sighted, we do have to give him credit for resilience and determination in the face of adversity.

Charles Brown never doubted he would achieve his ambition. In the summer of 1854, his dream finally became a reality.

(1)   Charles Henry Brown, Notebook.
(2)   Brown to Wise, undated.
(3)   This is the earliest mention of Joseph Dean in Charles Brown's records.
(4)   *The Leeds Mercury* 5 June 1852.
(5)   Ibid
(6)   Bradford, Brown to Wise 7 August 1850.
(7)   Ibid.
(8)   Brown to Hampton, 18 June 1849.
(9)   Hampton to Brown, September 1849.
(10)  Bradford, Brown to Hampton, May 1850.
(11)  Bradford, Brown to MacSweeney, undated.
(12)  Bradford, Brown to Hampton, 6 July 1850.
(13)  Dublin, Hampton to Brown, 13 July 1850.
(14)  Brown to Wise, 4 August 1850.
(15)  Wise to Brown, 10 September 1850.
(16)  Ibid.
(17)  Letter, *Builder* magazine, November 1850.
(18)  Bradford, Brown to Delcourt, December 1850.
(19)  Paris, Delcourt to Brown, February 1851.
(20)  Brown to Hampton, 20 January 1851.
(21)  Hampton to Brown, 22 January 1851.
(22)  Wise to Brown, January 1851.
(23)  Brown to Wise, undated.
(24)  Wise to Brown, March 1851.
(25)  Bradford, Brown to Wise, 4 April 1851.
(26)  Brown to Hampton, undated.
(27)  Australia, Brown to MacSweeney, 24 October 1863.
(28)  Bradford, Brown to MacSweeney, 22 April 1851.
(29)  Ibid.
(30)  Ibid.
(31)  Unidentified letter.
(32)  Clapham to Brown, 19 September 1853.
(33)  Coxwell to Brown, 26 March 1854.
(34)  Wise to Brown, 23 September 1857.
(35)  Hampton to Brown, undated.
(36)  Brown to Wise, 7 August 1857.

# Brown and Dean

*"Once the aeronaut, in popular estimation, was little
less than a demigod and his apparatus was looked upon
with a degree of wonder almost approaching awe."*
*Herald* 1863.

Charles Henry Brown was born around 1826 in the West Riding city of Leeds, northeast England. His grandfather Joseph Brown had ten children, was a poet and famously became a Quaker 'martyr': he built a house in Lothersdale, Yorkshire which still exists. Charles' parents, Benjamin Brown, a bookkeeper, and Hannah Higgins were married in St Peter's Church, Leeds. Fourteen months later, the parish register records the christening of their first child, Edwin, but there is no record of Charles' birth or christening. No civil birth register existed in England until 1837; the churches kept records only of christenings. Only the eldest child of a family was christened in the mother church; subsequent children being baptised in the smaller, scattered chapelries. A check of the registers of these chapelries has revealed no such ceremony for a Charles Henry Brown, so it can be assumed that his parents neglected his baptism.

People of Leeds worked in the collieries close to the city boundaries, or in the farmlands, washing, carding and combing the wool in the fast-flowing Pennine streams, or worked as weavers; for Leeds had fast developed with the advent of steam power into a world centre for ready-made clothing. Leeds was only ten miles from the mills of Bradford and twenty miles from Haworth, famous as the home of the Bronte children.

The young Charles must have witnessed many balloon ascents, for Leeds was popular for such events. Perhaps as he fished in the Leeds Canal, the young Charles watched balloons pass overhead and dreamed of fame. When Charles Brown was only a lad of eleven, Mrs Graham made her 46th ascent there. Charles Green made his 336th ascent from Leeds; Stephen Chambers, Henry Coxwell, the Italian Brothers and William Green senior also ballooned there. It is certainly possible that Charles Brown was among the hundreds of spectators staring skywards. It may have been the visiting aeronauts who influenced his lifetime love of aeronautics. Certainly, he was not encouraged at home for he later wrote that, "My father, who was greatly opposed to ballooning, would never allow me to read anything on the subject - whenever a balloon accident occurred he would inform me of it." (1)

Perhaps the young lad was too shy to introduce himself to the aeronauts who ascended at Leeds. However, distanced by the pen, he felt he could approach them. Late in 1845, when he was only nineteen (two years after the first entries in his notebook of aeronautic events), he wrote to Henry Coxwell, the most renowned balloonist in England. Coxwell replied, "I am not sorry to find that like myself you are a young man. I am your senior by about six years, so you see, we are both young, enterprising and ambitious characters." (2)

Aged 22, Charles Brown, the postal clerk who worked alternatively at Leeds and Bradford, married Eliza Hartley who bore him seven children - two girls, five boys - over the next seventeen years. Brown recorded nothing of his wife's thoughts about his ambitions to fly or his spending their meagre income constructing balloons. Living in the heart of England's weaving industry area probably gave him access to lower priced materials to sew balloons. Neither marriage nor fatherhood made Brown waiver from fulfilling his dream to fly.

His new correspondent Henry Tracey Coxwell, was born on 19 August 1819 at Wouldham near Rochester Castle. As a schoolboy he became passionately interested in ballooning when he saw Charles Green ascend. It was not until the summer of 1844 that the 25year old dental surgeon made his first ascent as a passenger of John Hampton. Over the next 41 years Coxwell was to become a giant in ballooning circles. Coxwell often assumed the name Henry Wells when ballooning, to avoid anxiety among his friends (and patients no doubt).

He initiated and edited *The Balloon* or *Aerostatic Magazine* which was well written and well received but ran for only four issues. Brown was a contributor, sending for publication his plans for a parachute. In 1848 Coxwell bought the first of his many balloons, the *Sylph* and spent the next four summers ballooning in Europe, often with royalty, noblemen, governors and the military as his passengers. By 1852 he had given away making dental plates for a living in the ballooning season and had adopted ballooning as his profession.

Coxwell shared with Charles Brown a consuming belief that aerostation was destined to bring great changes to mankind. They abhorred the ludicrous feats of the ballooning showmen of the day and the damage done to the fledging science of aerostation. Undoubtedly Henry Coxwell had an enormous influence on Charles Brown; they exchanged numerous letters and opinions seeing themselves as serious believers in, and promoters of, the young science.

In 1850 in his book, *Through the Air*, American John Wise published a letter of Brown's which extended to five pages and lamented the slow progress of aeronautic science in England. What is particularly curious is Wise's introduction to that chapter,

> "Mr Charles Henry Brown, a young man of much intelligence and a great enthusiast in aeronautic matters, was a pupil of mine. He went to England with the expectation of being able there to gain more aeronautic experience and information than he could get in this country, and afterward located in Australia, where he made a number of fine experiments." (3)

There are many discrepancies in this: Charles Brown was a resident of England until 1857 when he left for Australia and as a poor postal clerk and family man, I'm sure he never visited America. Wise's School of Aeronautics began in Pennsylvania in 1839 when Charles was only thirteen years old.

Presumably Wise was either confused in later life, was making false claims, or mistook the other Charles Brown, the Sheffield aeronaut who was active at this time, made his own balloons and who ascended in Bradford, or his son (also an aeronaut named Charles) for Charles Henry Brown of Leeds. Due to this, rumours spread that he was the Charles Brown "who had several failures at Sheffield and Halifax some years ago." (4)

Records show a Mr C Brown ascending in Sheffield in 1824, 1827, 1838 and 1843 and Charles Brown, "son of the Sheffield aeronaut", ascending in 1858 in Wolverhampton - after Charles Henry Brown had arrived in Australia. (5)

To compound the difficulties in tracing the Leeds Charles Brown's aeronautic experiences, there was a Roger Brown who took up "older brother Charles Brown of Sheffield's place" at Wakefield in 1827; a J Brown's aerial machine was listed in the catalogue of the 1851 Great Exhibition in London and a Mr Brown as proprietor of the Portsmouth Recreation Grounds when Coxwell ascended there in 1863. The latter was possibly Charles' brother Edwin, who was described as "employed in the ballooning season" although "opposed to ballooning". (6)

Monck Mason listed the following Brown ascents,

"Mr Brown ascended London 5th July 1802
Mr Brown ascended Wakefield 6th October 1827
Mr S. Brown ascended Pontefract September 1827
Mr Brown ascended Dewbury 1829
Mr Browne ascended Manchester 11th August, 1831" (7)

All these 'ballooning Browns' added complications to my research, however Charles Henry Brown's own account of his first ascent in a balloon is beyond dispute. Brown's first aerial voyage was Coxwell's 237th; it was the first "nocturnal trip" ever made in a balloon at Leeds. In the moonlit gardens at 9.30pm that Monday night, Charles Henry Brown at last climbed into the basket of a balloon, the *Sylph*, "amidst a blaze of brilliant coloured fires" suspended on a wooden frame beneath the car. They touched down gently in a cornfield, disturbing "a covey of partridges, and also some cattle, which ran about furiously". Their "delightful and interesting excursion" had lasted 1¼ hours and covered 5½ miles. They left the balloon in a farmer's barn and walked back to the gardens, arriving at 3:30am. So excited was Brown that he wrote of it to the *Leeds Intelligencer* which published his account on 9 August 1854. (8)

In a letter to his Irish correspondent Mr MacSweeney, Brown says he kept exclaiming "How delightful! How charming! Magnificent!" Coxwell was not quite as enthralled, as he "does not like fireworks at all; he was very fidgety" but a different man when they ceased, for "he took my hand and said, 'Mr Brown I am glad I have had the pleasure of being your first pilot' and opened a basket of refreshments, quite at ease." (9)

Just three years before Brown left for Australia as chief aeronaut, he had realised his dream; he had finally flown in a balloon, albeit as a passenger. It is quite likely that Coxwell let Brown pilot the balloon for a time on this gentlest of flights. Whatever took place on that journey, we do know that Coxwell and Brown emerged as friends. Winter set in but Brown's letter-writing and chronicling continued. Coxwell the dentist wrote of "tooth making against time" and giving attention to "neglected patients". (10)

The summer ballooning season of 1855 came and went without further flights by Brown. By summer 1856 Charles Brown was acting as agent for Coxwell and also Clapham, arranging engagements and gas supplies; in return Coxwell asked Brown to accompany him on his flights. Their ascents were usually part of entertainment for the public. They flew from Leeds in Coxwell's balloon *Sylph* on March 24 and 25. Both flights were successful: the first reached 8000 feet in forty minutes and covered eight miles; the second went to 6000 feet and was of 32 minutes duration. Together they flew from Sheffield to Brighton in Derbyshire, over eight miles in distance, in July and again in August.

Brown went to great lengths to help people with aerostatic information, even to the extent of copying by hand, newspaper reports to send them. His enthusiasm remained unabated; he would have been delighted when Coxwell lauded him, for "you have established a character for perseverance...you have given undoubted proof of friendship." The great aeronaut, wintering back at Aerial Cottage Tottenham, was under siege from two sources, his patients and his wife. He wrote candidly to Brown of getting "into such disgrace with my patients" and of his thoughts of giving up ballooning as "it interferes with my business so fearfully, that I get into bad odour at home". These comments were the first of many on his wife's opposition to his ballooning. Ironically, it was to be Mrs Coxwell's interference and domineering personality which inadvertently paved the way for Brown's journey to Australia. (11)

Coxwell invited Brown to spend Christmas that year with them but unfortunately Brown had to decline as he could not afford the 5/- train fare each way.

In July 1857 Brown compiled and printed *The Aeronautic Remembrancer* which contained news of the previous month and a few advertisements. Whether the personal expense was too great, or interest lacking is unknown, but no further issues were printed.

Coxwell, miserable at home and "rather busy in the tooth line", complained, "when anything goes amiss in the ballooning way, I have no consolation at home, but rather exultation at misfortune." Brown's letters cheered him "instead of the set that surround me." (12)

Surprisingly, Charles Brown does not record his first flight as pilot of a balloon but described himself as a pupil of Coxwell's and of having made 85 ascents in England. Brown was uncharacteristically vague here, failing to record whether he was in command or a passenger. Unquestionably they flew together but, for the understanding of future events in Australia, it would have been advantageous to have had a log of Brown's actual flying hours.

The origins of Joseph Dean - who flew in Australia in 1858 - have proved elusive. I have been unable to discover where and when he was born, where he lived and died, even if he married and had children. He was not on Brown's mailing list. The earliest reference I found on Joseph Dean, for 1819, was in a book by balloonophile JE Hodgson. It stated that the Cuthbert Collection in London - the finest collection of balloonmania in England - had "a small piece of fine linen with the following note, 'Dean's Rarefied Air Balloon' which was exhibited at the Belvedere Gardens, Islington, 1819. Presented by himself to John Cuthbert'" (13)

Dean apparently used this balloon in an unsuccessful attempt to ascend "on the practically obsolete Montgolfière, or hot-air, principle". Hodgson spoke disparagingly of Dean's attempt, and of his personality: "a more futile scheme of a retrograde character was that projected by Dean," but he does appear in Hodgson's roll of the first 500 aeronauts. (14)

That same year, on 23 June 1825 he ascended with George Graham, which Monck Mason recorded as the first for a Mr Dean. (This flight took place a year before Charles Brown was born, so Dean was considerably older). Mason also records the flight of a Miss Dean in London in 1837, but whether she was a sister, daughter or no relative at all of Joseph Dean (often erroneously referred to in the press as William Deane) is difficult to ascertain.

Many of Joseph Dean's ascents are officially recorded, but in total are nothing like the figure of 119 he later claimed to have made. The number of flights made by both Dean and Brown (and whether in the capacity of pilot or assistant) was to be of great relevance in Australia when the two aeronauts argued over who should make the country's first historic flight.

Brown himself noted many Dean ascents and wrote of him as "well known in England for having made 119 ascents from the Vauxhall and Cremorne Gardens in London and various towns in England." According to Brown, Dean was a pupil of Charles Green, who occasionally flew under the assumed name 'Captain Bedey'. Of the eighteen ascents mentioning Dean in Brown's books,

"9 were made solo
4 were possible solo flights
2 listed him as assistant
3 were made in the company of others:-
    *one with C Graham
    *one with JD and JE Godard
    *one with Henry Coxwell as pilot."

Presumably he acted on these flights as assistant or pupil. (15)

As no other documentation of Joseph Dean's flights has come to light, it is possible he exaggerated the number of his ascents or chose not to reveal that he was not always the pilot. It is also possible - given Brown's later animosity towards Joseph Dean - that he deliberately falsified the accounts and did not credit Dean with his full number of ascents.

It has to be said that not every flight made was entered in Brown's accounts; only the more remarkable or those reported in newspapers or to him in by other contemporary aeronauts. He could also have written his accounts much later in his life, after all the events of the next decade and a half but, having studied his books, I doubt this, for I consider that Brown, as a chronicler of things aeronautic, recorded the events soon after they came to his notice.

Dean flew regularly in the summer and autumn ballooning seasons in the years 1854-1857, by which time he had turned professional. He flew multiple times from the Bellevue Gardens in Manchester in 1854, scattering handbills over the 8000 spectators; one flight being hailed as "the best ascent witnessed at Belle Vue this season" and "made in fine style." (16)

In 1856 Dean assisted Godard in a flight from the ruins of the thirteenth century Dudley Castle; in 1857 Dean flew in a double race against JE Godard in London which featured three events. Dean in the *Prince of Wales* balloon won all three over Godard in the *Aurora*. Godard and Joseph Dean replaced Adams when the Royal Cremorne Gardens dismissed him after the death of parachutist Henri Le Tour, when he took him up under his balloon.

Dean flew many times from the Gardens. The *Era* of 28 June 1857 described him as a "daring aspirant for aeronautic fame" and reported that, "he was surrounded by his numerous friends, who immediately christened him the hero of the evening in bumpers of champagne". His liking for alcohol was to become an increasing problem in his aeronautic career; perhaps it was already so, for that year Dean was involved in several mishaps, considerably damaging the balloon. Dean travelled back to London, perhaps to have the balloon mended. While there, he flew over the Crystal Palace with Coxwell, in command of his *War Balloon*. Dean's next ascent met with disaster. Filled at the gasworks, the balloon broke away during attempts to move it to the zoological gardens, was dashed against a tree and burst. Two days later 'Captain Bedey' made a successful ascent, "his 104th aerial excursion". (17)

The year 1857 is the first in which the *Tavistock* balloon - which travelled out to Australia with Brown and flew over Sydney - was mentioned. Pear-shaped, of muslin blue and white stripes, it had been constructed by Coxwell and originally named *Napoleon*, possibly to insult the English government which, unlike the French ruler, had expressed no interest in Coxwell's ideas for the use of balloons for military purposes.

In June, Coxwell made an epic voyage in the 24 000 cubic foot balloon, when he travelled for five hours, setting out from Woolwich and landing in Tavistock in Devonshire. So pleased was he with his reception there, and with his small balloon, that he re-named it *Tavistock*.

Charles Brown and his mentor Henry Coxwell, unaware of forthcoming historical events which would involve them both, continued to mail letters to each other when apart. Coxwell, in quaint, almost poetic language, wrote of their love of "...aerostatic mania, for whilst I conceived the child, you assisted me at its birth, (and) have a natural affection for the little cripple." He also referred to them as "balloonatics", an apt term perhaps. (18)

Neither man knew that Coxwell was to play a major part in their permanent separation, for Charles Brown was soon to leave England for Australia, expressly to undertake that country's first flight and balloon ascent. Nor was Coxwell aware that his little balloon, *Tavistock*, was destined for a much longer journey before the year was out.

(1)  Brown to J MacSweeney, 24 October 1863.
(2)  Coxwell to Brown, 16 October 1845.
(3)  John Wise, *Through the Air*.
(4)  Charles Brown, Notebook.
(5)  Ibid.
(6)  Charles Brown, *Aeronautica*.
(7)  Monck Mason, *Aeronautica* 1838. (Later Brown published a pamphlet entitled *A Letter to a Friend Descriptive of Two Excursions With Mr Coxwell's Balloon which ascended from the Leeds Royal Gardens, March 24th and 25th, 1856*).
(8)  *Leeds Intelligencer*, 9 August 1854.
(9)  Brown to MacSweeney, undated.
(10) Coxwell to Brown, 4 October 1854.
(11) Coxwell to Brown, 1 October 1856.
(12) Ibid.
(13) JE Hodgson, *History of Aeronautics in Great Britain*. (In 1917 Hodgson bought the collection of balloon books and prints first started by John Cuthbert about 1820. He donated it in 1848 to the Royal Aeronautical Society.)
(14) Ibid.
(15) Brown, *Aeronautica*.
(16) Ibid.
(17) *Manchester Examiner*, 31 July 1857.
(18) Brown, Notebook.

# Antipodean Attempts and Accidents

*"When the ingenious contrivance is made known,*
*it will transcend all present speculation, like the*
*chameleon in the fable, the creature when turned out*
*will be unlike all the visions which our theorists have had of it."*
Editorial, *Sydney Morning Herald*, 28 June 1843.

Australia was no different to other nations: flight had fascinated her earliest inhabitants, the Aborigines, perhaps as long ago as 40 000 years. Like other ancient people, the Aborigines had myths of spiritual ancestors. One, Baiame, is depicted on a cave painting at Milbrodale, near Byrock in New South Wales. The arms of the Ancestor Being are extended the width of the granite cave. It is easy to imagine that this huge arm span represented an early effort to fly.

For many thousands of years Australian Aborigines had utilised their own aerodynamic skills in a most practical application: when they used the boomerang, they showed an understanding of certain principles of flight. The apparently simple, curved wooden structure is aerodynamically complex: the weapon spins and arcs through the air to return to the thrower. In fact, the boomerang was possibly the world's first successful aerofoil.

The antipodes were never forgotten in England and Europe, after Cook's voyage of discovery in 1770 and second voyage of 1772 - 1775 finally proved the existence of a great south continent. There was much curiosity and interest in the huge new land in southern latitudes. Imaginary writings were published about voyages to a utopian southern land.

One of the best in terms of imagery and fantasy is *La Découverte Australe par un Homme-Volant*, (translated as *The Austral Discovery by a Flying Man*, or *The French Daedalus*) by Nicholas Restif de la Bretonne. Published in 1781 in troubled France, it contains a depiction of what is possibly the first reference to human flight in Australia. - that of Victorin, who encourages his male descendants to use wings to leave France and discover an archipelago in the southern hemisphere, inhabited by weird combinations of man/monkeys, man/bears, serpents, frogs, elephants and more. Bretonne's imagined land features a vast, isolated utopia.

Australia's existence in the Pacific had already been established and partly mapped by the time of Bretonne's publication, just eight years before the French Revolution, a strong indication of the resentment felt by the populace for the privileged aristocracy. Unrest for economic, social and political reforms was the spur which led Britain to settling Botany Bay in 1788; and France to the Bastille in 1789.

As late as 1830 a watercolour appeared in Vienna satirising Charles Green's penchant for ballooning away from England. It shows the veteran aeronaut introducing his passengers, on descent, to the antipodean natives.

After the first British convict settlement in Sydney New South Wales, there followed a time of discovery and settlement in the new colony, as people left their homeland and sailed to Australia to start anew. The ensuing decades were filled with endeavour, principally domestic, exploratory, commercial and administrative in nature. Little thought was given to research or the sciences; the main sources of recreation became entertainment and sports.

News of the exploits of early aeronauts travelled to the colonies and was read months after the events. Amongst the news of politics, royalty, and social life in the mother country, this obsession with the science of aerostation back home, meant little to them. Later arrivals may have already witnessed balloon ascents in England and were blasé about them; those who had not witnessed such events were enthusiastic.

The first interest in ballooning from Australian soil appeared in 1843 - fifteen years before Brown and Dean's arrival - in a 'letter to the editor' by one who signed himself 'Aeronaut':

"Twenty years ago I invented and made known to a few scientific friends a new species of balloon." It was a powered balloon kept aloft by hot air supplied by "portable gas and argand burners". He was convinced "that a mere balloon would not accomplish the great end of periodical or exact transit." This gentleman and his friends desired, as many before them, to make air currents "subservient to our wishes" rather than being at their mercy. (1)

Although 'Aeronaut', in a subsequent letter, did not expand on his scientific invention, he proposed a "mechanical contrivance" to make the balloon more than "it has been for the last half century, a philosophical toy." Acknowledging that the result would be limited by the fifteen horsepower generated, he suggested that the power needed was "electricity". (2)

There were several responses to his initial letter. One man, 'Ives' had a dream in which he saw aerial carriages used in war between France and Russia. "After this, war was declared amongst all nations" and the aerial cars carried "men and munitions and many I saw were dashed to pieces by broadsides of cannons...many men were killed and fell." Almost a hundred years before the eventuality, this man, prophesied that over water "every man was provided with chutes and life-preservers; so that in falling into the water, there was still a chance of being saved" and picked up by a ship. (3)

Published in the same issue was a letter from Francis Forbes of Skillatur, near Muswellbrook. announcing that he had constructed a working model of an aerial carriage, using "the Archimedes screw-fan." Forbes obtained better balance by revolving "two rotatory screw-fans ....in opposite directions. The screw-fans or vanes must turn on an axis lying in the plane of the kite and they must be placed behind the kite, or at the side, to propel it forward." (4)

It is likely that Forbe's carriage was the "model of an ellipsoidal balloon (intended to be propelled by the Archimedian screw) exhibited at Adelaide gallery" that same year, 1843. (Forbe's advanced proposal was similar to the box-kite planes which the Australian inventor and aviator, Lawrence Hargraves, flew in the early 1900's.) (5)

Influence on the history of Australian aerostation shifted to the island colony of Tasmania, settled after NSW to receive convicts from England. A new arrival from England Mr Thomas Rea, persuaded his employer in Launceston to publicly testify to his abilities as a gunsmith. The obliging Major Wellman complied, saying Mr Rea's "work is far superior to any I have seen in this country. His charges are moderate; and I recommend him as a tradesman." (6)

Thomas Rea's fortunes must have increased as a result of the reference for, a mere two years later, the newspaper ran an advertisement to the effect that Rea - now elevated to 'Professor' - was to make a "GRAND AERIAL TRIP" in an "IMMENSE BALLOON" of his own making; on the "first fine day of the Launceston Races". It stated, "PROFESSOR REA WILL POSITIVELY ASCEND", but encouraged the public to help with the great expense involved, especially as 'the feat' is in this country a heroic one." (7)

Rea was already selling tickets from his gun-maker's shop for the princely sum of 4/-. Business must have been slow for, three days before the planned event, tickets were reduced to 2/6 and an advertisement placed promising "to return every farthing of the money to everyone if he does not, in truth and reality, perform." Rea calculated that "this leviathan balloon, 60 feet high, by 129 feet in circumference will not take more than twenty minutes in inflating." The public were assured Rea "will not leave the balloon unless by necessity he is obliged to descend in his patent parachute." (8)

Rea apologised for failing to get off the ground on that Friday March 7 and decided not to charge for his next attempt but "to leave it to the public to give what they think proper." Upwards of a thousand people assembled at the appointed place in John Street, to witness Australia's first balloon ascent. Only a hundred paid for admission to watch the inflation behind a curtain "which concealed the apparatus from vulgar gaze." The fire was lit under the calico envelope to fill it with rarefied air, but several hours later it was apparent it would not fill that night and the crowd dispersed. (9)

The week following, Mr Rea twice attempted ascents. The envelope was torn on a shingled roof and finally "the calico split to pieces" when a wind squall hit it. Lacking the funds, or the conviction, to construct a new balloon, Rea must have patched up his balloon as best he could, for he continued daily attempts to ascend. "The balloon did once ascend a few yards, but the professor was left in his basket on the ground." Finally, this convinced him of the balloon's incapability to lift and "he resolved to build another on improved principles." (10)

Rea exhorted the public to donate £100 towards the cost of a new silk balloon. The aeronaut was to raise the remainder and a tradesman pledged to supply gas gratis. It is doubtful he ever made another balloon, as no one seems to have seen it: although the *Launceston Examiner* reported Rea as having, "taken great pains in constructing the balloon," from calico, painted with "common beach oil." The same article told of the storage shed being gutted by fire and "the machine was reduced to tinder." (11)

It sounds suspiciously like a fire of convenience to cut Rea's losses, or to save his pride. As no records exist of Rea ballooning - or parachuting elsewhere - it is assumed that his driving force to be the first aeronaut in Her Majesty's Colonies appears to be but pecuniary.

Perhaps Thomas Rea was hounded out of Tasmania as a charlatan, for he established a business in Geelong Victoria. It was announced that "Mr Rea, a gunsmith of this town" - who also exhibited marionettes - intended to fly an oiled calico balloon on Boxing Day. Rea's petition to the magistrates grandly stated his intention "of furthering the advance of science and rendering it practically useful to mankind." The bench, probably unaware of his failures in Tasmania, "willingly gave consent" and Police Captain Fyans personally contributed ten shillings towards construction and appealed to the public for financial assistance (12)

The astute reporter of a Melbourne paper that carried the article doubted Rea. He demanded to know "what year" his intention was to be honoured, why Rea was to use a clothes basket for a car and about Rea's statement that "he contemplated a Launceston ascent." (13)

Years later, pioneer Australian balloonist Charles Brown, wrote of Rea that "parties who have known him intimately upwards of twenty years in Tasmania and Victoria say positively that he has only sent up paper balloons inflated by burning straw." (14)

Tasmanians were to wait 33 more years to be treated to the spectacle of a balloon rising majestically above them: until Thomas Gale's flight on 6 February 1878, almost 22 years to the day after Australia's first ascent.

A major influence, and the first person of significance in Australia's aviation history, was Dr William Bland: medico, author, inventor and politician, who spent years studying the problem of aerial navigation. In March 1851 Dr Bland MLC, designed his *Atmotic Ship* (from the Greek 'Atmos' meaning vapour); so named as he intended it to navigate the atmosphere. His was a serious attempt to produce aerial direction by a combination of balloon and steam engine; a lighter-than-air proposal. (15)

Drawings show a large, elongated balloon or float, filled with hydrogen in separate gas-tight compartments to reduce the effects if one burst. The passenger/cargo float was 100' long by 30' wide and contained stove, boiler, water and coal storage. The steam produced would activate two screw propellers fore and aft: sails acted as a windmill for extra impetus. Spark arresters provided safety from fire, as did a six-metre distance between gasbag and steam generator. Bland installed other safety measures as well: to lessen the effects should a float burst, he provided a net over the float and designed escape valves to let gas out as needed.

Ballooning for pleasure, adventure or remuneration did not interest Dr Bland: he regarded it purely for navigational and travel purposes. He estimated it would take a mere four to five days for his *Atmotic Ship* and its Australian passengers (3½ tons in mechanics plus 1½ tons of passengers and cargo) to reach England, calculated on an approximated speed of 50 kmh. The route to England - which took two to three tedious months by sea - would be cut 6,000-12,000 miles by travelling over land. The payload (income-producing cargo) could be increased by lengthening the balloon without detrimental effect in the air.

London's Crystal Palace exhibited Bland's models and plans of the *Atmotic Ship* in 1852, as did the Paris Universal Exhibition of 1855. Interest was expressed by Emperor Napoleon III but he was restrained from placing an order by his Finance Minister. Queen Victoria and Abraham Lincoln also declined offers to purchase. Undaunted, Bland continued to make practical experiments for several years and to write letters to fellow scientist James Glaisher and to the Aeronautical Society of Great Britain (of which he was a member), to no avail.

Newly elected as the Australian Medical Association's first president, Bland published a booklet, The *Atmotic Ship* in 1855 and expounded his theories on Atmotic Navigation at lectures delivered to the NSW Philosophical Society and at the Mechanics School of Arts (which he had co-founded) in June and September of 1859. The paper advertising these evenings described Bland as a "well-known highly scientific character." (16)

Hoping to gain official recognition for his invention, he reprinted his paper in 1865. Still it attracted little attention or success. Dr Bland's brilliant ship of air - never constructed - was years ahead of its time. Many credit it with being the precursor of the airship - to which it bears a remarkable resemblance; others say that Count von Zeppelin incorporated Bland's ideas in his dirigible fifty years later.

Although a man of stature in Australia, William Bland had not always been of exemplary character; possibly the memory of his conviction for murder lingered overseas and negatively influenced prospective customers of his brilliant invention.

William Bland, the second son of Dr Robert Bland, was born in England on 5 November 1789. After graduating in medicine, Bland joined the Royal Navy and was rapidly promoted to naval surgeon. It was in India in 1813 that Bland's life took an unexpected turn and fate steered him to Australia. The *HMS Hesper* docked at Bombay late in February 1813. On board, an argument broke out between purser Robert Knight Case and Lieutenant William Randall. According to Bland's account "drawn up for posterity" he attempted to calm the aggressors and restore order. Case called him "a contemptible fellow" and Bland, unable to let the slight pass, "threw his glass at him". The crew from a visiting Royal Navy ship supported Bland's conduct against Case, who had been previously described by the Captain as "a coward, a scoundrel and a villain." The purser challenged Bland to a duel and the doctor entered into it, without reluctance, despite efforts of "accommodation". (17)

The ill-fated transaction took place at dawn on 7 April with both parties firing together by signal. Case fell, shot in the lower abdomen by Bland, who then rendered assistance. They laid the injured Case on the bottom of a boat and rowed him to the nearest ship, where hours later he died. The following day Bland and the seconds of both duellists were committed for trial on a charge of 'Wilful Murder' and jailed immediately. A previous, similar incident had resulted in three months jail for the offender, and the expectation on board *HMS Hesper* was for the same, so the ship awaited the outcome of the trial of 14 April; however, Bland was found guilty and sentenced to seven years' transportation. The *Denmark Hill* transported him to Hobart Town, Tasmania in January 1814, and the *Frederick* to Sydney six months later.

There, Governor Lachlan Macquarie's policy of utilising convicts' talents ensured that prisoner Dr Bland cared for the inmates of a mental asylum in Castle Hill. In October 1815 he received a pardon and became the first full time private medical practitioner in Sydney. Two years later he married twenty year old Sarah Cover but they later separated. Bland's second wife died; he then married widow Eliza Sweathman in 1846 and settled in Newtown.

Bland, a flamboyant but stormy character, argumentative by nature, ran foul of the law again and was imprisoned at Parramatta for lampooning Governor Macquarie. He returned to private practice and spent much time and energy serving the community; he began a long association with the Benevolent Society. His philanthropic ways led him to assist the sick, the poor, writers and church builders alike and to help develop the colony's education system.

His status as a citizen rose to the level where he ventured into politics; here also, as in medicine, he held an admirable record. Dr Bland supported many significant ventures: emancipation of convicts and the struggle for a jury system to be introduced. He demanded legislation by representation and encouraged self-government for the colony. In 1843, in NSW's inaugural election, he became Sydney's representative and, the following year, a trustee of the NSW Savings Bank. He had several terms of office as a Member of the Legislative Council and retained his prominent position as a skilful, progressive surgeon.

He published medical articles and designed two inventions. The first - the use of carbonic gas circulated in the holds of wool ships to suppress spontaneous combustion - became widely used. His second invention, the *Atmotic Ship*, fared less well and Dr Bland's fortunes declined.

Six months after the first balloon ascent in Australia in 1858 (of which, no doubt, he read accounts with interest) Bland's services to the community were acknowledged by a gift of money and a candelabra. In 1861 plans for an annuity for him were rebuffed; in the same year he was declared bankrupt, although once he had owned large tracts of land at Hunters Hill in Sydney and in Prospect Hill, Gerringong and Yass.

Bland still wrote: "aerial navigation has long since appeared to me beyond doubt practicable, and if so is calculated to confer many highly important benefits on man." He died (79 and intestate), of pneumonia on 21 July 1868, ten years after Australia's first successful lighter-than-air flight and just ten years before Lawrence Hargrave began his experiments. (18)

A Dr Evans once described Bland as "brave, consistent and accomplished...an elegant, scholar, a man of science" and as "one of the earliest founders and patriarchs of liberty on this continent." It could have served as his obituary. (19)

Attention in England was directed towards Australia by inventor JJ Oddy Taylor who, during a visit to London by the NSW Surveyor General, Sir Thomas Livingstone Mitchell, (renowned in Australia as the explorer Major Mitchell), wrote to him. Taylor's letter of introduction, told of discussions held at London's Polytechnic Institute between aeronaut Charles G Green (son of Charles Green), the lecturers, authorities and himself about the feasibility of an aerial survey of the interior of Australia, "still a terra incognita." He diplomatically sought Mitchell's views on "the usefulness of such an Expedition", as he considered the surveyor to be "more competent than any other gentleman to give an opinion upon this subject." (20)

Mitchell honoured Taylor by visiting him and discussing his geographical survey plans for Australia. Taylor demonstrated on his model - previously exhibited in London - the action of his propellers and other fittings; Mitchell expressed doubts associated with running out of gas and ballast should the balloon, surveying at 100', need to rise over a 12,000' mountain range and then return to its previous level. The gas Mitchell thought, "would be exhausted, and you would have exiled yourselves for life." (21)

According to Taylor, in the letter Mitchell sent five years later in 1858 to his successor as Surveyor General, Mitchell was convinced that, in theory, Taylor's ideas were correct, for he exclaimed, "Taylor you are right! Thank God I have been permitted to live to know that this survey can now be practically accomplished." Taylor claimed Mitchell had promised to lay the project before the Legislative Assembly, "but unfortunately death overtook him." (22)

Taylor proposed taking to Australia Green as aeronaut, himself as co-ordinator and the *Royal Nassau* balloon, "which could be navigated as easily as a screw ship at sea." He intended to complete the survey "from East to West or North to South...in about a month." Taylor's letter on his project was passed on to the Honorary Secretary for Lands and Public Affairs in February 1859, then returned to the Surveyor's Office to gather dust. (23)

The newspapers in England had picked up the story of the "novel scheme...propounded for exploring the vast unknown interior of Australia." One reporter thought that if "the interior of this immense continent is not to be exploited by man, with the aid of a horse, and ox, and camel" then a "scientific combination" should render such a purpose indispensable. (24)

In Australia, Sydney newspapers used Taylor's idea for a general discourse on aerial navigation. An editor, although critical that neither aeronauts themselves, nor "men of inventive genius" had done little more than propound ideas for such exploration, did not regard the concept as "dreamy or absurd". (25)

In the years between JJ Oddy Taylor's two letters to the Surveyors General, a ripple of aeronautic interest lapped the shores of Sydney.

A paper fire balloon was let loose on Christmas Eve at 7.30pm "The wind blew fresh, and it travelled across the harbour at a great elevation, at a rate of about 30 M.P.H., passed over Balmain" towards the inland river town of Parramatta and out of sight. (26)

Toward the end of 1856 newspaper advertisements announced that Frenchman Pierre Maigre, "of aerial fame in France, US, East Indies, Mauritius and other places" intended to thrill the crowds with a "climb to the heavens." Of course, such claims of experience were not necessarily true, but they lent an air of professionalism to such events. (27)

The French consul in Sydney took Monsieur Maigre to meet the NSW Governor, Sir William Denison, who echoed the enthusiasm and excitement of Sydneysiders and offered the use of the Domain - a large area of public land adjacent to Sydney Harbour. In readiness was the 100' high calico balloon, tactfully named the *Sydney*, a small car - 4' long, 2' wide and just 18" deep - and a steamer to render assistance should the balloon and Maigre drop into the sea.

The events of 15 December 1856 are well documented. On that day, a crowd of 12,000 paid the admission price and surged through the entrance gates at 2pm, for the commencement of the four-hour process of inflating the balloon. The ascent was billed for 6pm. Tension and excitement mounted during the afternoon, as the inert balloon, suspended from a rope stretched between two 70-foot poles and tethered by twelve guy ropes, gradually inflated. Maigre explained that he used 'spirits of wine' to soak the straw on the brazier before firing it.

Governor and Lady Denison arrived at 5.30pm; shook Maigre's hand and together they inspected the straining balloon. People heard the governor express doubts that such a large object could be lifted with hot air. Maigre replied that he would stake his reputation on it and ordered the basket - bedecked with ribbons and two fluttering French flags - be attached. Loud clapping and a rendition of the *Marseillaise* accompanied Maigre as he stepped into the basket and raised his top hat to the audience. Twelve men pulled on the restraining ropes: one became too enthusiastic and tore a hole in the fabric; the hot air hissed, the balloon shrank.

Within an hour the balloon was repaired, and the slow process of inflation began again but, before his dwindling supplies of straw and spirits had supplied sufficient lift, some of the crowd, boisterous, sceptical and impatient, rushed at the balloon. As it began to collapse, Mr Ainsworth the publicity agent, quietly disappeared.

Maigre, less intuitive, stayed on, pleading with the crowd to let go their hold on the balloon. Someone pulled his hat from his head and threw it to those behind; "with a wild yell this was seized upon and demolished". (28)

The luckless Maigre suddenly took flight across the Domain, pursued by 4,000 of the mob, screaming with rage at his failure to fulfil his contract. Shrewd police grabbed Maigre and hid him in Government House on the edge of the Domain. The frustrated mob - deprived of their quarry - vented their anger on the balloon. Sailors from *HMS Juno* - a Royal Navy ship visiting Sydney - led by a huge man who'd been drinking rum all afternoon, grabbed the French flags and threw them on the brazier, which he then kicked over onto the envelope, causing it to catch fire. The crowd - fuming at paying out heavily for no entertainment - added the wicker basket and hundreds of chairs and fencing to the bonfire, then ripped down the grandstand to feed the fire. Two hours after the riot began, word spread that Maigre was at Government House. Many threw stones and broke windows in their attempts to gain entry but, by this time, mounted police charged the scene and quelled the riot.

During the melee, two boys were injured when the tall masts that had supported the envelope crashed to the ground. They lay moaning and bleeding until taken to hospital. Only one recovered. Eleven year old Thomas Downes died from a fractured skull. His body was buried in a corner of Camperdown Cemetery in the grounds of St Stephen's Church Newtown; the same church that Dr Bland helped build. Little Thomas' grave lies among many early pioneers of the colony. His moss-covered tombstone remains today; the engraving of a balloon still visible upon it. Indirectly, Thomas Downes thus became Australia's first aerial fatality.

On 16 December, four sailors and a civilian appeared before Magistrate Dowling, charged with riotous behaviour. He ruled that, although their behaviour was not acceptable and the defendants were implicated in the riot, public patience had been severely strained and so he dismissed charges. He was satisfied Pierre Maigre was no imposter (he produced certificates showing he had flown in Nice and in different French towns) and that the balloon would have at least flown over the Domain, had the crowd not interfered. Dowling believed Maigre's intention was not to deceive the crowd, as "he would surely not have gone to the great expense he did". Maigre's expenses amounted to £500 and the gate taking to less than £300. (29)

Despite "the riot, incendiarism and bloodshed," the Domain was again made available to Maigre. On Christmas Eve 1856 a second, free attempt failed when the cords holding the balloon snapped. A third attempt also failed. A reporter vividly described Maigre's balloon as "swaying to and fro like a dowager duchess seized with cholic (sic)" and decreed that Maigre never intended to go up but "acted the disappointed man to perfection." (30)

Pierre Maigre, his credibility destroyed by his earthbound disasters, left the colony and was not heard of again.

So it happened that inventors and aeronauts in New South Wales had to yield to Victoria, the honour of first place in antipodean aerostation.

(1)  *Sydney Morning Herald* 1 June 1843.
(2)  Op cit 9 June 1843.
(3)  Op cit 28 June 1843.
(4)  Ibid.
(5)  Francis William Forbes was the son of Sir Francis Forbes, the first Chief Justice in NSW. He occupied Ellangowan Station on the Darling Downs in Queensland in 1847 and died in 1866. This information appears in the *Australian Dictionary of Biography* which states that FW Forbes' interest in flight took shape in the early 1800's - obviously a mistake as he was not born until 1817

and did not arrive in Sydney until 1843, when he was only seven years old, according to the Forbes papers, Mitchell Library.

(6)   The *Launceston Examiner* 21 January 1843.

(7)   Op cit 22 February 1845.

(8)   Op cit 10 March 1845.

(9)   Ibid.

(10)  The *Launceston Examiner*, undated.

(11)  Op cit 25 May 1845

(12)  *Geelong Advertiser* 25 December 1849.

(13)  *The Melbourne Daily News* 25 December 1849.

(14)  Charles Brown, *Aeronautica*.

(15)  Bland's *Atmotic Ship* differed to that of Forbes, whose powered flying machine was heavier-than-air. They may have discussed aerostation together for Forbes' father, with Bland, established a free Grammar School and the Sydney College (later part of Sydney University). Both were involved with the discontinuation of convict transportation, although held opposite views. In the Forbes papers is a tribute to the judge by Dr Bland.

(16)  *Sydney Morning Herald* 20 December 1859.

(17)  Dr Bland, MSS relating to Dr Bland's duel, trial and transportation. Angus and Robertson Sydney, 1892, limited edition of 33 copies; one is held in the Mitchell Library, Sydney.

(18)  Bland, Letter to *Empire*, 1860.

(19)  *Empire* 21 January 1862.

(20)  Letter JJO Taylor to Sir TL Mitchell 2 February 1853 - Mitchell Library Papers of Sir Thomas Livingstone Mitchel.

(21)  Ibid.

(22)  Letter JJO Taylor to subsequent Surveyor General 4 December 1858 - the Ernest Crowe Collection National Library, ACT.

(23)  Ibid.

(24)  *The People* 30 May1857.

(25)  *Empire*, undated.

(26)  Ibid.

(27)  Ibid.

(28)  *Melbourne Herald* 20 December 1856.

(29)  *Argus* 26 December 1856.

(30)  *Bell's Life in Sydney* 31 January 1857.

# Setting Sail for Australia

*"By land. Let them travel, as many as list.*
*And by sea, those who like the hard fare,*
*In an airy balloon, whilst I sit at my ease,*
*And pleasantly glide through the air!*
*Round this globe, the farthest they can reach,*
*Let them travel night, morning and noon;*
*Such excursions as these are but bagatelles,*
*When compared with a trip to the moon!"*
*Literary World* London 1840.

In August or September 1857 George Coppin, the noted actor, entrepreneur and later politician, arrived in London from the Australian colonies, in search of new talent for the Cremorne Gardens Amusement Park. Coppin and actor GV Brooke co-owned and managed the 10 acres of pleasure park in Richmond in the newly separated (from NSW) colony of Victoria.

The actors had purchased Cremorne in 1856 for £11,500 from Jack Ellis, a former proprietor and caterer for Royal Cremorne Gardens in London, who had gone to Melbourne to create a similarly exotic park on the northern bank of the Yarra River, 1½ miles from the city. Originally known as Wright's swamp, it seems to have been a billabong of the river. Ellis' enterprise had failed, largely due to lobbyists, who had procured a prohibition on drinking alcohol in the grounds on Sundays, causing patrons to stay away in droves.

The new owners spent over £10,000 on improvements to the pleasure gardens, set in acres of landscaped ground. Under Coppin's management, the swamp was transformed into a lake, for which Coppin imported the first white swans and goldfish in the Australian colonies. He constructed a replica of the Pantheon theatre, a bar and zoo which held two lions, an elephant and a giraffe; backdrop scenery depicting a panorama of Rome was placed behind the dance floor and band stand. Visitors to the Gardens in summer could feast on an array of opera singing, ballet, theatre, military bands, mardi gras, fancy dress balls, flower shows, river regattas and fireworks displays.

The Gardens' river setting made access easy for visitors, who preferred to ride on one of the steamers Coppin owned, rather than risk travelling on the dirt road from the city and being held up by bushrangers. (No railway existed in Melbourne until 1859.)

The fortunes of Cremorne Gardens Amusement Park in Melbourne - like its royal sister in London and sister in Sydney - fluctuated. A constant stream of new amusements and talent was necessary to offset flagging public interest; this then was the reason for George Coppin's visit to England. It was a rushed trip, for he disliked leaving behind his wife who was three months into her pregnancy.

Coppin knew England well, for he had been born in 1819 in Norwich, to actor parents; Coppin learnt his acting skills at Dublin's old Abbey Theatre and commanded great admiration and affection. In five short weeks in England Coppin engaged fifty artistes and contacted balloonist Henry Coxwell with a proposal to make balloon ascents in Australia.

"Mr Coppin, from Australia, is very anxious to take me out with him", Coxwell wrote to Charles Brown, but "I have refused." Coppin then proposed that Coxwell make him the two balloons he required but as usual, Coxwell's wife was less than enthusiastic for, as the balloonist/dental surgeon so succinctly stated, "this Mrs Coxwell sets her face against." (1)

George Coppin then asked John Hampton to accompany him to Australia, but he "heard of it too late", according to James MacSweeney. (2)

Coxwell wrote suggesting Charles Brown undertake the contract,

"as Mr Coppin told me you have written to him and as your estimate of a Muslin Balloon exactly coincided with mine, can't we do business together, and you undertake the affair? I will strike the pattern, and probably get Chambers to make the nets...Could you undertake to get the balloon made, unvarnished (which would be better for going out) within the month...Mr Coppin leaves on the 15th of October." (3)

At this stage Henry Coxwell was asking Brown only for help to supply the balloons. Days later he again wrote, expressing surprise,

"When I recommended you to Mr Coppin to make balloons, I had no idea you would like to undertake a series of ascents, and leave home, business, and so forth, to engage upon them. I thought from what you said to Mrs Coxwell and to me that you had abandoned any idea of that sort. I wish I had known that you would like to undertake the thing, as I could have at once proposed you in my place. Now I will do so directly." (4)

The more experienced aeronaut gave him advice as he was wont to do occasionally: "You must mind what you are about - for remember all the ascents are to be made from seaports, and passage money and living will amount to a high figure. If you make a proposition, have so much for each ascent; and passage money in advance." (5)

Coxwell again asked Charles Brown to solely undertake the making of the balloons, "I could send you the pattern, and I should think you could manage the rest, or else I might as well fight it out at Tottenham." (6)

The tyrannical Mrs Coxwell was to remain uninformed of this development, with her husband pleading with Brown not to mention his part in the affair, "Mind - if he gives you the order to make the balloons, you must not allow him to suppose that I have anything to do with it!" (7)

The oft-sensitive Brown had taken offence at Coxwell's advice and patronising tone. Brown makes it clear that he has had more experience than Coxwell in balloon construction, "I built two large balloons several years previously, in 1851 - at the date of the above letter Mr Coxwell had only built one, *Napoleon* or *Tavistock* in May 1856." (8)

Often headstrong, Brown may have ignored Coxwell's friendly advice, for he later complained of his contract with George Coppin. In his haste to get to Australia and make his name as an aeronaut, Brown overlooked important financial aspects of the document, an oversight he later regretted.

True to his word, Henry Coxwell wrote to the Australian entrepreneur on Brown's behalf. His curious statement, "I have not worded it too strong, and yet confined my recommendation to strictly correct statements", I interpret to mean he covered up the fact that Brown was a fairly inexperienced aeronaut. His words speak for themselves,

"All I can say is, you won't find anybody upon whom you can place so much reliance; and I am certain we have no aeronaut in the present day who has made aeronautics so much his study. His experience with me has not been extensive, but he had had a balloon of his own, and has associated with other aeronauts. Of his trips with me I can speak highly, and I have no doubt he will prove a credit to you should you engage him." (9)

In reply to Brown's mentioning his ballooning 'fever', Coxwell gave his protege further advice, "I am quite certain by my own experience, that the only way to cure the mania is, to allow it full scope," assuring him, "I wish you luck, and...I am not personally the least displeased, jealous, or offended" that Brown was going to Australia in his place. He graciously wished, "that your path may be as fortunate as mine...You can always draw upon me for sincere advice, and I have no doubt you will deserve success." (10)

After this flurry of mail, events moved quickly. Brown constructed the *Australasian* envelope from 500 yards of material. "The netting was made expressly for it is of the best Indian hemp. The car is one in which Mr Brown and Mr Coxwell have frequently ascended." (11)

Due to time constraints the *Tavistock* balloon was procured as the second balloon to journey to Australia. Coxwell described its basket as "the best my man has ever made." He made no mention of the condition of the balloon envelope, which later was to become a contentious issue. (12)

It is unclear who recommended Joseph Dean as assistant. It is unlikely that Brown had, for he wrote, "such a character is sure to be distasteful to Coppin. He is of intemperate habits." Dean's love of liquor was to increasingly become a problem in the colonies. (13)

With a contract hastily drawn up between them, Coppin booked passages for himself and Brown on the expensive 'overland' route, taking "a minimum of luggage" and "a smelly steamer" from Marseilles to Alexandria. There followed a trek across the Egyptian desert to Suez where they boarded the *SS Simla* after a long delay. This route was designed to cut the journey by many weeks, (the Suez Canal only opened in1869) as it avoided the lengthy trip around the Cape of Good Hope. A steady stream of military and civil service personnel used this route to several of England's Commonwealth countries. (14)

Brown appears on the shipping lists as 30 and single, whereas he was actually 31 or 32 years old and married. (Joseph Dean travelled separately.) Brown's wife, Eliza was to follow with their children Annie 9 and twins Frederick and Eugene aged 14. (Their youngest child Herbert had died as an infant and they were never again to visit his grave; nor was Charles Brown ever to see his parents or brother Edwin again.)

As he sailed towards Australia, Brown must have reflected on what lay before him and on his reasons for leaving behind all he cherished in England. Why had he taken on this journey? Was it simply an adventure, or was it a good opportunity to gain fame and glory as Australia's first airman? Or did he turn his back on the poor, dirty conditions of Leeds in post Industrial Revolution days in the hope of finding a better future? Was he aware that his passage to the antipodes was one-way only?

We will never know his reasons, for he did not record personal data; or if he did it has not survived. There is a gap in Charles Brown's records, from 1 October 1857 to 15 February 1858; a time when he was busy packing in England, travelling to and settling in Australia.

The name of their ship - the *Simla* - was a familiar one in the nineteenth century. Simla was a hill station in British India, 7000 feet up a spur of the Himalaya, where officials and the military spent summers, "It was a dream of coolness in a very hot land; a hope of healthy rest...a solace for the wounded and the desolate...above all, a bitter-sweet memory of home - cuckoos and thrushes, pines in the mist, honeysuckle and roses in the rain." (15)

The *Simla* was also carrying British troops to help quell the Indian mutiny of 1858 - 1859. Other passengers bound for Australia probably had thoughts of gold, for it was less than a decade since gold had been discovered, and only three years since the momentous rebellion of miners at the Eureka Stockade at Ballarat in Victoria. The passengers were oblivious to the fact that the gold industry was in a steady decline, and that they were heading for probable unemployment and hardship following a period of deflation from 1854 to 1856. By 1857, unemployment was almost double the figure for 1856, with the migration from Britain that year of 43 000 people. The year 1858 was "notably a year of suffering." (16)

In the daily struggle to establish themselves and survive in a new country there was little thought of such ethereal events as balloon flights. The colonists were caught up in the excitement, disappointments, new wealth or hardship that the 1850's goldrushes had brought to Australia. As historian Geoffrey Serle states, "many thousands at last retired from the goldfields which had previously concealed much unemployment." There were insolvencies in plenty; Geelong and Melbourne were hit hard by the economic crisis; the government was "bankrupt of policy, powerless and suspect of continually advancing their private business interests" and brawled constantly with the conservative opposition. (17)

This then was the scene when Charles Henry Brown berthed in Melbourne. It was not a good time to be arriving in the colonies.

(1) Coxwell to Brown, September 1857.
(2) Cork, MacSweeney to Brown, 8 February 1859.
(3) Coxwell to Brown, September 1857.
(4) Coxwell to Brown, 12 September 1857.
(5) Coxwell to Brown, 12 September 1857.
(6) Ibid.
(7) Ibid.
(8) Charles Brown, Notebook.
(9) Coxwell to Coppin, 14 September 1857.
(10) Coxwell to Brown, 14 September 1857.
(11) *Illustrated Melbourne News*, 6 February 1858.
(12) Coxwell to Brown, 30 September 1857.
(13) Brown to Coxwell, undated.
(14) Bagot, *Coppin the Great*.
(15) Pat Barr, *Simla: A Hill Station in British India*.
(16) WP Worrell, *The Gold Rushes Chapter* VIII.
(17) Geoffrey Serle, *The Golden Age: A History of the Colony of Victoria, 1851-1861*.

# First Ascents, Melbourne

*"I don't see how we can avoid looking to a man with*
*respect, who in the discharge of his professional duties*
*is perpetually looking down upon his fellow-beings,*
*who in his eyes, at such time appear nothing more*
*than the minutest specks of animated nature."*
*My Note Book* James Neild

The journey to Australia proved to be less expeditious than Coppin wished for as the ship stayed in Egypt for five weeks. Coppin was irritated by these delays, not helped by the *Simla* arriving within Port Phillip Heads at 10pm on Thursday 7 January 1858. "It had anchored so that no one could get ashore until the following day." Coppin was desperate to see his wife. He arrived just in time, for Harriet gave birth eleven days later, to Blanch Brooke. (1)

Charles Brown settled in Fitzroy, where he lived at 6 Marion Street, since demolished. Nearby inner suburbs Collingwood, Fitzroy and Carlton were collectively described as each having about 10 000 residents in an "extraordinary number of small, mean habitations." (2)

Within three weeks of their arrival, Brown and Coppin had organised and advertised Australia's first balloon ascent to take place. It was well known that Coppin held charity functions at the Cremorne Gardens, to support causes such as the Deaf and Dumb Institution, orphanages and victims of tragedy, flood and fire. Information was conveyed in the handbills, or advertisements in local newspapers, "Cremorne Gardens Grand Gala Night, Balloon Ascent, Pyrotechnic Display, Cosmoramic and Biscenoscope Views etc." (3)

Preparations began the night prior to the ascent at 1.30 am. The plain white, varnished muslin balloon *Australasian* was partially inflated at the City of Melbourne Gas and Coke Company's gasworks at Batman's Swamp where, "it gleams dazzlingly in the clear moonbeams." The cost of the lighter-than-air coal gas was sizeable, 22/6 per thousand cubic feet, a heavy outlay for Coppin. The partially inflated balloon was conveyed to the Gardens at 4 am by horse and cart, with the aid of thirty men, much rope and ten bags of ballast. Someone with a sense of humour and a clever use of words described what he saw after the two aeronauts (Dean had obviously arrived in Melbourne) lifted the balloon, "To speak truly, the balloon seemed a little the worse for its night out. It had a decidedly dissipated, used-up sort of aspect. As the great sphere swayed about in the light wind, it was as strongly suggestive of the rolling gait of an intoxicated reveller as could be supposed." (4)

The balloon - topped up with gas from 2pm onwards - held 35 000 cubic feet when fully inflated. (There were many privately-owned gas works at the time, producing gas from oil or kerosene. Coppin had his own gasometers, principally to supply his theatre with gaslight.)

After many unsuitable weeks during which "dreadful heat...has prevailed" the chosen day dawned; 1 February 1858 was fine with a breeze blowing from the southwest and away from the sea and its dangers. Charles Brown, as the aeronaut specifically selected to command the *Australasian* on its inaugural Australian flight, had checked the meteorological reports from the newly established Melbourne Observatory on Flagstaff Hill. (5)

Thousands of people converged on Cremorne that summer's day. Coppin's steamer *Pride of the Yarra* and the *Iron Export* left Prince's Bridge (opened to celebrate Victoria's 1851 separation from the colony of NSW) ferried people hourly from 9am to 6pm,

> "The roads leading to Cremorne were thronged with vehicles, and the cars with foot-passengers from 3 until 5 o'clock, and when the latter hour arrived the environs of the gardens were thronged with curious spectators. The steamboats and the smaller craft on the river had contributed to swell the crowds." (6)

Newspapers described the "pleasant holiday scene" in ecstatic terms and spoke of "joyously anxious faces" on those come to see history being made and "an exuberance of life,"

> "...Every eminence from which a view of the gardens could be obtained was dark with human beings. The parapets and verandahs of the neighbouring houses were occupied by anxious sightseers; the banks of the river were lined with them, and they assembled in thronging numbers everywhere but in the grounds themselves" (7)

Disappointingly for the launching of aerostation in Australia, there was little fanfare: no gold trimmings, national flags or the sipping of champagne by nobility, as occurred in Europe and England. This first ascent on Australian soil may have lacked the grandness of the first French ascents: nevertheless, it was a spectacular occasion. Charles Brown must have felt pride and happiness as he viewed the balloon he had constructed, standing 60 feet high and 40 feet in diameter, ready to take him into the clear blue of the Australian sky; to become the first aerial voyager in this country to be lifted by balloon: to view its land from above.

At the appointed time for the ascent, it was obvious there was not enough gas in the balloon to take up both Brown and his assistant Joseph Dean. There are varying accounts as to the reason for the balloon being insufficiently charged. The *Argus* blamed "some neglect of the valve" causing "a considerable quantity of gas to escape". *The Illustrated Melbourne News* of 6 February 1858, stated that "owing to the great heat and violent breeze, the needle-holes at the seams were greatly stretched and a good deal of gas escaped." (8)

Yet another account said the strong southerly wind which blew all day and "the oscillating motion of the tethered balloon caused a considerable loss of gas." (9)

Whatever the cause, it was impracticable for more than one aeronaut to make the historic flight. A heated argument broke out between Brown and Dean. The former claimed the privilege as the maker of the balloon and the person chosen specifically for the task; the latter on the grounds of his superior experience of 119 ascents.

The *Argus* said that "Mr Brown generously gave way and Mr Dean took his place in the car." Others that "Brown jumped out before the stays were released", and Dean seized his opportunity to lift off in the *Australasian*. (10)

Another paper stated that "Mr Brown conceded to Mr Dean what he as the constructor of the balloon might fairly have claimed as his right viz. the credit of being the first to explore the aerial realm of Australia." (11)

George Coppin's biographer said it was the impatient owner who silenced them and made the decision for the quarrelling aeronauts. It was this extraordinary quirk of fate which gave Joseph Dean - and not Charles Brown - the honour of being the first aeronaut in Australia. Not for Brown the dream of glory, for his biggest moment in history was cruelly thwarted. From the time that Brown stumbled out of the basket in a disbelieving

De Lana's Idea 1670

The birdlike *La Passarola* Portgual 1709

Montgolfiere Brothers' invention, the fire balloon 1783

Marquis d'Arlandes and Pilâtre De Rozier, the first two humans to fly in the *Montgolfiere* 21 Nov 1783

Fanciful early ideas

Blanchards Channel crossing attempt 1816

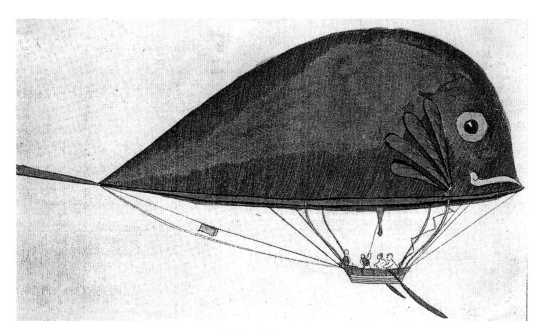

Dirigible design 1816-17

American aeronaut and mentor John Wise

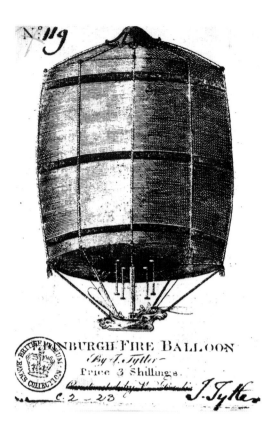

First flight in Britan - Tytler, 1784

Sadler ditches in the Irish sea

Actress Mrs. Sage, the first Englishwomen
aloft 1785

Widow Madeleine Blanchard's fatal fall 1817

Nadar's *Le Géant* 1802

Cocking's parachute 1836

Parachute death of Cocking

Victorin's half beast, half man

Victorin's flying man

Cartoon of Charles Green in the Antipodes

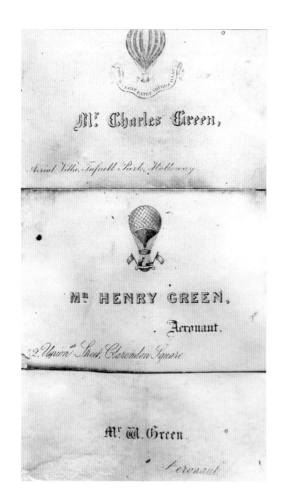

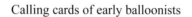

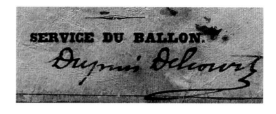

Calling cards of early balloonists

John Hampton's *Erin go Bragh* balloon

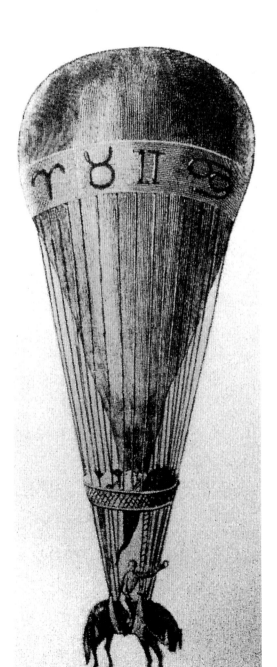

Showman Poitevin on pony 1850

Henry Coxwell, aeronaut, scientist, mentor

Charles Brown's first flight, Leeds 1854

Poster for the Italian Brothers' show,
aeronaut William Green 1854

Transportee and MP, Dr William Bland

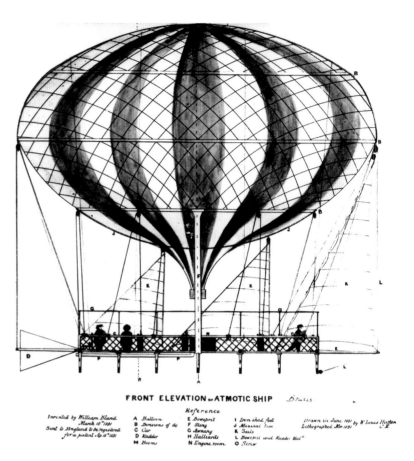

Bland's brilliant Atmotic Ship 1851

Riot in Sydney's Domain, Maigre 1856

Eleven year old's grave, Newtown

Melbourne actor/entrepreneur George Coppin

Antipodean aeronaut, Charles Henry Brown

Coxwell recommends Brown for Australia

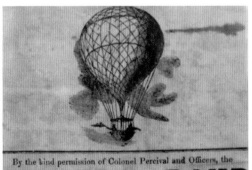

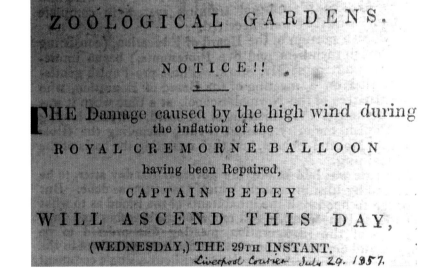

Ascent of Capt. Bedey (Jospeh Dean) 1857

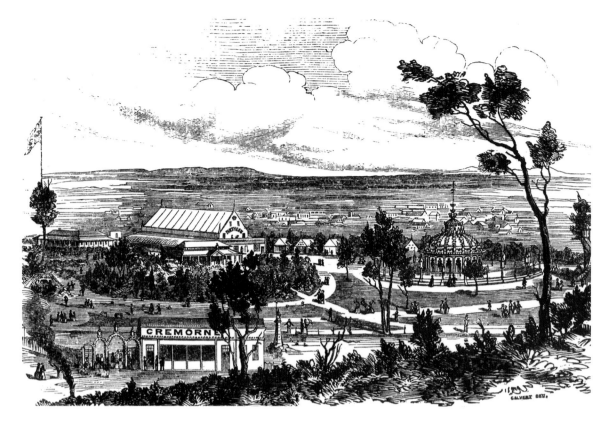

Cremorne Gardens Amusement Park Melbourne

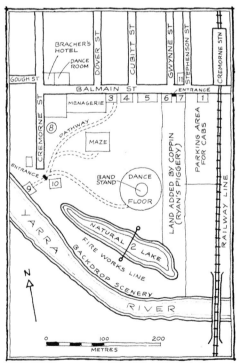

CREMORNE GARDENS, RICHMOND 1856.

1 PANTECHNICON        7 CRYSTAL BAR
2 TRAPEZE             8 GASHOLDER
3 COPPIN'S RESIDENCE  9 LANDING STAGE FOR BOATS
4 SIDE SHOWS         10 PEACHMAN'S HOTEL

1856 map of the Gardens

Mr Coppin, from Australia, is very anxious to take me out with him, and would not stand particular for a few hundreds, more or less. I have refused, however, for various reasons, which I cannot now explain. Next he proposed my making him two balloons: this Mrs Coxwell sets her face against, and as Mr Coppin told me you had written to him, and your estimate of a Muslin Balloon exactly coincided with mine, can't we do business together, and you undertake the affair? I will strike the pattern, and probably get Chambers to make the nets, also another party to make the valves. Could you undertake to get the balloon made, unvarnished (which would be better for going out) within the month – and if so, what share of the profit would you propose to give me out of the £160? Mr Coppin leaves on the 15th of October

Brown copied all correspondence into his Notebook

First Australian flight, above the Yarra
River 1 Februrary 1858

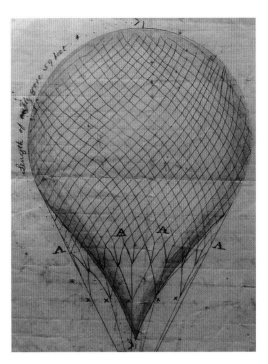

Brown's sketch for the *Australasian*
balloon

Brown the balloon maker

**THE NEXT MORNING.**

Shocking condition in which a respectable Balloon was recently brought home at four o'clock in the morning, after "a blow-out"
at Cremorne.

Punch cartoon after the first flight

Coppin's balloon medal that Brown donated

*All England Eleven* balloon, named for the first cricket test match

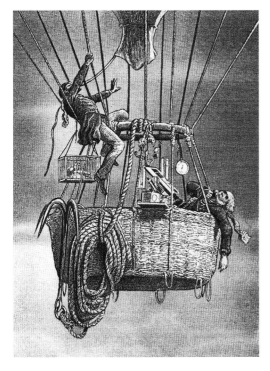

Coxwell suffered hypoxia on a high altitude flight 1862

In setting out on an exploring voyage, the aeronaut _ take advantage of a strong wind, so as to travel a g distance in a short space of time. However, to base o_ calculations on the mean rate of 25 miles an hour, the e_ breadth of this continent, from south to north, would_ traversed in 80 hours by a balloon. What other known mode of transit could compete with this?

The exploring balloon should be of great size and capab_ of retaining its gas a considerable length of time. _: forming it of two layers of silk, or other material close texture, both layers varnished and then cemen_ together, it might be kept floating for weeks. The ca_ should be a seaworthy boat; but so constructed as no_ to be liable to injury by a descent on land. A crew _ four persons, two to manage the balloon, and two to ma_ observations, would be able to rest and refresh themselv_ in turns. It would be well to secure the provisions in wat_ proof bags fastened to the car.

Starting with a favorable wind, the balloon should n_ be allowed to ascend above that wind. By means of a rope suspended from it, and trailing along the ground, the balloon could be kept at such an altitude as would allow it to clear trees { _ _ _

The insertion of this in the columns of the Argus will oblige your humble servant — C. H. Brown, aeronaut. Melbourne September 4. 1858.

Brown's letter to the *Argus* proposing exploration by balloon 1858

## EXPLORATION OF AUSTRALIA BY BALLOONS.

"Firstly,—The balloons which are now at Melbourne were never built for the purpose of scientific experiment or exploration, but simply for public amusement. The aeronauts, however, who went out in accordance with my recommendation, were particularly requested to make frequent meteorological observations, both in the higher region and lower currents, especially with a view of observing how far it is likely a balloon would be influenced by inland and return breezes. Mr. C. H. Brown, a gentleman of acute observation, assisted by Mr. Dean, are now making the required observations, and from the accounts already received there appears to be good grounds for believing that certain reliable currents will facilitate the undertaking. As a matter of course, an expressly built machine, of ample dimensions, will be requisite, together with every conceivable appliance, to afford a return journey by a diametrically opposite wind to that embraced at the outset. The party will also be provided with an improved and gigantic fire balloon, in a collapsed state, which can be inflated in the most desolate interior locality without gas, a reserved expedient, which in the event of injury or exhaustion to the parent machine, will provide the means for a second trip.

Coxwell backs balloon exploration in Australia 1859

EA Crome painting of flight across Sydney Harbour

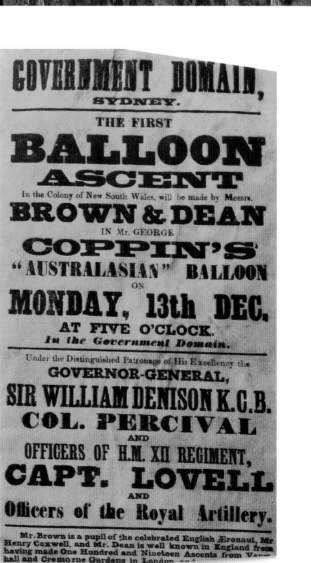

First Sydney ascent advertised

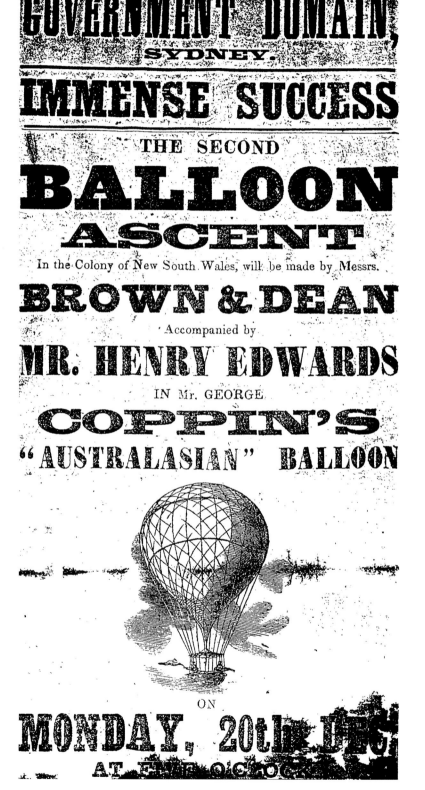

Brown & Dean's second Sydney flight

Green's disaster at Sydney Inn

Dean's Bombay accident

Dean and Madame Marian in Calcutta
1862

Triple trapeze act beneath balloon

that the public be called on to subscribe so much each, say Rs. 2 or 3; that the sum so collected be left in the hands of a stakeholder (say yourself,) to be handed over to Mr. Johnston on his completing his performance to the satisfaction of some nominee on the part of the public. We have some guarantee then for the due performance of the exploit, but if there should be a failure, then let him be paid his expenses out of the fund collected, and the balance might be made over to some charity. *But you will see that some of these observations is not very* Yours obediently, VOX.
27th December 1862. *Creditable to Dean management*

The Ascent from the Eden Gardens yesterday afternoon was accomplished successfully, but we regret that in a pecuniary point of view, the spirited Projector has been a heavy loser. The vicinity of the Gardens was literally crammed in every direction by Natives, anxious to catch a glimpse of the inflated monster, but in no wise eager to contribute anything towards the heavy liability incurred by the owner. This is peculiarly a failing among the lower order of Natives, but we were glad to find that the superior class mustered inside in large numbers. From the character of the entertainment much risk is necessarily run, and a very wide margin has to be allowed for those who take advantage of house-tops, and other means of obtaining a view of the ascent,—anything in fact instead of paying. The weather was not altogether favourable, occasional showers compelling a hasty retreat to the various places of shelter. The inflation was successfully managed, but some little delay took place, in the hope, as we were informed, that more spectators would arrive. Shortly before 5 o'clock, the ropes were let go, and the balloon rose steadily, drifting with great rapidity across the Maidan. To the surprise of all, it soon began to descend, and scarcely ten minutes had elapsed before it safely alighted again on *terra firma*. The elevation attained was very inconsiderable. A lady and gentleman, in addition to Mr. Deane, the Aëronaut in charge.

Brown's caustic comments about Dean scrawled across news reports

Brown's death certificate 1870

Inquest findings

Fred Brown with his ancestor's memorabilia

His descendants, plus author and son at graveside

Cremorne Gardens Mural, Richmond

Brown's grave, Melbourne General Cemetery

150 years since Australia's first flight 2008

daze, events moved swiftly. "It was obvious from the business-like manner in which Mr Dean set about his work that he was a practised aeronaut, and that no fears be entertained on his account." (12)

At eight minutes to six on that 1 February 1858 day, Joseph Dean gave the word to start; the assistants at the restraining ropes let go and "the huge machine slowly arose amidst the cheers of the assembled multitude inside and outside the gardens - cheers which were repeated and re-echoed by the spectators in more distant localities. As he cleared the Pantheon Theatre, Dean discharged bags of sand en masse and the balloon rose to a considerable altitude, drifting towards the north-west until "in twenty minutes she had become a mere speck." (13)

We can only imagine the anger and extreme disappointment that Brown must have felt by this bitter twist of fate that had befallen him, as he watched Dean float triumphantly away in the balloon he had made, taking Brown's rightful place in Australian aeronautical history. From that time on, Brown's relationship with Dean soured considerably. It seems he never forgave him.

For Joseph Dean it was another story, his flight was successful and without further incident. He lost no time in contributing his narrative of the excursion to the newspapers for publication the following day. Dean's wondrous, first person account of his Melbourne flight is also the only record of his writing in existence. It is reproduced here in full,

"Once clear of the buildings in the garden, and having discharged a bag of ballast, the balloon arose with some rapidity, and I had barely time to acknowledge the cheers of the crowd below before I had attained an elevation at which they almost became inaudible. But at times I could catch a sort of hum or murmur, and looking down, I saw thousands of upturned faces in every street and road surrounding the place from which I had taken my departure. After emptying some more sandbags, I attained a sufficient elevation to enable me to command an extensive field of vision without altogether losing points of detail. Nothing could be easier than the motion of the balloon, or pleasanter than the temperature of the atmosphere at that height; and persons unaccustomed to such excursions in the air would have been thrown into raptures of delight by the magnificent spectacle which I witnessed below me, of the setting sun and the rising moon at opposite ends of the globe, both luminaries looming through the haze the one like an enormous warming pan, and the other like a shield of gold I once saw at Windsor Castle.

What chiefly struck me, besides the difference in the feel of the atmosphere, was the different color of the earth's surface as compared with what I had been accustomed to see in making balloon ascents at home. There, in the very height of summer, the face of the country looked as green as a billiard table, though variegated with patches of yellow corn. Here it assumes a dirty budd (sic) color, mottled with a greenish brown wherever trees abound.

I could make out the rectilinear outline of Melbourne very well, the streets running north and south being particularly well-defined, owing to the strong shadows cast from the houses by the setting sun. But the most beautiful terrestrial object seen from the elevation at which I then was, were the Bay, and the ranges of Mountains lying to the east and north-east of the city. The Bay resembled a turquoise in color, and the curvature of the shores at that height resolved itself into the most graceful and undulating lines imaginable. The mountains on that side of them, which was not opposed to the setting sun, were of a rich purple color, while there were fissures in them which were perfectly black, and also great masses of sombre shadow, which I suppose were caused by the forests which in some places completely covered the slopes to the very summits.

I saw bushfires burning in several directions - very little flame, but a good deal of smoke being visible. I must not forget to mention another circumstance which struck me very much - the extraordinary circuitous course of the river Yarra. Anything more fantastic or erratic than the meanderings of this stream I never saw; and not having previously seen it depicted on a map, I was the more amazed when I surveyed all its turns, and windings, and sinuosities, from my observatory in the car.

As Mr Coppin had expressed considerable anxiety that I should return to the ground and report the success of the experiment (of which neither he, nor I, nor Mr Brown had ever entertained a doubt) on the same evening, and as I am as yet imperfectly acquainted with the country, I prepared to descend after having been travelling steadily in a north-westerly direction for almost 5 and 20 minutes, and accordingly commenced discharging gas. On nearing the earth I perceived that plenty of assistance and numerous vehicles were at hand, and having effected a safe landing near what I was informed was the Plenty road, between 7 and 8 miles from Melbourne, I returned to town with my machine in perfect safety. I hope to have an early opportunity of becoming better acquainted with Victoria from a birds eye point of view." (14)

On landing, Dean found himself embroiled in another quarrel, this time over the £5 reward offered by Coppin "to any carter or other person who shall convey the balloon to the gardens after descent. "The reward was exceptionally generous when one considered that Brown and Dean's weekly earnings were only £3/5/- each. Dean returned to the city in time for George Coppin to announce from the stage at his Theatre Royal, following a performance, that the first Australian flight had been safely and successfully concluded. (15)

The ascent, although a triumph, was not a pecuniary success. The public had shown their resentment at the doubling of the usual admission price, by watching the event from outside the boundaries of the Cremorne Gardens. One journalist commented caustically that,

"The public seemed to have arrived at the conclusion that Mr Coppin had imported balloons and aeronauts, and incurred a heavy outlay in the purchase of the requisite gas, and in the transport of the balloon to and from the works at Batman's Swamp, with no other object than that of providing the assembled thousands with a gratuitous spectacle, and the car-drivers and boatmen with a rich harvest." (16)

Two weeks later, Charles Brown made Australia's second ascent and his first flight in the colonies. He sent this handwritten account of the eventful voyage to the *Argus*,

"At Mr Coppin's request, permit me to lay before your readers some account of my ascent from Cremorne gardens this evening with Mr Coppin's balloon, the *Australasian*. At 48 minutes past 6 by my watch, I left the ground with a good ascending power, and was much pleased with the picturesque scene (at once displayed) below me. I first ascended in a north west direction, which was continued until I arrived over the Eastern Hill, at which time I attained my greatest altitude, more than two miles. Here I was seized with a most violent pain in my right-ear, which induced me to open the valve in order to descend. The heat of the sun rarefied the gas so greatly, that I was compelled, in order to cause my descent, to open the valve no less than 28 times. From time to time I threw out hand-bills...I got into a gentle current, which, if it had continued, would have wafted me out to the bay; but as there was little day light remaining, I thought it prudent to descend...I arrived over a spot which I thought favourable for landing. I drew the valve string and came down in the most gentle manner possible on the road between Collingwood stockade and Brunswick, about four miles from Cremorne, after a voyage of 44 minutes. On my descent I was treated in a most brutal manner by the people assembled. Why I know not, but they tore the hair from my head, bruised, pushed, and almost suffocated me, besides damaging the balloon by tugging at and trampling on it...Mr Needham, of the gasworks, assisted in extricating me from the savages. In conclusion, I must express my regret that the ascent took place at so late an hour in the day, as if time had permitted, I could have made experiments and observations connected with the southern hemisphere which would have been regarded with interest by the admirers of aeronautics in England." (17)

This flight was notable for two reasons: it was the first in Australia on which advertising leaflets were dropped and was the first to be violently attacked in this country.

The *Australasian*, with both Brown and Dean aboard, ascended again on 15 March for a night ascent, lifting off at 10.05pm. "Three minutes after we left the ground, the fireworks suspended below the car burst forth, presenting a most beautiful sight." They drifted over Prahran towards Port Phillip Bay and "in various directions for 3 hours and 20 minutes and travelling at least 40 to 50 miles." (18)

They landed in a paddock in Spring Vale at 1.25am so they slept in the basket until morning, when the proprietor of the Spring Vale Hotel, Mr Mathew Bergin, gave them a hearty breakfast and sent them off in a dray. They arrived in Melbourne at noon. (It was a courtesy in England for aeronauts to publicly name and thank the owner whose property they landed on. (This may have been a tradition, but it highlights the indisputable fact that good farmer relations are essential to balloonists.)

One mischievous writer for the *Melbourne Punch* (1 April 1858 - April Fool's Day) accused his "contemporaries of rendering fictitious accounts of this night flight" and published an "authentic narrative" from "the enterprising aeronauts,"

"...we were not unmindful of the claims of science upon us. Yet, rapidly as we neared the stars, we did not observe any great change in their appearance, nor were we able to discover any traces of human life in the moon.
...we had been for some hours drifting in the direction of the "Gulf of Carpentaria", and were hovering over the Straits of Malacca.
...when we reached earth we were astonished to find ourselves within a few miles of Canton. We immediately conveyed ourselves and our apparatus to that city which we found to be suffering from the effects of a mighty bombardment but which was altogether in the hands of the British. We were hospitably received by the inhabitants."

A further two ascents were made that season from Cremorne Gardens by Brown and Dean. That of 29 March was a cool, moist evening on which the moon shone so brightly that they could read their watches and the compass by it. During the hour-long flight they passed over the Botanical Gardens but had problems with crowds assaulting them at Batman's Swamp, so flew on to Emerald Hill (South Melbourne). Four soldiers "towed the inflated balloon, with us seated in the car, over the Princes's Bridge...and deposited us, at 12 o'clock, on the identical spot from whence we had ascended, amidst immense cheering." (19)

The last flight for the summer season took place on 5 April. It took the two aeronauts high above Melbourne - away from "the earth studded with lights" and into dense cloud, mist and intense cold. Twice they tried to descend but wind drove them into the trees. At midnight they landed safely and again spent the night in the basket, "well provided with the good things of this life." (20)

The five flights of Brown's contract with Coppin were now complete. To the entrepreneur who had organised Australia's first aerial journeys, aerostation had proved a rather unsatisfactory enterprise, for it had not produced the projected profits.

Coppin's interest had already begun to wane due perhaps to his pre-occupation with personal tragedies, family matters and political aspirations. For, just three weeks after the historical flight his first child by Harriet his second wife, little Polly Bishop Coppin, died on 21 February. April that year saw Coppin elected a councillor of the Municipality of Richmond. In June he retired from the stage, shrewd enough to realise that his ambition to serve in Parliament could be achieved, not as an actor, but only as a respected citizen and councillor. In August that year his wife gave birth to a daughter, Amy Maude. A week later on 2 September, unrecovered from the birth Harriet died.

George Coppin had two medals struck in honour of Australia's first balloon ascents, thus following a tradition laid down in Europe to honour outstanding aeronautic achievements. He presented one to Charles Henry Brown (and presumably another to Joseph Dean) who later donated it to the Melbourne Public Library. For many years, a Coppin Balloon Medal dated 1858, was displayed in the (then adjoining) State Museum. I feel sure this is the medal that Coppin gave Charles Brown, and which is now held by the Melbourne Museum.

During that first winter Charles Brown, with time to spare and an axe to grind, wrote numerous letters of complaint. Brown's concept of himself was as a scientist and he felt slighted by the inability of others to acknowledge him in that role. He regretted being unable to conduct experiments on his flights. Perhaps Brown was naive, or had an inflated opinion of his aeronautic importance, to think that George Coppin would value the balloonists he had sponsored, otherwise than in amusement and monetary terms.

Again, discussion raged in the dailies, as to the usefulness of the balloon to mankind. Sections of the press viewed ballooning seriously. Others would like to have been more positive, "...wishing we could indulge in some sanguine expectations and that there was any rational prospect of mail, which would satisfactorily supplant the present tantalising service". (21)

Important as Australia's first ascent was, it took second place in Australian newspapers to despatches from London telling of the British Army's conquest of Delhi during the Indian mutiny. *The Illustrated Journal of Australasia*, in its March 1858 issue, was scathing in its comments. "In the old country, balloons are now too common to excite any especial furore."

Brogden echoed these sentiments, "...the shrewd pioneers realised that the balloon had no future. As a sport, ballooning was - and is - wonderful. As a method of transport, it did not exist." (22)

Even Brown himself, in an article he collected, written in 1858 or 1859, noted disillusionment creeping in. "Beyond their employment for war purposes by the French, and for meteorological observations, balloons have rendered but little service to mankind, and most persons regard the balloon merely as a philosophical toy." He also reminisced, rather poetically, on the joys of ballooning,

> "In ten minutes I have experienced the warmth of spring, the cold of winter, and the heat of summer. The shadow of the balloon with its car, cords etc; is sometimes seen on the clouds surrounded by an Iris of the most beautiful prismatic colours." (23)

Brown indulged himself in another area of interest: exploration by balloon. This idea had again been mooted in the press, "Perhaps it remains for Australian aeronauts to discover some new and valuable application of the art; and we really think it not at all impossible that a balloon, as our 'ship of the desert' might be found of service in solving of the great problem of the 'terre incognite Australis'." (24)

Brown was keen to see the unknown inland of Australia himself,

"Much has been said and written on this subject...I am firmly convinced, from frequent observation of the currents of air prevalent at Melbourne during the last eight months, that there are, almost invariably, two opposite currents blowing inland and seaward at the same time, and that it is therefore quite practicable to go from Melbourne into the interior, and to return, perhaps not exactly to Melbourne but certainly to the neighbourhood of some civilized spot...his elevated position enables him to survey at one glance a vast extent of country...the entire breadth of this continent, from south to north, would be traversed in 80 hours by a balloon.

The exploring balloon should be of great size and capable of retaining its gas a considerable length of time. In forming it of two layers of silk, or other material close texture, both layers varnished and then cemented together, it might be kept floating for weeks. The car should be a seaworthy boat, but so constructed as not to be liable to injury by a descent on land.

A crew of four persons, two to manage the balloon, and two to make observations, would be able to rest and refresh themselves in turns...

By means of a rope suspended from it, and trailing along the ground, the balloon could be kept at such an altitude as would allow it to clear trees, etc, and also retain it in the current of air blowing near the surface of the earth. A long piece of whalebone fastened to the end of the rope, would prevent its lashing round trees.

Having proceeded as far north as desirable, a landing may be effected in a valley, or under shelter of trees, to protect the balloon from southerly winds...The direction of the upper current of air may be ascertained by means of a small balloon let off from the car: should that current prove unfavourable for the return voyage, the balloon may remain at anchor awaiting a favourable wind...the final landing may be effected, or the balloon may be allowed to proceed to the coast, whence the travellers would be enabled, by their sea-worthy boat car, to sail for the nearest port."
(25)

His letter provoked discussion and drew disbelieving responses from some, "Many enthusiastic aeronauts have spoken with confidence of the practicability of exploring the unknown interior of this country...any attempt to quit the settled districts of Australia or Africa, and float away over the far interior, would be simply madness."
(26)

In London, Henry Coxwell also became alarmed and wrote,

"Firstly, the balloons which are now at Melbourne were never built for the purpose of scientific experiment or exploration, but simply for public amusement. The aeronauts, however, who went out in accordance with my recommendation, were particularly requested to make frequent meteorological observations, both in the higher region and lower currents, especially with a view of observing how far it is likely a balloon would be influenced by inland and return breezes. Mr CH Brown, a gentleman of acute observation, assisted by Mr Dean, are now making the required observations." (27)

Coxwell, in his *Aerostatic Magazine*, published further details of a plan to explore by balloon. A few years later, on 1 July 1861, the Burke and Wills Expedition of Exploration left Melbourne for the interior, taking with it camels provided by George Coppin's Cremorne Gardens Zoo. Charles Brown had proposed accompanying the explorers with a balloon, but his proposal - and his later submission to aid Mr Howitt's search party for the doomed explorers with "a Montgolfier, or fire balloon" and without remuneration - was rejected. The Hon. John Macadam as Honorary Secretary of the Royal Society declined his offer as impracticable. Unbeknown to Brown at the time of his writing, Burke and Wills were already dead, the official date of deaths registered as 30 June 1862. (28)

Looking back on this from the twenty first century, in fully mapped Australia; it is easy to mock these seemingly naive and fanciful notions.

In that first winter in Australia, Brown turned to John Wise in America who encouraged him to strike out on his own. To his friend in London, Henry Coxwell, he complained of the state of the second balloon, the *Tavistock*, purchased from him in England. Unhappy with such criticism Coxwell replied,

> "When I packed it up it was certainly not in the condition you complain of - and I can only account for it by supposing the increased temperature and fearfully close folding have tended to rot it. I question whether a silk one would not share the same fate, and I should not be surprised if you report the *Australasian* to be unfit for service at the termination of this season." (29)

Brown told Coxwell of his contract problems with George Coppin; Coxwell, although powerless to help, was more sympathetic to this complaint. He offered advice, but also admonished Brown for lack of due care,

> "It is rather odd that you only so lately discovered the omission in your agreement: as a professional man you should have been sound in this respect and had a second stamped edition drawn out on Australian soil, in the event of detecting any flaw in the first hasty memorandum. I quite thought there were to be at least 20 ascents, as any less number would not compensate you for your services. As to the living costing twice as much, that I am not surprised at: but I considered it an understood thing that you were to be boarded at the establishment, or how would it be possible for you to keep yourself, wife and family out of a pittance from five ascents. However, if Coppin breaks the Agreement, you must fight hard to keep you position." (30)

Brown, keen to redeem his reputation with Coxwell (after being robbed of the title 'first to fly in Australia'), bemoaned his misfortune to his mentor. Coxwell's comments on Joseph Dean illustrate that aeronaut's character, "I regret to hear that Dean has been ill, but it being the result of intemperance, one cannot pity the foolish fellow. You are quite right in maintaining your dignity and playing first fiddle; never mind what he says - do your duty steadily, and even he himself will acknowledge you his superior." (31)

William Green, a member of the English aeronaut family of Greens, was in the colony at this stage. Brown - considering setting up in business himself - had asked Coxwell about Green's ability. Henry Coxwell's reply was far from encouraging. "As regards Bill Green. I should not recommend you to be any sweeter in that quarter than with your present associate. Low men, depend upon it, will always study to best you- selfishness and cunning I have nearly always found to be part of their nature and they will show it as an instinct, being hardly conscious of the possession of such meanness themselves." (32)

Yet again Brown stubbornly or foolishly, ignored the advice, for he later went into partnership with William Green.

(1)   Bagot, *Coppin the Great*.
(2)   Meredith, *Over the Straits*.
(3)   Brown, Notebook March 1858.
(4)   *Argus* 2 February 1858.
(5)   Ibid.
(6)   James Neild, Ed. *My Note Book* March 1858. (a weekly, not to be confused with Brown's Notebook entries).
(7)   *Argus* 2 February 1858.
(8)   Brown, Notebook.
(9)   Ibid.
(10) Greg Copley, *Australians in the Air*.
(11) *The Illustrated Melbourne News* 6 February 1858.
(12) *My Note Book*.
(13) *Argus* 2 February 1858.
(14) *Evening Mail* 9 February 1859.
(15) *The Herald* 13 February 1859.
(16) Brown, Aeronautica.
(17) Ibid.
(18) Ibid.
(19) Ibid.
(20) Ibid.
(21) *Journal of Australasia*.
(22) Brogden, *Australians in the Air*.
(23) *The Origin and Progress of Ballooning* unknown.
(24) *The Herald* 1 February 1858.
(25) *Argus* 14 September,1858.
(26) Brown, Aeronautica.
(27) *Lloyd's London Paper* 30 January 1859.
(28) *My Note Book*.
(29) Coxwell to Brown 1 November 1858.
(30) Ibid.
(31) Coxwell to Brown 1 November 1858.
(32) Ibid.

# Partnership Problems

*"In happy freedom, pleased to feel the wind,
And wonder in the luxury of air."*
Chester Courant July 28, 1858.

There are no details of how Brown or Dean survived financially that first winter in Australia. It is reasonable to assume Brown's family struggled as he received little remuneration from Coppin. The following summer both aeronauts and the *Australasian* balloon left for Sydney to make ascents there. Perhaps Coppin extended their contract in the hope that the venture would be more profitable with a larger population and a more predictable climate. Perhaps Brown had prevailed on Coppin to review the contracts, for they parted on good terms, as if they had come to some agreement. Brown was reinvigorated.

Having travelled by coastal steamer the 600 miles to Sydney, the pair were met on 3 December by Coppin's business partner, the eccentric GV Brooke, who'd booked them into a Hotel in Castlereagh Street and organised a tent to store the balloon.

The trustees of the cricket ground in the Outer Domain entrusted their enclosure to the aeronauts, a generous gesture considering the damage inflicted during the riot there two years before, after Pierre Maigre's failed attempt.

Coal gas was supplied by the Australian Gas-Light Company, but during the two hour inflation Dean almost asphyxiated himself by inadvertently inhaling gas. At 4.30 pm on 13 December 1858, His Excellency the Governor "and his entourage were ushered to a handsome tent, decorated with flags. Governor Denison - who had witnessed Maigre's downfall - closely inspected the balloon and concurred that the inflation "was quite sufficient." (1)

Brown recorded that the balloon rolled about in the windy conditions and "came right down on the Governor's head." Despite understandable nervousness, Brown and Dean together ascended in a strong wind; the balloon "went off with the greatest eclat and rose steadily and majestically. Loud cheering broke out to which the aeronauts responded by waving their caps and throwing out handbills; even the Governor was seen to throw his hat in the air. The *Australasian* floated across Sydney Harbour and landed gently in a gully at Neutral Bay, having completed the first flight across a large body of water in Australia." (2)

Searchers only found the aeronauts in the sheltered hollow after shouts of 'coo-ee' back and forth. Brown described the searchers as "a motley lot" which included "a Chinaman, a Negro and a New Zealander". They caught a ferry back to the city where GV Brooke took them to the Prince of Wales Theatre, which was showing a farce entitled *You Can't See the Balloon*. Brown wrote of his experience on stage in the crowded theatre, "I never knew of any actor hailed with such cheers and clapping as we received. After bowing to the people for some time, I was glad to get away, I assure you, for I was disgusted with it." (3)

Fame did not ride easily on Brown's shoulders; however, his employers were delighted with the day's takings of £500, with expenses tallying £127.

At this point it is interesting to note major differences between early and modern balloonists. Only paying customers were allowed into an enclosure to observe the balloon inflation and ascent. Today's commercial balloonists charge only the passengers they fly; anyone is free to watch a balloon inflation and ascent. For safety reasons, the majority of balloonists avoid flying over the sea or large tracts of water; it is only relatively recently that we have seen the most experienced pilots attempting such feats.

Charles Brown's letter to the only other aeronaut in Australia William Green, reveals his reactions to his new celebrity status and to his troubled relationship with Joseph Dean. He described a visit to the Lyceum Theatre in Sydney,

> "I was alone, as Dean was drunk. I sat in the boxes; and the moment I did so every eye was turned on me, and I was pointed and stared at by everybody. Not being able to bear it, I got into a back seat, out of sight. I have received invitations to dine with several gentlemen, who requested me not to take Dean along with me, as he was such a blackguard: but I cannot pay these visits, for Dean follows me wherever I go. We have quarrelled twice since our arrival in Sydney."

Even at their lodgings, Brown was embarrassed by his assistant. "Dean sits at table with his shirt sleeves rolled up, eats with his knife, etc to the disgust of all at the table." (4)

*Bell's Life in Sydney* reported on 1 January 1859, that a fire balloon was sent up on Christmas Eve and passed over Balmain and the inland town of Parramatta, and another went up from York Street. It is likely that these were small unmanned balloons, for the next flight Brown recorded was on 30 December when he took aloft an American comedian friend of Coppin's, Harry Edwards, who thus became Australia's first passenger. Their 55 minute journey ended in an orchard at Kissing Point near the Parramatta River.

A reporter was Brown's only passenger on his next Sydney flight in January and Brown, ever meticulous in gaining press attention, wrote his account of the flight. They proceeded along the southern shore of Sydney Harbour, over Woolloomooloo Bay and Garden Island. A gentle current bore them on, and they landed in a grass paddock at Rose Bay near South Head Lighthouse. Although a sea breeze had now sprung up and could have carried them back to Sydney, Brown decided against re-ascending as, "I thought it too hazardous a venture, as I was but a short distance from the sea." (5)

Scientifically minded as always, Brown had pointed out to his passenger a curious feature, "the revolution of the balloon on its vertical axis." The reporter was so "content" with his flight he sent Brown "a substantial token of acknowledgement". (6)

Brown's fourth ascent was the only night ascent made in Sydney; it took place on a humid evening, 17 January 1859. Brown realised when the envelope was only half filled that the 28 pounds weight of fireworks suspended beneath the basket would diminish ascensional power. He was thus "compelled to dispense with the grapnel which, from the calm state of the weather, I thought would not be required." (7)

No sooner had the balloon cleared the ground, than the fireworks attached to the car burst forth with a deafening roar. Dogs barked and the large crowds in the Domain and Hyde Park shouted as he passed overhead. At great altitude, and "feeling quite secure," Brown looked around him: the city of Sydney presented a beautiful sight. Suddenly, as often happens on a humid Sydney summer's night, lightning flashed on all sides of the balloon; "at times the lightning appeared to form a complete and immense circle around me". (8)

Brown opened the gas valve while over Coogee Bay just as a current of air swept him seawards. Without the grapnel, the terrified aeronaut could not halt the balloon's trajectory. "I felt sure I should lose my life somehow, but I was determined to get down on land, if possible… you will be able to judge of the awful smash with which I struck the ground…having no grapnel, the balloon rebounded to a great height, and it seemed certain that I should be carried into one of two strong post and rail fences, but I cleared both." Brown dragged through the scrub "at a terrific rate, the car cutting through the bush like a knife" for at least a mile. He knew he had to save himself before coming down in the dark in the water. "The wind was strong, and I was bumped a good deal over the rocky ground - I held on till my hands became powerless, and then I dropped over the side of the car in front of a large bush which broke my fall - an hour afterwards my hands remained closed, I had not power to open them. Beyond having my shoulder slightly grazed I had received no injury." (9)

He had staggered to his feet and chased the balloon for 3/4 of a mile before losing sight of it. He located it, considerably torn, the following day, near Botany Bay.

He had been in the air only twenty minutes but covered four miles. He wrote of his frightening flight to Coxwell, saying his narrow escape had scared him, "that was indeed a close shave - then I did think my hour had come." In the letter, written nearly two years after the event, Brown's perception of the flight had changed radically from that provided to the press, for he blamed Joseph Dean for trickery over the fireworks, delaying the take-off and for leaving behind the grapnel, and accused his assistant of attempted murder, with these words: "as long as I live I shall never think otherwise than that Dean intended me to be killed." (10)

Apparently, he made no such official accusation to police as no charge was laid against Dean. According to Charles Brown, Dean was rarely sober in Sydney, but he did attempt several ascents. One ended in failure with "two holes in the balloon envelope, one by an umbrella and the other by a policeman's baton." (11)

GV Brooke and Harry Edwards, the American comedian, later accompanied Joseph Dean on a frightening but farcical flight, during which the balloon struck a church spire and chimney pots in Macquarie Street and ended up with the grapnel caught in a windowsill and its occupants tipped out onto the roof. They fell into the street, the car swinging almost into a butcher's shop and Dean cut his leg badly. With malice and unfettered glee Brown wrote, "what a 'go' it would have been if they had been impaled on the butcher's hooks." The balloon was badly torn, but Brown complained that "Dean did not render any assistance either in overhauling or repairing it, all was left to me," for Dean was again drunk. (12)

In fairness to Dean it should be noted that Brown was the maker of this balloon and others, so had the requisite knowledge and expertise to work on balloons, and therefore it was reasonable to expect him to undertake any repairs.

By accusing Dean of un-cooperativeness and attempted murder, Charles Brown may have been displaying signs of paranoia, first evident in his letters to Henry Coxwell, complaining about Dean. It is difficult to judge if Brown was justifiably bitter with his past complaints and future dealings. Certainly, luck was rarely on his side and his situation improved little in his subsequent years in Australia, but then his perfunctory and righteous personality was given, not to tact and diplomacy, as much as to criticism and confrontation.

In typically defensive style, Charles Brown dashed off a letter to the *Era* newspaper, refuting a reader's claims that he was "a bungling aeronaut" and that his Sydney ascents were "more or less failures."

While in Sydney Brown wrote a pamphlet - Brown's Balloon Manual - 11 or 12 pages long. He recalled that it was "only a paltry affair and was never intended by me to be sold, but to be given away". However, GV Brooke saw an opportunity and had it printed and "is selling it at sixpence." None of the pamphlets has survived. (13)

With the only balloon in Sydney torn, the aeronauts returned to Melbourne where George Coppin refused to foot the bill saying, "he would not spend a farthing in repairs." (14)

They brought out from storage the *Tavistock* balloon to be used for the first time on 8 February 1859. Once again arguments erupted. Coppin had laid 3" gas piping in the Cremorne Gardens in their absence, although Brown had told Coppin all along that it was useless to fill a balloon with anything less than a 4" diameter pipe. Dean disagreed, stating he had done so in England. Brown countered that Dean could only have done so with a better balloon than the *Tavistock* and in cooler temperatures.

What transpired that day in the hottest part of summer - the thermometer was 120 degrees F in the shade - proved Brown's point. The *Tavistock* had "hundreds of slits in her top, and the repairs done at Woolwich were very bad." At the point of half-inflation, "the gas escaped as fast as it went in." (15)

A further attempt three days later in the cool of early morning also failed; in six hours the envelope was only half-full, so it was stowed away in favour of the repaired *Australasian*. On this occasion, as on others, Brown's wife flew with him.

The next ascent - the seventh from Cremorne - Brown and Dean made together. After towing the inflated balloon to the gardens, "there came on a storm of thunder, lightning and rain - the wind blew fearfully, but the *Australasian* weathered every blast". The determined aeronauts went up at 10 that night and flew 4 or 5 miles in 22 minutes. Brown recorded in his notebook, somewhat sadly, "there were but eight visitors to the gardens that night, so Dean and I made the ascent cheaply - for nothing." (16)

That was the last balloon ascent at the Cremorne Gardens. Its brief affair with the enchanting balloon and the fantasy of aerostation was over. In a bid to keep the Gardens financially viable, Coppin and his partner installed billiard tables; balls, exhibitions and fetes continued, and attendances briefly increased with the newly opened railway and station at Richmond.

Despite the varied program, the Gardens became a financial burden on its owners, partly due to Melbourne's fickle weather. The partnership was dissolved; of their joint property, Brooke kept the Theatre Royal as his share and Coppin received Cremorne.

During that summer of 1862 the clowns, acrobats and circus animals performed; the side shows opened as usual; the gardens, fountains, swans and statues looked as splendid as ever and the trapeze artists performed high above the ornamental lake. The last grand spectacle was a fireworks display, then the Cremorne Gardens closed forever in January 1863. For ten years they had been an integral part of Melbourne's social and cultural life; a place of amusement and entertainment for many. Cremorne had also substantially supported the community, with benefits and charity days held annually to help those in need.

Coppin put the Cremorne fittings and equipment up for auction. The buildings and gardens he sold to a Mr Harcourt who established a lunatic asylum (the only such place in the country for the next twenty one years), until it was bought in 1884 by land boom speculators and sub-divided. Streets were laid down; factories and workers' cottages sprang up; the ornamental lake was drained into the river. Today the only section of the Cremorne Gardens that remains, is a tiny melancholy park jammed against the Monash Freeway and completely cut off from any view of the Yarra River.

After that last humiliating ascent, Brown wanted to be independent of Coppin and to be freed from further engagement. He had written of an approach by an American in Sydney who offered to pay the passage of Brown and family, and an advance of £100, if they would go to California for one ascent. He was also to pay for a new balloon.

In a subsequent conversation with George Coppin on the subject, Coppin wanted to know what would happen if he was left with two balloons. Brown replied that Coppin had Dean and that one aeronaut was sufficient, particularly as the operation was not making a profit. "Dean be ----!" said Coppin. "I have no confidence in him." (17)

The American trip never eventuated, (Brown may have concocted the story to persuade Coppin to release him from his contract). Brown remained in Australia and purchased the balloons from Coppin for the stated amount; £50 of his own money, the remainder to be paid back in three months by himself and new partner William Green, who had been assisting the firework maker at Cremorne Gardens.

William Green junior was born on 7 March 1814 and adopted the profession of most of the male members of his family. For a time, he was his Uncle Charles' assistant in England. On an ascent with him and nine others in the *Nassau* balloon in July 1849 they struck a house roof and two were thrown out. The balloon rebounded then rapidly descended. Charles Green blamed his nephew for holding the valve line so tightly it opened, causing gas to escape and the balloon to elongate and crash.

In 1852 William Green had flown from Munich in Germany with cousin Charles George Green. William Green made several ascents from Leeds in his *Royal Victoria* balloon, with the renowned Italian Brothers (Edouard and Jean Bouthellier) who performed extraordinary manoeuvres beneath the car.

Once, in 1854 his balloon was only half-inflated on take off and consequently almost came to grief. Insufficient inflation seemed to be a speciality of William Green, for he repeated this in Sheffield in 1855 when the balloon, on rising, oscillated and caught in adjoining trees.

His dubious record made him a particularly poor choice for Charles Brown's new venture. Coxwell had advised Brown against a partnership with Green in November 1858, but the letter may well have arrived after they had drawn up the legal documents, in the March of the following year. The whole agreement was fraught with intrigue. Brown had previously confided in George Coppin the need for a respectable person to join him in the payment of the three month bill, but kept secret the person's identity, aware that Coppin disliked William Green. When Green's attendance was required, before Coppin would discharge Brown's contract and sign over the balloons Brown,

> "took him on dark, when I thought Coppin wouldn't recognise him. The dodge was successful - I got my agreement cancelled, handed over the money and bill, and then sent Green outside the gardens, that he might be seen as little as possible. In a few minutes Coppin discovered the trick, but it was too late: he told me that if he had known that Green had anything to do with it he would not have let the balloons go." (18)

A few days after the deception, Green and Brown left for Sydney taking the *Australasian* with them. All went well for two or three days, when Brown began to take umbrage at Green "when he began to 'blow' quite as much as my old associate (Dean) had done: he even went so far as to say that the Sydney people had never witnessed an ascent, but that they had then got a man (meaning Green) who knew how to make one." (19)

It was decided that Green should make the ascent and take a paying passenger; a young man offered £20 to Green for a flight but only paid £3. Brown's confidence in Green was strained, for he suspected Green of pocketing the difference.

It was a fine day, what little wind there was blew inland. Green ascended from Pitt Street; the balloon slowly turned in the direction of the Pacific Ocean, then rapidly dropped, reaching the ground only thirteen minutes into its flight. Brown, fearing something was amiss, raced to find the balloon had descended "on the horns of some bullocks in the yard of a public house, the Woolpack Inn, in George Street." Brown wisely decided not to venture into the yard as the balloon was close to a blacksmith's fire and he feared an explosion. All may have been well if a man sitting on the roof of a shed, after lighting his pipe, had not thrown down a lighted match. The gas caught fire, the balloon envelope swelled with the heat and rose above the house tops, "a great globe of fire." Shrieks, screams and scorching heat filled the air. People, chiefly young children with "faces horribly disfigured and their hair burnt off," ran from the yard as the helpless Brown watched. Firemen were quickly on the scene and prevented the fire spreading to the surrounding wooden houses. (20)

Police stopped the rush to the gate and thus prevented deaths. Seven people including two children were badly burnt and a nearby doctor's surgery treated several others. A crowd collected around Brown who was "known to almost everybody in Sydney." Fearful of violence from the excited mob, Brown took the advice of a friend and caught a cab to his hotel. Hours later Green arrived, "very ill, and complaining some of his ribs were broken" but he received no sympathy from his partner. (21)

The hapless Brown had now lost to fire the only usable balloon in Australia, "even William Green said the *Australasian* was as fine a balloon as he ever saw - and the Greens are notorious for praising their own and condemning others." Sympathisers organised a public subscription and raised £60, but a scoundrel fled to California with part of this; the remainder went in paying the bills they had accumulated in five weeks in Sydney. (22)

The *Australasian* had made thirteen ascents in all: seven in Melbourne and six in Sydney. Back in Melbourne, Brown swallowed his pride and took a job at Coppin's Olympic Theatre as "money-taker and box office keeper," later leaving this job to become a solicitor's clerk. About this time, he received an offer of £100 to make ascents in the prosperous gold town of Bendigo, from a Mr Joseph Field, "an intimate acquaintance of young Pritchard's (Hampton's assistant.)" When Field arrived in Melbourne to arrange matters, he encountered Green, "who presented the *Tavistock* as his own balloon." Green impressed Field unfavourably for "the party at Bendigo would have nothing more to do with either of us." It seems Joseph Field decided to attempt an ascent himself, for Brown informed Coxwell that "Field was killed at Bendigo, by falling from a great height, when fixing an 'ascension rope'. I believe he left a widow in England." (23)

Green failed three times to respond to Brown's demands for an explanation of his conduct. Brown had for some time thought he would "like to get rid of him (Green) - now I was determined to cut the connection; so I advertised in the papers that the partnership was dissolved, and sent copies of the notice to William Green and Coppin." (24)

Coppin threatened to sue Brown and Green for his unpaid £50, so Brown hastily filed a schedule in the Insolvency Court. Brown offered to assist Green through the same court (as Brown understood insolvency business) to save him expense, but Green would not listen and instead "called me vile names and threatened a good deal". He later apologised saying he was drunk at the time; nevertheless, it cost Green £19 in court fees and Brown only £3. (25)

Brown, writing of his legal troubles to Coxwell, mentioned that Green had borrowed money from his boarder, Joseph Dean, and had not repaid it. He also told Coxwell that Dean had missed his footing when stepping down from the mail coach and had broken his leg. He spent time in hospital where, surprisingly, Brown visited him, noting that "he is quite a changed man in his disposition towards me, and I believe he is sincere!" Dean had even offered to labour with a balloon for Brown, "for his victuals." (26)

Brown had to surrender the refurbished *Tavistock* as part of the insolvency action and it was offered to Coppin, who said he would buy it back if Brown would consent to make four ascents. Determined to recommence ballooning, Brown proposed making four ascents for £10 each and to make a new balloon to be called *Brown's Balloon*, which was to remain his property. Ever the businessman, Coppin refused to pay more than £5 an ascent; Brown declined, and Green offered to make ascents for £2 each.

At this stage, Brown determined to take steps to prevent the *Tavistock* falling into Coppin or Green's possession. He intended to put in a higher bid for the balloon, "make one ascent with it at the opening of some new gasworks here in February (1861), and then destroy it, preserving the net which I believe is in good condition." Vindictively he wrote, "I will prevent the celebrated aeronaut (the 'veteran Green' as he calls himself here), making another ascent this side (of) the globe." (27)

No doubt Brown wished he had heeded Coxwell's advice, "which warned you against partnerships, which are the worst ships you can sail in," and had steered clear of Green. (28)

Brown's bid for the *Tavistock* was successful; he stated later that he had torn it up. Ever seeking to make further ascents, Brown wrote to newspapers in Launceston and Hobart Town trying to attract public subscriptions to ascend there, but his overtures proved fruitless; nor did the offers Brown says he received to balloon in China, Java or India eventuate.

Stoically, Brown set about making a new balloon of silk and linen for a Mr JF Johnston, entrepreneur. This balloon was the first constructed and the first painted balloon in Australia. Brown agreed to build it for nought except the sole use of the balloon and half the profits. Unbelievably and foolishly, he had no written agreement with Johnston, the senior pyrotechnician and caterer at Cremorne, who reneged on the deal. When he threatened to give the construction to Joseph Dean, Brown scoffed, "Dean knows nothing of balloon-making," so the task remained his. (29)

In a letter to *The Age*, Brown described the balloon: "on one side of it is a medallion portrait of Her Majesty Queen Victoria and on the opposite side the Australian Arms, (the Emu and Kangaroo)." Johnston commissioned this balloon specifically for Australia's inaugural international cricket match, played in Melbourne, between the distinguished English Eleven team and a Victorian side gathered from city and country cricket clubs. Johnston, as the proprietor of the match, named the new Brown-built balloon *The All England Eleven*.

After a journey of 64 days on the *SS Great Britain*, the visitors arrived for their initial match at the Melbourne Cricket Ground (MCG) on 4 January 1862. At the end of the game with the local team outclassed, the new balloon named in honour of the touring side, made its debut in the presence of the Governor, Sir Henry and Lady Barkly and 25 000 spectators. (30)

Dean helped with the inflation that day,

"I detected him tying the springs down the wrong way, but do not think he did it intentionally - had they remained so, the inflation of the balloon would have been an impossibility - the valve would have remained open, and the loss of gas would have been equal to the supply. The thermometer was 131° F - the burning sun parched up the varnish, and the loss of gas was enormous." So much so that the balloon raised six people initially but an hour later only three. The governor, according to Brown, "said it was the most beautiful ascent he ever witnessed." (31)

In the basket that historic day were Mr and Mrs Brown. As it rose higher, they noted "fifty or more bushfires in the east." They came down in Albert Street, allowing Brown and his wife to walk the short distance to their home. Brown was paid £10 from the £40 Johnston received. Although unaware of it at the time, this was Charles Brown's last flight. (32)

Mr Johnston wanted Brown to make more flights, for £10 each but Brown, for reasons unknown, had decided against ascending for him again. Johnston wished to take the new balloon to Calcutta in 1862 but Brown steadfastly refused to take on any engagements under £20, effectively pricing himself out of further work. It is feasible that his wife, again pregnant, may have argued against her husband giving up steady work as a lawyer's clerk, to travel to a foreign country to make a precarious living out of a few ascents.

Whatever the reason, Johnston engaged Dean to accompany him to India, but first took Dean and the balloon to Ballarat, 80 miles from Melbourne, to appear before the residents of this gold mining town (known as "the rich and respectable man's diggings"), at a gala event at the Copenhagen Gardens, a European styled pleasure park. Dean was paid only £5 an ascent. (33)

The event was to be managed by "the veteran Aeronaut Professor J. Dean." Filled with 25 000 cubic feet of gas at the local gas works, the balloon was to be conveyed fully inflated to the gardens for an ascent at 7 pm. The doors opened at 6 pm and the townsfolk and farmers danced to polkas and watched the fireworks display but were ultimately deprived of the magnificent sight of a balloon rising into the evening sky. At the earlier inflation, two of the workmen were laid out from inhaling the gas and the balloon would not float. Dean cut away the basket and "proposed to convey it via Dana Street to avoid telegraph wires, but before they ascended the hill near the Church of England, the balloon fell to the ground and was injured by the quartz stones." (34)

Dean placed the blame squarely on the Ballarat Gas Company, stating that the gas was too heavy to lift the balloon, which had previously risen and floated at the Melbourne Cricket Ground with passengers, sandbags and less gas. Threats of legal action flew through the air; the engineer asserting that the balloon leaked, which Dean denied.

According to Charles Brown, Joseph Dean had proved again to be "remarkably ignorant for a man of his age" and should have been aware that the Ballarat gas was too heavy as it was made from cannel coal which is "nearly as heavy as atmospheric air". Brown wrote of Dean,

> "laid prostrate through inhaling the gas. He has had several narrow escapes through inhaling the gas - twice at Sydney, when the supply of gas was not so quick as we wished, did he disconnect the balloon from the gas-pipe, put his nose into the pipe, and sniff, to ascertain whether it contained gas - on both occasions I thought he would have died - the public, looking on, thought him intoxicated." (35)

Ascents Dean was scheduled to make at the gold towns of Sandhurst (now Bendigo) and Castlemaine were consequently abandoned. Although Johnston, packing to leave for India, had paid no money to Brown for the construction of the balloon, the ever-willing - or guileless - aeronaut gave him "written instructions in balloon management (as I had promised)." In August 1862 Johnston left, "intending to make ascents himself. I advised him to take Dean as an assistant, which he did, but regretted afterwards." (36)

Calcutta was the city of choice as it was the only place in India using gas for lighting. The *All England Eleven* balloon became the first Australian-made balloon to fly in another country. It was renamed the *Victoria*, either for the reigning British monarch, or for the colony of its origin in Australia. As Johnston became too ill to fly, Dean made India's first flight from Calcutta's Eden Gardens which Johnston owned.

Advertisements in India declared Dean as "the First Veteran Aerial Navigator of the Antipodes, formerly Assistant to the great Green and Coxwell of London." The Oriental Gas Company filled the balloon for its flight. The drawcard was Madame Marian, "the intrepid lady aeronaut" and the first British woman to ascend in India. 'Madame Marian' could hardly be hailed as an aeronaut, for this was her first ascent as far as I could ascertain. In fact, the intrepid lady was J Johnston's wife. (37)

She accompanied Joseph Dean on that "fine and calm" Boxing Day in 1862. An immense crowd of spectators was dissatisfied at the flight's duration of a mere ten minutes. *The Age* in Melbourne reported that the "lower order of natives" did not pay to enter the select circle to watch the inflation, but stood on rooftops to glimpse the balloon, whereas the newspaper was glad "to find that the superior class mustered inside in large numbers." (38)

According to Johnston, Dean was "shaking like an old woman" and "was white in the face, and as nervous as possible." He told Brown with annoyance of Dean's 600 - 700 yard flight and ended his letter on a disgusted note, "so much for the drunken, filthy hog this time." Johnston thus confirmed the opinion held of Joseph Dean by both Henry Coxwell and George Coppin. "Mr Joe Dean has turned out one of the most shameful drunken pigs you ever heard tell of...every week since he has been here he has overdrawn his wages and spent every shilling in drink with all the filthy old soldiers and sailors he can pick up in Calcutta." (39)

Not only was the first ascent at the Eden Gardens a pecuniary loss, so was the second, when Dean took up several locals for 5 rupees each, to gain a panoramic view of Calcutta.

*The Bengal Nurkaru* newspaper of 6 March begged the public to pay and go inside the gates of the grounds: only one in five were doing so. Cuttings detailing the financial losses are pasted in Brown's scrapbook and across them, scrawled in Brown's handwriting, are his bitter comments, "so much for Mr Dean's pluck," and "But you will see that some of these observations is (sic) not very creditable to Dean's management." (40)

Two balloon ascents took place over Calcutta before Johnston discharged Dean as being "nothing more than an assistant labourer to an aeronaut." Greatly assisted by the instructions Brown had given him before leaving Australia, Johnston flew the balloon himself, as did his wife, 'Madame Marian'. One flight had crossed the Ganges and settled in the small village of Gooserie, where the alarmed inhabitants ran in all directions. (41)

Dean stayed in Calcutta for a time - he was hospitalised for weeks, after being kicked in the abdomen by a horse. Never one to let an opportunity pass, Brown wrote, "he was intoxicated, went to lay down in a stable, and was then kicked." (42)

Dean returned to Australia and again went to Ballarat, aware that the inland cities were still prosperous, due to increased wool production, agriculture and population; gold having declined in value.

The unprofessional Dean's 1863 attempt to ascend there failed and he subsequently disappeared without trace. Perhaps he retired to the nearby town of Maldon - also built in the goldrush days - for 1864 records list a J Dean, as a general storekeeper in Main Street. Maldon played an interesting role in my research for this book. It led me a merry dance in my choreography of ballooning dates and records.

For many months I chased records of a balloon flight, said to have taken place in Maldon in 1857, that is, pre-dating Joseph Dean's Richmond ascent in February 1858, accepted as being Australia's first ascent and flight.

Information on the earlier Maldon flight came from newspapers which reported that in October 1976, members of the Pegasus Balloon Group flew during Maldon's Spring Festival, to commemorate a flight from that town in the year 1857. The *Castlemaine Mail* had earlier reported the 1976 balloon flight was "to celebrate what is thought to have been the first balloon flight in Victoria in 1862." The same paper wrote that the modern-day balloonists ascended from the Maldon oval, as "Derby Hill (near Main Street), the original take-off site, was thought to be too rough for the delicate nylon fabric of the balloon." (43)

I turned to a copy of the *Bendigo Advertiser* hoping to discover the original aeronaut's identity. I was startled to read, "In 1857, a balloon flight, believed to be the first in Victoria, was made from the Penny School at Maldon to mark its opening." (44)

The five year discrepancy in those dates was of vital importance to this book, so I began sifting through piles of old newspapers and local histories in search of the truth.

An ex-member of the Pegasus syndicate informed me that the original flight had travelled a distance of 4 or 5 miles and ended in Clunes, where a monument existed with the date and names on it relevant to the flight. I haunted local historians for knowledge of such a monument but found none: a visit to Clunes shed no light on the matter either. The book I had been referred to for photographs of the Clunes monument and its inscription proved to be non-existent.

Was it still possible that a balloon ascent could have celebrated the opening of the school in 1857, or its re-opening in 1862, four years after Dean's first Australian aerial voyage?

I turned to the history of Maldon and Clunes in general and to that of the Penny School specifically (so named because students paid a penny a day for lessons). The Maldon Penny (Denominational) School was a brick and wooden building on the corner of Camp and Church Streets, renowned for its bell tower. Building commenced in 1856 and about one hundred people were present at its official opening on 16 February 1857, this being the first permanent school to be located on the Maldon goldfields. Reports in the newspaper of the day - the *Mount Alexander Mail* - did not mention a balloon ascent. (45)

It is possible that a balloon ascent was planned for the official opening of the school. Local historian, Frances Gray says that the Church of England ran out of money when building the school - which doubled as a church - so a generous citizen put up £100 of his own money to complete it. She doubts there would have been any money to spare for a balloon ascent.

The town of Maldon underwent a population explosion after the gold rush of 1851; men worked not only as prospectors, but as wheelwrights, coach builders and blacksmiths. The building of brickyards, foundries, butter and cordial factories, engineering works and a flour mill quickly followed. Maldon even had a public amusement park, Spencer's Cremorne Gardens but there was no mention of a gas works. Author Patsy Adam-Smith, in an article entitled "Maldon - A Museum Piece", mentioned a proposal in 1859 to light the streets with kerosene lamps. From this I have deduced there was no gas available in Maldon in 1857 to inflate the balloon that was said to have flown from Maldon to Clunes. (46)

As there were no roads in the area in 1857, it would have been difficult and costly to transport a balloon on a bullock wagon from Ballarat or Geelong. No gasworks existed in nearby Clunes in 1857, but by the time of the second date given for the balloon flight - September 1862 - the Clunes Gas Company had commenced operation.

On 18 December in 1861 the school had blown down in a huge storm, leaving it partially demolished. The second school building was formally opened in September 1862. *The Tarrengower Times* reported the event but made no reference to a balloon ascent.

I concluded that no manned balloon made an ascent in Maldon in 1857, but that it was feasible one had in 1862, inflated by Clunes gas and transported to Maldon for the re-opening of the Penny School. Joseph Dean was in the goldfields area in 1862, but Charles Brown himself had stated that the Melbourne 1858 flight with the *Australasian* was, "the only balloon which had ascended with an aeronaut in the Australian colonies." The phrase, 'with an aeronaut' suggested to me that balloons, made from paper or cloth and filled with smoke or hot air from a fire, *may* have been sent aloft unmanned, above the goldfields. (47)

I then discovered newspaper reports of specific balloon ascents in the gold town of Bendigo. The releasing of "a very pretty balloon" took place at a picnic at Emu Creek in 1858; it was "about 10' high, manufactured by Hogg, (and) ascended in most admirable style." (48)

An advertisement appeared on New Years' Day, "a balloon similar to that which was launched...on Thursday last, with such success, will ascend...at 4 o'clock this afternoon. The balloon is about 20' in height, and manufactured by Mr Hogg, the pioneer of Sandhurst ballooning." (49)

Perhaps this planned ascent was an early advertising gimmick associated with the plethora of candidates jostling for positions at the Sandhurst municipal elections being held at the time. The height of these small balloons - just 10 and 20 feet - were unsuitable for carrying a person aloft. It is likely that Mr Hogg - unknown in aeronautic circles - made them from paper or cloth, filled them with hot air from a fire, and let them go to fly solo over the goldfields, purely as a novelty for public amusement.

If indeed, a manned balloon *did* fly from Maldon to Clunes, it could have been piloted by Joseph Dean, who had a balloon in the general area earlier that year and may have returned on request to the goldfields before leaving for India.

Then again, it may have been flown by a colourful local identity, Jonathan Moon, described as "a versatile and rather tragic ex-merchant, traveller, balloonist, artist, photographer, reporter and manufacturer's agent." Moon, a wealthy West Indian merchant, had made balloon ascents "with Green and other prominent balloonists." (50)

He preferred adventuring to attending to business in England, which failed, so travelled to Australia in 1852 in search of a second fortune, leaving behind a wife and son. Jonathan Moon worked as an entertainer in

Sydney and lectured on his aerial flights and travels. He tried life as a miner on the Victorian goldfields, both in Castlemaine and in Maldon, where he was settled by 1858. The educated Mr Moon became a jack-of-all-trades. He delivered lectures at Maldon (then Tarrengower), was appointed town librarian, wrote a local guide and business directory, reported for *The Tarrengower Times* and opened a photographic studio.

His chance discovery in a London newspaper that his wife had divorced him and remarried, led to an exacerbation of a chronic lung ailment and he died, aged 52 and impoverished, in Maldon Hospital. Although there is no definite proof of his being engaged in ballooning activities in the goldfields, nevertheless he appears to have had the knowledge and experience to do so, thus it must remain a possibility. (51)

(1)   *Sydney Morning Herald*, 14 December 1858.
(2)   Brown to William Green, 16 December 1858.
(3)   Ibid.
(4)   Ibid.
(5)   *Era*, 14 January 1857.
(6)   Ibid.
(7)   *Sydney Morning Herald*, 18 January 1859.
(8)   Ibid.
(9)   Ibid.
(10)  Brown to Coxwell, 24 November 1860.
(11)  Ibid.
(12)  Ibid.
(13)  Ibid.
(14)  Brown to William Green, 16 December 1858.
(15)  Ibid.
(16)  Brown to Coxwell, 24 November 1860.
(17)  Ibid.
(18)  Ibid.
(19)  Ibid.
(20)  Ibid.
(21)  Ibid.
(22)  Ibid.
(23)  Ibid.
(24)  Brown, Aeronautica.
(25)  Brown to Coxwell, 24 November 1860.
(26)  Ibid.
(27)  Ibid.
(28)  Coxwell to Brown, 25 March 1860.
(29)  Brown to Johnston, 21 December 1861.
(30)  This event was commemorated 126 years later when *The Age* journalist, Keith Dunstan went up in a balloon from the MCG.
(31)  Brown to MacSweeney, 24 October 1863.
(32)  Ibid.
(33)  *Ballarat Star*, 6 March 1862.

(34) Ibid.
(35) Brown to MacSweeney, 24 October 1863.
(36) Ibid.
(37) Ibid.
(38) *The Age*, 26 February 1863.
(39) Calcutta, Johnston to Brown, 8 January 1863.
(40) Brown, Aeronautica.
(41) Johnston to Brown, 8 January 1863.
(42) Brown, Aeronautica.
(43) *Castlemaine Mail*, 6 October 1976.
(44) *Bendigo Advertiser*, 18 September 1976.
(45) Information from The National Trust of Australia.
(46) *Walkabout* V35 (2) February.
(47) Brown, Notebook.
(48) *Bendigo Mercury*, 30 December 1858.
(49) Op cit 1 January 1859.
(50) Miles Lewis, *The Essential Maldon*.
(51) Ibid.

# Regrets, Death of Brown

*"There was no leaf in motion,*
*The loud winds slept,*
*and all was still."*
Chester Courant, 1858.

Charles Brown was leading a sedentary life with his family in Melbourne, not much to his liking. His chronicling of the aeronautic happenings of others only served to make him reflect on his life; to become resentful and dissatisfied. Brown's complaints reveal him in a somewhat pathetic light, as a sad and lonely man, either the victim of circumstances or of his own misdoings. In a self-pitying tone he wrote, "my leaving England has deprived me almost entirely of aeronautic correspondents" and although, "there is another aeronaut here, I might just as well be alone. I allude to William Green, who only speaks of balloons as an amusement...Even Mr Coxwell who was in the habit of writing to me once or twice weekly, has addressed but four or five letters to me since I left England." (1)

In a further rambling letter, Brown dredged up all the old grievances, against the Leeds aeronaut Russum, who had warned him off ballooning as too dangerous, and against John Hampton, who had told Brown his crippled arms would prevent him becoming an aeronaut. "I have made more ascents than Russum without ever striking a building. I did not break my arm on my first ascent, as Hampton did, nor have I ever fallen in water as he did on his second and fourth ascents, though nearly all my ascents have been made from seaports." (2)

Coxwell must have tired of Brown's litany of grumbles and betrayals and was "afflicted with the old chronic complaint, dislike of letter writing", for he responded no more to Brown's correspondence. (3)

Brown also opined on aeronautic safety: "A balloon under the sole management of an intelligent person is quite as safe as any other vehicle. Many of the accidents that have occurred have arisen from the use of intoxicating liquors: I always, on a balloon day, abstain totally." There followed more self gratification, "though a very nervous man myself I have frequently been surprised at my coolness in 'ticklish affairs balloonatic!'" (4)

The zealous Brown - an expatriate more by mismanagement than design - never saw his mother or brother again, but stayed on in Melbourne industriously providing for his wife Eliza and their seven children. He continued to work as a solicitor's clerk, isolated from the ballooning fraternity and reliant on his brother, now a merchant in Yorkshire, and a regular correspondent, "...who sends me the newspaper paragraphs relating to aeronautics, which come under his notice, and but for him I should know little of what is going on in Europe - he is greatly opposed to ballooning, and has frequently said he hoped he should hear no more of my doings in that line." (5)

Edwin had never been much "interested in the subject" of ballooning, although he had a "taste" of it one night with Coxwell. It had been Edwin who had written after the Sydney accident, concerned for his brother. "I do sincerely hope that thou wilt give up the idea of obtaining a livelihood by aerostation, and settle down in some other employment, as it would have been a sad affair for the family if thou had lost thy life in the late affair." (6)

It was to Edwin now that Charles Brown turned; a disappointed, bitter man; his letter is tinged with regret, even jealousy,

"Every time I see an account of a fresh ascent being made in England, or elsewhere, it makes me long to be 'up and doing' - Coxwell's success is rather annoying to me - not that I am sorry to hear of his success - on the contrary I am delighted: but I think I acted very foolishly in coming out here, to a field too limited for remunerative ballooning. I think if I had remained in England I should have done well - much better than I do here." (7)

It is likely had Brown remained in England, he may have shared some of the scientific successes he craved, and that his mentor Henry Coxwell enjoyed. Partly due to Coxwell's constant harping on the subject of science in aerostation, the British Association for the Advancement of Science (BAAS) was born. In 1859, a year after Brown and Dean's first ascents in the Australian colonies, it initiated a program of scientific and meteorological observations to be made from balloons at high altitudes. The Association nominated Henry Coxwell as pilot and James Glaisher FRS, an eminent astronomer and meteorologist, as scientist.

Glaisher was Superintendent of the Meteorological Department of the Royal Observatory at Greenwich and a member of the Balloon Committee of BAAS, when chosen for his new scientific post. As a team, Coxwell and Glaisher made their first ascent in the summer of 1862, and their 27th and last ascent in mid-winter of 1866. During these four years, they studied the atmosphere and physical properties of clouds (even measuring the size of raindrops at different elevations) and created the first world altitude record - 37 000 feet (7½ miles).

James Glaisher proved to be a thorough researcher: he took aloft cameras and scientific instruments to measure air temperature, moisture and oxygen content; magnetic vibrations, electricity in the air, types and density of clouds, and wind direction and velocity. On these trips Glaisher made many important discoveries: that air temperature drops with increasing altitude; that upper currents of wind move more rapidly than lower and in different directions, and that lower atmosphere is denser than the thinner stratosphere.

On one memorable high altitude flight in 1862, Glaisher became insensible with hypoxia, but Coxwell - although also affected by lack of oxygen - with hands black and frozen, was able to open the gas valve with his teeth and bring the balloon safely back to earth.

Coxwell and Glaisher initiated the releasing of pilot balloons prior to an ascent, to ascertain the strength and direction of air currents: a practice still used by modern aeronauts. This great team pushed beyond the boundaries of known science. More than that, they renewed public interest and enthusiasm in atmospheric science.

Coxwell had two other areas of interest in the practicability of balloons. He considered captive balloons would be of great value to exploring parties in reconnoitering and was first to demonstrate the war balloon to the English public. The distinguished Coxwell was hailed by the press as the 'Columbus of the Skies' and even called 'Admiral' Coxwell. (8)

Little wonder then, that Charles Brown, reading of such doings, had pangs of regret and jealousy. To make matters worse for Brown, a hotel but a few yards from his home had hung a portrait of Coxwell ascending from the Crystal Palace in his *Mammoth* balloon. Australian newspapers devoted more space to overseas events such as Glaisher's experiments, Coxwell's military balloon and to the Aeronautical Society of Great Britain, than to local ascents.

York was the scene of Coxwell's last public ascent, in 1885, chosen because he had ascended in this town for 28 consecutive years. He died at home just five years later, aged 81. James Glaisher - born ten years before

Coxwell - survived him for 3 years, and died at the grand age of 94, in 1903, just as the era of aerostation ended and aviation history began.

Charles Brown's own days as an aeronaut were over, although of this he was unaware as he pursued every opening. He told his brother of a party who wanted to take him to China, Java and India - "the thing is not yet decided." (9)

Brown ended his poignant letter to brother Edwin in England - the last copied into his notebook - by penning,

"Sometimes I think I will make an effort to get back, just for one summer; but the expense of the voyage and having to provide for my family during my absence I cannot manage. If I were single I would be with you very soon. I should have no desire to leave here at all if I could only make an ascent occasionally, for I like Australia very well - the climate of Victoria just suits me. Thy affectionate brother
Chas. Hy Brown." (10)

It was from Brown's last letter to his brother, dated January 1864, that I began to search public records for his death. I felt certain he had remained in Australia for in the State Library in Melbourne was his book Aeronautica, the handwritten, word-for-word account of letters Brown had sent and received. The bound book had been donated to the library in 1939, but by someone with a different surname.

In their files was a letter from a V Brown, published in *The Age* on 8 October 1932, answering queries about Australia's first balloonist, whom he identified as his father. (I later established the writer as Vincent Brown, the son born to Charles and Eliza in 1860, their first Australian child, and 72 years old at the time of his writing.)

I determined to find Charles Brown's descendants; with a common surname like Brown, I realised it would be quite a task. At times I got close, only to find barriers. One family had moved from their recorded address; the new owner spoke little English and knew nothing of the family. Neighbours gave vague clues that "they went to Queensland in a caravan," or "they live somewhere in Reservoir."

After much perseverance, and help from door-knocking friends, I finally traced them. The Brown family proudly showed me the treasure trove that once belonged to their ancestor: his huge scrapbook of handbills, calling cards and newspaper cuttings in several languages, dating back to those printed in 1783, informing people of the aeronautic achievements of the Montgolfier Brothers. There was another book in Brown's handwriting: a history of major ballooning events around the world, his photograph (the original long lost) from a 1970s newspaper article on Charles Henry Brown and his descendants.

Paul Brown, Charles' great, great, great grandson and other family members thought Charles Brown had died in the Yarra River around 1870. They could give me no further details.

I was surprised that six years had elapsed between Brown's last recorded letter and his death. He must have been disheartened at the absence of further opportunities, for he neither wrote to his aeronautic compatriots, nor recorded ascents overseas, unless such records have not survived. It is also likely that Brown's widow - surely left in poor circumstances after her husband's death - sold some of his collection, including his handwritten books.

At Melbourne's Public Record Office, I checked files on 1870 inquests. When I came across records of three Charles Henry Browns who had drowned in Victoria that year, I thought it would be almost impossible to ascertain which was the aeronaut. For, until I saw his death certificate, all I knew of Charles Brown, was that he was from England, had a brother Edwin and was married: at that stage I did not know his wife's name or if he had children.

I need not have worried; one file I discarded immediately, for he had drowned in country Victoria. The other two had both drowned in the Yarra, but as I read through the lists of their personal belongings, I knew which was my man, for the policeman who discovered the body came across a "piece of wood produced with the name of Brown engraved in a balloon." (11)

A carpenter, James Brown (no relation) had been fishing in the Yarra River at Richmond on the evening of Tuesday 18 January 1870. He became the last person to see the 44 year old alive. It was about 9 or 9.30 pm that a light breeze blew and the temperature (at 4pm) was 97 degrees, perfect for bathing in the river, as many were. James Brown heard a splash, ten yards upstream and saw a man in the water who sang out, "I say Sam", then floated under the iron railway bridge and sank. James walked upstream and found a hat containing a pipe, pencil, tobacco and quill, "placed apparently so as to attract attention on top of a rail." The carpenter alerted the police station to his find. (12)

Three days later, Constable Titus Nelson discovered the body of Charles Brown floating in the middle of the river, "dressed in respectable clothes." There were no signs of violence and he determined the body had been in the water 3-4 days. It was he who discovered the wooden balloon engraving in his pocket. (13)

The aeronaut's widow, Eliza Brown, identified her husband's body. In her statement to the coroner, she said she had last seen him between 8 and 9 on,

> "Monday morning last the 18th instant (She meant Tuesday the 18th) at his own house," given as 193 Carlton Street, Carlton. She revealed that "he was not well - the result I think of too much drink. He was occasionally of intemperate habits. He was very low and dispirited after drinking. I saw no more of him alive but I traced him to some public house up to 6 o'clock that evening. He had no money with him." (14)

It was a melancholy end for the virtuous Brown, who had always spurned drunkards. He had continued in his mundane job as a solicitor's clerk, gradually despairing of ever ballooning again and thus, apparently, took to drinking in excess, ironically the same habit for which he had so often castigated his rival, Joseph Dean. Ironic too, that just twelve years after arriving in the colony of Victoria with his head full of aeronautic dreams, Brown's body was found floating in the Yarra River, not far from the scene of his greatest disappointment, the Cremorne Gardens.

It was unclear whether Brown's death was suicide or an accident. Doctor George Graham who conducted a post-mortem, conservatively stated, "death was caused by syncopal asphyxia from drowning, I believe." (15)

The Irish journalist Edmund Finn - better known as 'Garryowen' - was a supporter of the theory that it was easy to become a victim of drowning in the Yarra River. He wrote,

> "I was an expert swimmer, and, one hot summer day, jumped into the Yarra in the vicinity of the now Punt Road ferry. The River was deep, and down I went, but was astonished to find that my ascent to the surface was impeded by a kind of suction drawing me downward, and it required all the muscular power in my body to get up again...Several instances have occurred where some of the best white swimmers in the colony suddenly and unaccountably lost their lives in this river." (16)

As was the custom at inquests, a jury of twelve men sat before the coroner, Samuel Curtis Candler, on 24 January. They could not decide whether Charles Brown had committed suicide or drowned accidentally and presented an open finding to the Chief Commissioner of Police, who thought the death was "either a case of accident or suicide. I think the later the more probable alternative." Despite his remarks, Charles Brown's death certificate kindly gave the cause of death as "accidentally drowned" on 18 January 1870. (17)

A perfunctory report of the inquest appeared in the Age on Tuesday 25 January 1870: no mention was made of his having been a pioneer aeronaut in Australia. Just eight years since his last flight, Brown had already been forgotten. The burial took place in the Church of England section of the Melbourne General Cemetery in Carlton, the plot being already occupied by his son Frederick who died in childhood. Subsequently, Brown's wife Eliza and another child Eugene were buried in the same grave.

When I unearthed Charles Henry Brown's grave it was a forlorn, weed covered mound, unmarked except for a number, 327. He was overlooked in death, as he was in life. (18)

Although the year 1870 found Victoria "rich in all the elements of property" with provisions cheap and the harvest abundant, it must have been a time of struggle for the new widow and her children, Annie 21, Eugene 16 (born in England) and the Australian born Vincent 10, Miriam 7 and Walter 4. (19)

With Charles Henry Brown, the observer and experimenter of aerostation as science, died the brief age of the serious aeronaut in Australia.

It was to be almost a decade between the last successful flight, (the MCG ascent of Brown's in 1862) and that of Tom Gale in 1870. In between, the aerial showmen had been born and nurtured: and the unknown writer of the following prophecy, was proved correct,

*"Although born by the spirits of public*
*interest and adventure, the balloons' future*
*lay in entertainment."*

(1)   Brown to MacSweeney, 24 October 1863.
(2)   Coxwell to Brown, 1 November 1858.
(3)   Op cit, 24 October 1863.
(4)   Ibid.
(5)   Ibid.
(6)   Edwin Brown to Charles Brown, 10 August 1859.
(7)   Charles Brown to Edwin Brown, 25 January 1864.
(8)   *The Times*, London, 6 July 1865.
(9)   Charles Brown to Edwin Brown, 25 January 1864.
(10) Ibid.
(11) Sworn statement at Coroner's Inquest, 24 January 1870.
(12) Coroner's Inquest papers.
(13) Ibid.
(14) Ibid.
(15) Ibid.
(16) Margaret Weidenhoff, Ed, *Garryowen's Melbourne* 1835-1852.
(17) Genealogical Society of Victoria, *The Genealogist* June 1989.

(18) On 22 May 1994, descendants and members of the Australian Balloon Federation, the Balloon Association of Victoria and the Aviation Society of Australia, gathered at Charles Henry Brown's graveside, to hold a Commemorative Service that finally acknowledged his achievements. A plaque to his memory was unveiled and gratitude expressed that he had made that long journey to our shores and pioneered ballooning in this country.

(19) TW Leavitt, *History of Victoria and Melbourne* Vol II.

# PART TWO

# THE SHOW GOES ON

# Touring Australia by Balloon

The early aeronauts in Australia - Charles Brown, Joseph Dean and, to a lesser extent, William Green - had experienced the hazards and tribulations that beset most pioneers. They overcame public opposition in various ways but failed to influence people to take aerostation seriously.

Australians perceived balloons as a source of amusement. They surmised that, because early colonial flights did not 'go' anywhere specific, then obviously aeronauts were mere thrill seekers, fascinated with being airborne and at the mercy of the winds. Despite Brown's efforts to promote aerostation as a science, Australian ballooning, from 1870 onwards, was to be exploited both by showmen for the applause and by promoters for remuneration, who inadvertently discredited serious aeronautic endeavours.

The 'up and down' method of ballooning complementary to an exhibition or fete was to be popular for many future decades. Perhaps it was as well Brown was dead, for he would have found abhorrent the level to which the balloon was doomed to sink for the next 42 years. The pioneer Australian aeronaut had ignored the evidence that aerostation really did have nowhere to go, except in the direction of giving pleasure.

In the 87 years between the official launch of the manned balloon and Brown's death, there had been few advances in aeronautics. The balloon still could not be directed or steered from one point to another but was totally reliant on the prevailing wind.

A feature of the remaining three decades of nineteenth century ballooning in Australia was the large number of ascents by professional showmen for their gratification, who arrived from other shores to tour the country in a clockwise direction and exit via Asia, hopefully with pockets sagging under the weight of their lucrative earnings.

Balloonists were not alone in travelling this route, for it was a defined circuit followed by other entertainers: actors, musicians, circus performers and the like. The route could never be described as well-worn or the going easy, for the remote roads were tiresome lengthy dirt tracks, often winding through punishing country. To be a traveller with a show in those days was to be absent from home and family (in America, Europe or England) for years and to live in rough conditions with few comforts.

The isolated communities along the route turned out in their entirety to witness the latest spectacle or entertainment. Their welcome and hospitality was immense and all-encompassing - they vied with each other to offer the entertainer a comfortable bed and then plied them with food and drink, questions and conversation.

Unwittingly, the pattern of Australia's cultural life was being set, whereby entertainers from overseas were deemed worthier of esteem than the home product. Australia's so-called 'cultural cringe' conceivably arose from such innocent beginnings, yet the term and its effects have proved impossible to shake off. As early as 1859, Brown's Notebook had complained about "the prejudice which exists...against aught of colonial origin." (1)

The scene was now set for the arrival in the colonies of Thomas Gale, who proved to be a link between one era of aerostation and the next, for he just pre-empted the showbusiness era of Australian aerostation. He was one of nine children born to professional aeronaut, lecturer and actor, Lieutenant George Bercher Gale of the British Royal Navy, and his wife (who John Hampton had criticised for going aloft on many occasions.) George Gale and Charles Brown were friends in England, and it was to Gale senior that Brown, years earlier, had written offering to supply balloons to the Admiralty, but the venture had fallen through.

Tom Gale appeared in the colonies barely two months prior to Brown's demise. Sir Joseph Banks' Gardens and Hotel in Botany was the setting for Tom's first ascent on Boxing Day 1869. Inexperienced ground handlers caused the balloon to be holed, and Gale to be ejected from the basket. Disgruntled by what it construed as a hoax the crowd jeered the young aeronaut. No one was more disappointed than Gale himself who, to prove his bona fides, announced his intention to ascend from Sydney's Domain on 5 January 1870, without charge.

Employers had declared a half day holiday, in order that they and their workers might view the novelty. The general air was of festivity, "The Domain presented the appearance of a great fair. A merry-go-round was erected...and fruit stalls and carts were stationed (all over)." (2)

Inflation was very slow, due to the gas pipe being too small for the purpose. By 4 o'clock the balloon was only half inflated, but Gale decided ascent was possible; climbed into the basket only to find his weight caused the balloon to settle and refuse to lift. To prevent further disappointment for the 20 000 onlookers, "he speedily decided on his course of action - (he) detached the car, grapnel and ballast, tied the ends of the netting together, seated himself thereon, and gave the signal to let go. The balloon at once rose above the trees, and its solitary occupant raising himself on the hoop, took his position on it." (3)

After barely missing contact with the Sydney Mint and nearly striking a steeple, Gale drifted over the city on a light breeze towards Glebe Point, where he began to descend in a garden, but became entangled in a mulberry tree and was stained by the fruit. Finally, he descended in the University paddocks at Pyrmont. He "touched a fence, to which Mr Gale held on with one hand while he opened the valve with the other." With the aid of onlookers, Gale secured the balloon on the road where it had rolled, until it emptied. Gale's remarkable flight, on such a precarious perch, made only of twine, was hailed as the most daring witnessed in the colonies. (4)

Almost a year later, on 7 January 1871, Gale made his second Sydney ascent with passenger John Allen. In the interim Gale had supervised the construction of his new balloon, the *Young Australian*, easily the largest in Australia, being 72' high and 112' in circumference. Built at his personal cost, its 32 000 cubic feet of gas gave a lifting power equal to half a ton. Three thousand people assembled at Victoria Park. Very few paid at the gate, preferring to scramble over neighbouring fences. After a rapid 1½ hour inflation, the balloon "released from its bonds, rose rapidly into the air, and took a north-westerly direction." (5)

As it soared to an amazing altitude of 2½ miles over Sydney University, Five Dock, then Cockatoo Island, the balloon and occupant were lost to sight in cloud. Having remained two hours in the air, Gale made his descent. Fearing his aerial ship might catch in trees, Gale "preferred lowering it into Delange's Bay, in the Parramatta River, between Kissing Point and Tarban Creek," where it stuck fast in the mud. Fortunately, nearby fishermen helped him out of his predicament, and he was able to pack up and return to Sydney - somewhat mud bespattered - by dusk. (6)

The editor of the *Illustrated Sydney News* was so inspired by the event that he wrote eloquently of man's ongoing attempts to conquer the subtle element of air by wielding, "his sceptre as monarch of the air." (7)

Six months later, during the winter of 1871, Gale appeared in Adelaide, a city less populous than Melbourne and Sydney. Gale advertised that he would introduce aerostation to South Australia by making a "Grand Ascent in honour of her Majesty's Ascension to the throne". (8)

The editorial on the day waxed lyrical on the subject of Queen Victoria, "thirty four years to-day, Princess Alexandrina Victoria, only child of Edward, Duke of Kent, a young girl in the first flush of womanhood, ascended the throne of England." (9)

The largest crowd ever experienced in SA - 15 000-20 000 - thronged the Exhibition Grounds. "The trains from the Port were crowded to excess, and not a few of our country cousins came in from miles around, all intent on witnessing the great novelty." The crowd sat patiently and waited unhappily, "as hour after hour passed away, and nothing was visible to the multitude except the top of the dingy yellow bag, rising two or three feet above some dirty tarpaulins, stretched across half-a-dozen poles." (10)

Due to miscalculations in the amount of gas required, the filling of the balloon was eventually abandoned, after 8 hours effort. Hope expired along with the sagging envelope, despite Gale in desperation, declaring he would repeat his intrepid Sydney ascent, and go aloft without a car, but simply astride the wooden hoop. Still it was impossible.

*The Advertiser* was caustic in its summary of the day's "Non-Ascension - a Grand Hoax", reporting that, "it was 'Queen's weather', but never was royalty so caricatured. The idea of a monster balloon ascending into the upper regions, as an emblem of Victoria ascending the throne, was good enough, but what a falling off in the execution! Victoria did 'ascend' the throne, but the commemorative balloon never left the ground." (11)

It mocked Gale's futile attempts, saying he "abandoned his intention of going up on the 'hoop' as the night was damp and chill, and he had a great dread of the 'hooping cough'." It was reported that some patrons whispered that, "the contents of the balloon were not gas at all, but merely foul air" and humorously joked that "the Gale was there, but the Gas was not." (12)

Four days later, on 24 June, South Australia's first balloon ascent took place from the less-than-savoury cattle market yards on North Terrace. A larger diameter pipe attached to the gas main ensured inflation within an hour. Rain saturated cords and ropes and diminished the buoyancy of the gas, so Gale took up only one passenger, a Mr Tyas. Mounted troopers cleared a circle around the balloon, a precaution in case the balloon did not rise perpendicularly - as often happened - but swept along the ground.

Tyas later wrote of the brisk wind blowing above the pens of the yards, the poor visibility and the need to hastily discard sandbags to gain height. With no ballast remaining, and hills looming, Gale opted to end their twelve minute flight. Tyas agreed "it would have been dangerous to have got among the timber of the ranges and the gullies" and was delighted enough, despite a heavy landing and uphill drag to exclaim, "the landscape looked wonderfully dwarfed and foreshortened." (13)

Two further flights took place from the cattle market on 7 and 8 July and up to forty people paid Gale for tethered flights, at the end of a 200' 'rope'. Just such an 'ascent' was made by Lavinia Balford, South Australia's first woman to go aloft.

Thomas Gale settled permanently in Adelaide, residing in Alfred Street, Parkside. He continued to demonstrate his flying skills: in the Exhibition grounds on 2 January 1878, he attached two baskets and thrilled spectators as he climbed a connecting rope ladder from the upper to the lower car. Landing was equally spectacular, for the rope attached to the holding grappling iron broke, causing the passenger to be unceremoniously dumped out and sprain his wrist. Gale was ejected and suffered severe bruising. 'Professor' Gale ventured away from South Australia just once to forward the cause of aerostation. He took his balloon by ship to Tasmania late in January 1878, where the *Launceston Examiner* wrote, "Mr Gale's widespread fame is so generally acknowledged that it needs no comment from us." (14)

Tasmania's first balloon ascent, on 6 February 1878, drew a large crowd at the Public Gardens, but the venture was a financial loss, for only 400 people patronised the enclosure, "the remainder thronging the Windmill Hill and the Elphin Road" and enjoying a better view, as did those on all the ships tied up at the Tamar River wharf. (15)

The *Young Australian* balloon with Professor Gale and naval man Captain Stourton, rose gradually. "Thirty feet from the ground the balloon was dashed against one of the gum trees near the fountain...but once clear of this obstruction it rose higher." It steadied on a south-easterly course over Newstead, Queechy and St Leonards where the grapnel was thrown out. "Some men in the vicinity seemed afraid of the balloon and instead of rendering assistance, would not approach it...at length a girl of about 14 caught the rope and made it fast." (16)

*The Examiner* suggested steps be taken to recoup Professor Gale's outlay, pleading with the Launceston public to express their "well-known generosity" and set about soliciting subscriptions from hotels, banks and businesses in the hope that people would "liberally respond to the appeal of the daring visitor." (17)

Gale's second ascent from Launceston, on 18 February, drew a paying crowd of one thousand, but the quantity of gas had been so scrupulously measured it was inadequate and the company refused to supply more. Captain Stourton again accompanied Gale, in the vain hope of reaching Hobart Town in the south and exchanging signals by flags with a fellow naval Captain, when in sight of the sea. The balloon had barely cleared the trees when it began to descend rapidly, "knocking the ball off the weathercock on the top of the conservatory, which, in its fall, broke a pane of glass." They touched down behind the conservatory, where Gale unloaded his disappointed passenger who watched as Gale rose rapidly to double the height previously attained. "After swaying and twirling a little," the balloon drifted southward in a light breeze and came down safely not far from the township at Franklin Village. Having lost his paying passenger's fee due to the insufficient supply of gas, the Professor once more sustained a heavy financial loss. (18)

*The Examiner* complained of the treatment from the Gas Company, "In every town Mr Gale has hitherto performed in, the Gas Companies have always allowed him a discount in price on the wholesale quantity of gas he uses, but here the Company charged him the full rate." (19)

The Company replied, stating Gale had expressed satisfaction when the arrangements were made and had received extra gas and labour for no charge, although they incurred a loss.

In the spring and summers of 1878 and 1881, further reports of Gale's ascents were published, one on 23 September 1881 at Gawler, with his *Young Australian* balloon filled with hydrogen. Thomas Gale planned new aerial pursuits until his sudden death at home from an aortic aneurysm, on 10 November 1884, aged only 43. According to his obituary, Gale's last aeronautic display a few years before had ended with his balloon being destroyed on tangling with a gum tree. The paper enlightened readers to the type of person he was, "he possessed some engineering knowledge, and was known as a simple-minded, industrious man, who was efficient in whatever he undertook." (20)

Thus, Thomas Gale became the second aeronaut from English stock to be laid to rest in Australian soil: he was buried two days after his death, in the West Terrace Cemetery.

By 1878 many American and English balloonists had begun to adventure abroad, seeking to earn a living in different climes and far flung regions of the world. Apart from Gale's ascents in South Australian and Tasmanian skies, Professor Emanuel Jackson flew in country Victoria and James Stewart had an unexpected flight in New South Wales, which resulted in the death of a man and a charge of manslaughter being laid against American aeronaut, Rufus Gibbon Wells.

Rufus G Wells was one of the most widely travelled aeronauts of his day. Born in St Louis in 1832, he had been apprenticed to Eugene Godard in 1856 and is said to have beaten a ballooning trail throughout South America, Egypt, India, Burma, the Dutch East Indies, Britain and Europe. He used both gas and hot-air balloons. Aeronautic historians believe he was the 'Richard' Wells who flew in a race over New Orleans in 1858, against AJ de Morat. Wells' balloon was the larger of the two and was "inflated by vapour of alcohol," the other with gas. However, the cold atmosphere caused the vapour to condense inside the envelope, which collapsed and fell onto a house. Wells "jumped from his perilous position", whereupon "the barbarous rabble hissed and hooted Mr Wells very savagely as he walked home." (21)

Rufus Wells lived in England between 1860 and 1872 and engaged in other races during that time. He tried to join a balloon corps during the Franco-Prussian war, but both sides rejected his application. The adventurer flew balloons in Europe and became the first to cross the Appenines. He wrote of being well received by the Italians, he believed because he, "had the courage to defy Pope Pius IX who had refused permission for him to wave the American flag over the Vatican." In written accounts of his travels, Wells states he flew in Mexico on sixty occasions and also in Buenos Aires and Rio de Janiero. (22)

This leading American aeronaut arrived in Sydney in December 1877. Unaware of the past difficulties and misfortunes that had beset Brown and Gale, due to sudden harbour breezes and the bewildering number of air currents, Wells made hasty preparations. He had already had profitable flights in Victoria, but "was impatient to get on with his New South Wales programme because it was rumoured that a second overseas 'professor of aerostatics' was about to begin an Australian tour." (23)

Wells had lost a valuable balloon in Melbourne, so he engaged a firm of local manufacturers to make him a new balloon, using calico instead of silk. The order was rushed: the balloon was sewn in record time, in under a day. On Boxing Day, 1877 the crowd in Sydney's Domain, when Rufus Wells took the rostrum in the late afternoon and gave an oration for twenty minutes on the wonderful changes to mankind the balloon had effected, and on his own feats. He finished by saying anyone could construct his own balloon in a backyard.

With the crowd at a high pitch of expectation, Wells climbed into the basket, but overlooked the inexperience of the volunteer helpers, who allowed a violent gust of wind to slew the balloon sideways, enveloping a dozen spectators in the billowing cloth. Onlookers held down the balloon as it surged and dragged all over the enclosure. Spying larrikins with cigars intent on igniting the envelope, Wells shouted to everyone to let go. The flight rapidly became a memorable one, as Wells floundered in telegraph wires, hit a chimney in Woolloomooloo and dangled upside down while bricks crashed around him. He escaped via a drainpipe, leaving the balloon to shoot skywards and disappear.

Wells, with bloodied face, apologised to the crowd and promised a New Year's Day ascent; however, on the day the vagaries of the Sydney gas supply re-emerged and the balloon, with a hole in its side, failed to inflate sufficiently. A few days later an alarming report from Victoria reached him: that rival aeronaut, Professor Emanuel Jackson from Derby in England, had made a successful flight.

The hero of an alleged 277 ascents in his home country had indeed made a New Year's Day ascent in Ballarat, having arrived in Melbourne with one of the five balloons he was purported to own. Its colour - alternate stripes of yellow and orange made it the most easily discernible balloon in Australia - glowed "against the blue sky like a golden cloud." The reporter excelled himself by playing around with metaphors and making bold statements, the "vast bag...looked like a great pear that had sprung from the ground by magic." The ascent from the Eastern Oval, was "the only thoroughly successful one ever made in the colony." I suspect the reporter was befuddled by the champagne consumed when, by his own admission, "they drank the Queen's health." (24)

On this, Professor Jackson's 278th ascent, he was accompanied by JT Drew, a young Ballarat hairdresser who was rowdily cheered by the miners. The "vast conveyance glided from the ground like a bird taking wing." Hastily, Jackson tipped ballast over the side to avoid striking the pavilion and headed upwards to a height of 2½ miles where they could view the entire district. (25)

Over Creswick, "the flying grapnel struck earth and gripped, and the swaying balloon was brought to a standstill at a spot about four miles this side of Clunes" after a journey of eighteen miles. A couple of confused farmers rode up to investigate the strange object; one had thought it "a crow", the other "an heagle" (sic). (26)

Few of the travelling aeronauts admitted to pecuniary success. If these are honest financial assessments, why then did they continue to travel to Australia for another three decades? Jackson is said to have failed to recoup expenses for his Ballarat ascent; nevertheless, he had succeeded in flying there, sixteen years after Joseph Dean's failures in 1862 and 1863.

In Sydney Rufus Wells increased his efforts against his perceived rival. He need not have been so concerned, for a fortnight later Jackson departed, explaining, "he only came to the colony for private reasons, as he has more business in England than he can manage." (27)

Having decided hot air from a furnace of straw and rubbish would be a more reliable source of lift than gas, Wells tested his theory on a 10 January flight in 1878 but struck a fence and the balloon collapsed. "The whole affair was a fiasco," said the press. (28)

Undaunted Wells, two nights later, cajoled the spectators to supply a volunteer to go up 1000' or so, on a tethered rope. The crowd pushed forward ex-seaman James Stewart who, "had some experience with Irish balloons." Amongst the noise and confusion, a misunderstanding arose which was to have dire consequences. Stewart later said he had expected Wells to go up with him. Instead, he had only another terrified youth for company who jumped out of the basket as they rose and slid down the rope to the ground. Several onlookers had foolishly hung on to the car as it lifted and then fell off. One of them, Charles Harden, was seriously injured. This was the first mishap. (29)

Freed of its burdens, the balloon shot up as the winch handle revolved wildly, spinning off rope at an alarming rate. Near its end the rope snapped, hitting Wells between the eyes and knocking him out. The jerk flung Stewart from the basket; fortunately, in the dark he seized and clung to the rope, then hauled himself back inside the gondola. He was whisked away on an involuntary flight over Sydney Harbour. Just as he neared the northern shore, the gusting wind veered and sent him back over the water to drop indecorously in the midst of a genteel garden party at Government House, where he scrambled down a tree to be met by Wells, running up and "sporting two black eyes and an ugly wound on his forehead." (30)

James Stewart affirmed the experience would not deter him. He told the *Sydney Morning Herald* he had "a startling yet beautiful view of the city and its surroundings" and "had no sensation of fear when he found himself alone in the car, beyond a slight apprehension that he might descend into the water." The worst part of it, he said, was losing his hat and a valuable gold watch. (31)

Less fortunate was Charles Harden, who died of his injuries at the infirmary - the second balloon-related death in Australia. The coroner found Rufus Gibbon Wells guilty of manslaughter, but luckily for Wells, "the Crown Law officers thought he had been sufficiently punished for any negligence he might have shown." (32)

The disastrous flight proved to be Rufus Wells' last appearance in Australia; he left in disgrace but continued to travel with his balloon, giving hundreds of competent performances.

Wells and Emanuel Jackson had unwittingly established a pattern which would be followed by others who journeyed to Australia; they put up balloons in various parts of the country, then exited to other shores.

Showman extraordinaire was Henri (also known as Harry) L'Estrange who became the first Australian-born balloonist and, inadvertently the first to use a parachute. The boy born in the 1840's in Melbourne was an unknown circus worker when influenced by the 1874 Australian tour of famous French wire-walker, Charles Blondin, who had thrilled the world by crossing Niagara Falls on a tightrope. The ageing Blondin did nothing as cavalier in Melbourne or Sydney, but still drew big crowds to see his acrobatic and tumbling feats and left with a reported £50 000 profit. There were many 'Australian Blondins' in the travelling circuses and Harry L'Estrange was another who decided to emulate the Frenchman.

Fired with ambition, L'Estrange dreamed up ideas to outshine Blondin and become the recognised master of the tightrope. Deciding no venue was suitable in Melbourne, L'Estrange departed for Sydney in 1877 and gave a performance to raise money for more daring future events. Before a crowd of 2000, L'Estrange crossed a tightrope in a suit of armour, then finally, blindfolded, he pushed a dog in a wheelbarrow before him. The show ended with a large fire balloon floating way on the night sky and sufficient money to finance his dream.

The Australian ropewalker boasted that he would walk across Middle Harbour, 340 feet up, on a tightrope much higher and longer than Blondin had ever attempted. L'Estrange was his own publicity manager, a born organiser and entrepreneur. He shrewdly spread rumours that the authorities were trying to ban the dangerous stunt; that he was really Blondin in disguise; that the 1400' rope was really two spliced together and would surely part under his weight on the swaying rope. He hardly needed to point out there would be no surviving such a fall.

Saturday 14 April 1878 dawned fine and sunny. Thousands trod the paths from Mosman and North Sydney to Middle Harbour and gladly paid an admission fee. L'Estrange had personally chartered 21 ferries and vessels to transport 8000 paying customers from Circular Quay. Sales were large at the liquor booths and refreshment stalls that he had organised on a profit-sharing basis; signed photographs were eagerly purchased by the crowd.

Theatrically at 4pm, a cannon fired from the cliff top and L'Estrange stepped onto the rope carrying a balancing pole. L'Estrange was resplendent in a colourful yellow tunic, black tights and scarlet turban, as he stepped nimbly along the wire. At the crucial, sagging centrepoint of the rope on the crossing, the showman stopped - a ploy to build suspense - then completed the crossing in just fifteen minutes. Ferries tooted and thousands laughed with relief.

The stuntman repeated his feat twice more that month, on the 15th and on the 21st. He walked away a rich man, having made £10 000. After a year of lesser tightrope walking, Henri L'Estrange retired from the profession. *The Australian Sketcher* of 10 May 1879 attributed his retirement, to a cancer in the leg caused by "the friction of the rope by which he used to mount his pedestal...and although he recovered he could not walk with the old facility."

L'Estrange turned his attention to ballooning to attract paying crowds. Some say he made his own gas balloon, the *Aurora*, others that he bought an old one. The Sydney trials proved a fiasco as the balloon refused to budge more than a metre from 'terra firma'. Again, the poor quality of Sydney gas was blamed and L'Estrange, in anger, returned to his native Melbourne, where he also created a sensation, albeit for a vastly different reason.

The ropewalking marvel attracted a huge following at the Agricultural Society's ground adjoining Victoria Barracks in St Kilda Road. The workers accidentally holed the calico which Mr L'Estrange repaired with sticking plaster then, unperturbed by the state of his balloon, he took off. L'Estrange and the balloon accelerated upwards with surprising velocity. Elated by his speed, the novice aeronaut waved his handkerchief to the crowd. According to one eyewitness, at an estimated height of 1 3/4 miles (9000') and without warning, "a rent appeared from top to bottom. Immediately it began its downward journey." (33)

The horrified onlookers witnessed a unique event, "Almost instantly the silk parachute attached to the centre of the balloon opened and checked the speed at which the balloon was descending." Australia's first parachute descent had been achieved, albeit inadvertently. (34)

It is open to conjecture whether the parachute was indeed an emergency one attached to the balloon, or whether it was, in actuality, the burst balloon contained by its netting to form a crude parachute. The aeronaut's own words support the former theory. L'Estrange feared the parachute would fail him, "it split in several places but still remained tolerably effective." He was however still in the basket "clinging on with both hands." Notwithstanding the braking influence of his parachute, Henri L'Estrange came to earth with incredible velocity. (35)

Those spectators who rushed to the scene just minutes after his take-off were amazed to find L'Estrange alive, although unable to extricate himself from the material, which threatened suffocation, and from the tangle of branches and netting. Miraculously, although red in the face, he was only slightly injured. He explained the incident by saying he had miscalculated the buoyancy of the superior Melbourne gas and had also thrown out ballast, "thinking he would meet with extra atmospheric resistance." The gas had expanded to such a pressure that it could not be contained within the envelope. The fault lay with the aeronaut's inexperience, not with the balloon. (36)

Intent on capitalising even on mistakes, Henri L'Estrange appeared that night on stage at a hall, telling the paying audience of his perilous and rapid return to earth, saying he felt death was inevitable but prayed to God that it was not. He could see Government House below him, appearing "the size of a walnut" and threw out bags of sand ballast without thought to the possibility of their injuring people below. (37)

With his reputation in tatters, L'Estrange made a further attempt to attract publicity, on a flight from Braybrook on 7 December 1879. Again, he took the *Aurora* to Sydney where he captured headlines in a final disastrous public appearance on 15 March 1881.

The balloon descended in Woolloomooloo. Its grappling iron became entangled in a roof, whereupon L'Estrange slid down a rope to safety. While the balloon, "was swaying to and fro, the gas escaping from it became ignited by a light in the house, and the balloon exploded. Several persons were scorched and bruised and received shocks to the system. Mrs Hawke, an elderly lady, was severely injured about the face, and is likely to lose her sight." (38)

The extroverted daredevil had flirted with death and bad publicity too often to risk further attempts and so dropped out of the public eye, to retire to a tranquil life.

(1)   James Neild Ed, *My Note Book.*
(2)   *Sydney Morning Herald,* undated.
(3)   *Sydney News* 20 January 1870.
(4)   Ibid.
(5)   *Illustrated Sydney News* 21 January 1871.
(6)   Ibid.
(7)   Ibid.
(8)   *The South Australian Advertiser* 20 June 1871.
(9)   Op cit 24 June 1871
(10)  Ibid.
(11)  Ibid.
(12)  Ibid.
(13)  *The South Australian Advertiser* 26 June 1871.
(14)  *Launceston Examiner* 30 January 1878.
(15)  Op cit 7 February 1878.
(16)  Ibid.
(17)  *Launceston Examiner* 13 February 1878.
(18)  *Launceston Examiner* 19 February 1878.
(19)  Ibid.
(20)  *The South Australian Advertiser* 11 November 1884.
(21)  Charles Brown, Notebook.
(22)  Rufus G Wells, *The Boys Own Paper.*
(23)  Ibid.
(24)  *Ballarat Star* January 1878.
(25)  Ibid.

(26) Ibid.

(27) Ibid.

(28) *Sydney Morning Herald* 11 January 1878.

(29) Op cit 14 January 1878.

(30) *Northern Territory News* 10 February 1970.

(31) *Sydney Morning Herald* 14 January 1878.

(32) Ibid.

(33) Emily Foster, letter to the Editor, *The Age* 27 August 1932.

(34) *Australasian Sketcher* 10 May 1879.

(35) *The Illustrated Australian* 12 May 1879.

(36) *Argus* 15 April 1879.

(37) Ibid.

(38) *Australasian Sketcher* 9 April 1881.

# Parachuting Becomes Popular

Of a very different ilk to the showmen balloonists in Australia in the last thirty years of the nineteenth century and first decade of the twentieth, was Harry Henden. It was in Dartford Kent that Harry Henden was born on 13 December 1847; he spent his youth chasing clouds and rainbows and was 32 years old when he eventually took up ballooning. An enthusiastic exponent and member of the august London Aeronautical Club, he made two hundred ascents in England, Wales, Ireland, France and Germany during the years 1879 - 1884. On one flight Henden reached a staggering 18 000 feet in altitude.

Harry Henden had other interests besides ballooning. In England his spare time had been devoted to the art of bell ringing; he was a life-long member of the Ancient Society of the London College of Bellringers and had won prizes for his pealing of the bells. (As a mark of esteem on his death, the Society pealed the bells, although he had been absent fifty years.)

He was an associate of aeronaut John Morton, who owned three balloons, and together they made many successful ascents which were reported widely in the newspapers. In 1883 the pair flew *The Pictorial World* balloon for the London newspaper of the same name and took aloft illustrators and photographers to record aerial aspects. At one stage Henden was "employed by the military and Government of England to take officials on errands of importance in his balloon." At Woolwich Arsenal he was an instructor in military ballooning. On the eve of his departure for Australia in June 1884, Henden took up two officers of the Horse Guards in order to carry out a trial reconnaissance. (1)

Henden's last ascent in England was in his own balloon the *Gem* in August 1884. The following month the family shipped to Sydney to join Mrs Henden's brother, CF Stratton, who became Henden's business manager for his first few Sydney ascents and who had contacted the newspapers in advance, "Mr Henden, the celebrated London aeronaut, is coming to Sydney...and he intends, with the aid of his *Gem*, to translate himself to 'purer climes.' " (2)

Although he arrived in Australia on board the *Lusitania* (on 21 November 1884) with his wife, four daughters and a son, with the express purpose of demonstrating his balloon, the *Gem*, he was not reliant on aerostation for his livelihood. Like his father before him in England, Harry was a watchmaker and jeweller by profession. Two weeks after his disembarking, the public were told more about the aeronaut,

"A young, dark, good-looking man was beside us. 'Mr H. Henden, Aeronaut' was on his card... sitting in front of us was a man who had been a dozen times up above the clouds higher than Mount-Blanc! 'Is it not very dangerous?' we said. He smiled. 'Not much more than going to sea when you know your work properly, he replied.
Look at the number of accidents, we remarked. 'There was that poor L'Estrange - always going up and always coming down head first. We were present when his balloon burst'. 'Well,' he said, 'it couldn't well help it considering he had its neck tied with wax-end. Don't you think something in you would give if your neck was tied that way?' Then the young man left, first telling us that he was going to make various ascents in Australia and show the people what ballooning really meant." (3)

That same day, several thousand spectators watched his first Australian ascent, from Prince Alfred Park, with his large yellow balloon, the *Gem*, said to be the largest ever seen in Australia. Henden rose to 7200' and landed in open space near Enfield. A day later, on 7 December 1884, he again gave pleasure and value to those who had paid to see the demonstrations. The papers heaped praise on Henden's performance,

> "Balloon ascents in Sydney have, in the past, been attended with so much want of skill, and consequent misfortune, that a thoroughly successful ascent is quite an exception to what has come to be looked upon as the rule in connection with such trips. Mr Henden may, therefore, be fairly congratulated upon the unqualified success of his ascent." (4)

Henden's first ascent in country NSW took place on New Year's Day in Bathurst. The crowd included the Mayor, aldermen and one puzzled Chinaman who inquired, "suppose he no can't come down, what he do?" (5)

His reputation as an aeronaut steadily growing, Henden travelled to Melbourne, where he made a successful evening ascent on 4 February from the East Melbourne Cricket ground, scattering advertising handbills before landing at Footscray.

Two days later, in Ballarat, he survived what must have been an unnerving experience, passing "through rain clouds a couple of thousand feet in thickness." One cloud "he cut into exploded like a thunderclap" and he became "completely drenched" with 5 inches of water in the car. Sensibly, he ended the flight due to pouring rain. One startled farmer from the Emerald Isle exclaimed, "Shure I thought it was the divil (sic) come out of the Heavens." Farmers assisted him and, with true country hospitality, he was invited to stay in a local hotel, where a dance was hastily improvised. He "thoroughly enjoyed himself." (6)

After a further Melbourne ascent on 14 February, he returned to Sydney to complete the summer season. Henden chose a clover paddock in which to land, on St Patrick's Day.

During the summer season of 1885/86, Henden gave more skilful performances in Sydney and over Orange in western NSW, where he had settled with his family and where two more children were born, a son and a daughter. He had established his own jewellery and watchmaking business in Summer Street, (which he ran for the next fifty years, only relinquishing it four years before his death at the age of 89).

With his business flourishing, Henden had less time to devote to ballooning. His workload, combined with waning public interest, resulted in fewer appearances of the *Gem* in the 1886- 87 season. Flying became an unprofitable sideline for Henden. The balloon came out of temporary storage at the end of 1888 at the request of one JT Williams who sent a telegram to Henden, offering to buy his *Gem*. Harry Henden declined to sell, but agreed to lend it to Mr Williams, for him to "attempt the daring feat of ascending with a balloon but without a car, then jumping into space and descending to the grounds by means of a parachute." (7)

Erroneously described by newspapers as an 'Australian' aeronaut, Williams was to make his mark on Australia's parachuting history. This first deliberate parachute jump attempt came nine years after Harry L'Estrange's reluctant use of the parachute, and 105 years after the world's first parachute jump in Europe in December 1783. Over the interceding years - due to mishaps and bans by authorities - the links between balloonists and parachutists had parted.

In the early years of parachuting, the aeronaut and parachutist were often the same person or, alternatively, the parachutist went aloft as a balloon passenger with his bulky equipment. As with the balloon, the earliest endeavours in this field were made by the French.

Sebastien Lenormand made the first parachute descent in December 1783, when he jumped from a tree, while holding on to two rigidly braced (to prevent turning inside out) parasols and landed safely. Inspired he made further experiments by dropping weights and even a cat and dog by 'parachute,' the name Lenormand gave to his invention.

Jean-Pierre Blanchard was also experimenting in 1783 in Switzerland, using a dog in a basket suspended below a ribbed parasol type of parachute of his own manufacture. Later, in 1785, Blanchard himself jumped but broke a leg.

Joseph Montgolfier witnessed these events and made parachute drops, at the Papal Palace in Avignon on 23 March 1784, using sheep in a basket on each of six occasions.

It was left to aeronaut André-Jacques Garnerin to perfect the manned parachute. His was the first successful parachute invention; he was also the first to parachute from a balloon, before the French Court at Monceau on 21 October 1797. His wife, said to be the first woman to fly a balloon solo, also took up parachuting. Garnerin made England's first parachute descent in London on 21 September 1802, landing safely despite the parachute oscillating violently. The sickening and frightening pendulum-like swaying of early chutes was eventually rectified but was daunting enough to deter the English from embracing parachuting for another 35 years.

It was then that an Irish painter Robert Cocking, designer of his own rigid parachute, could not be persuaded this was foreign to aeronautic principles. Accordingly, without so much as a trial Cocking persuaded Charles Green and Edward Spencer to take him up beneath their balloon. He insisted on releasing himself at an altitude of 2 miles for his 24 July 1837 descent. Cocking's parachute collapsed immediately, and he plunged into a field in Kent, where he died, thus becoming parachuting's first fatality.

A year later, on 7 June 1838 and despite opposition, John Hampton became the first Englishman to parachute. For legal reasons he had to jump from a tethered balloon, but when aloft he obstinately cut the restraining ropes and released himself from the balloon. Hampton, true to his nature and wary of competition, intentionally slowed the development of the parachute by erroneously stating that the rush of air was so great on descent, that a parachutist was almost insensible and thus had great difficulty controlling the device.

Monsieur Henri Le Tour, described as a decrepit deformed hunchback, turned to parachuting to seek fame, honour and fortune. After thirty descents in France, Le Tour tried his luck in England in 1854. High winds whirled his parachute about, resulting in his striking a tree, breaking his spine, ribs and arm. He died three days later on 5 July, leaving a wife in late pregnancy and family destitute in France, and causing England to outlaw parachuting.

In America, manned parachutes were first demonstrated by Frenchman Louis Charles Guille, who toured in 1819, but it was not until 1880 that American aeronaut Thomas Baldwin introduced the silk, collapsible parachute that was to revolutionise parachuting.

With the trapeze bar introduced by Monsieur Henri Buislay, the parachute was poised ready to swing into action. The 1900s would become the heyday for parachuting from balloons.

In Sydney in 1888, "Mr Williams...a quiet, unassuming man, 33 years of age, scarcely five feet six inches in height" was considering the parachute from a new angle. "For a considerable time he has been making small experiments with the parachute with a view to demonstrating that it is possible to afford the aeronaut a means of escape in times of danger." This indeed was a new concept, but one that was not to be fully realised for decades. (8)

The Birmingham-born Williams who had been a Sydney resident for twelve years, determined to put his knowledge into practice using the *Gem*. Williams hoodwinked the proprietors of the Ashfield Recreation Ground into believing he had previously performed the feat. The novice had constructed his own chute which, "bore a resemblance to the top storey of a Chinese pagoda. It consisted of two rings, one about fourteen feet and the other four feet in circumference. These were covered in fine Chinese silk, the smaller ring being at the top and being partially uncovered to permit of the free passage of air." Police warned Williams of the grave risk.

Undaunted, he assured the crowd of his absolute confidence stating, "even his insurance company might have no fear of having to make a payment to his executors." (9)

At 6pm Williams attached his parachute to the side of the *Gem*'s netting then took his seat in a sling beneath the unmanned balloon. When let go, the balloon shot upward; seven minutes later from an estimated height of between 5000 - 6000 feet, Williams "unfastened the valve of the balloon and the moment the gas began to escape, threw his weight on to the parachute and shot downwards...at a terrifying rate. The parachute then expanded and Williams, hanging on to a ring at the bottom of the parachute floated gracefully earthwards." The descent took ten minutes and was free of any tugging or jerking; the only movement was a gentle swaying, as Williams experimented with steering. Such control was made possible by "the vent or hole at the top, capable of being enlarged or decreased in size at the will of the operator." (10)

The plucky little man landed with the slightest of jolts at Homebush, and soon began to brag. So pleased was the amateur at his own success, he challenged Professor Thomas Baldwin (brother of Samuel Baldwin), smoke balloonist and parachutist, to compete against him.

JT Williams claimed in 1890 to have ascended to an incredible 20 000' in Sydney. According to one aviation historian, "the statistics were not checked by any experts, but there was no doubt that he vanished from sight of the onlookers and when he landed in the George's River he was numb with cold." (11)

One cynical reporter, writing of the challenge to Baldwin, "the eminent American who also scrapes the sky with his umbrella," wondered how the competition was to be judged. Would the winning parachutist take the purse of between £100 - £300 for being first down, longest up or for "grace and elegance in coming down?" (12)

Professor Thomas Sackett (or Scott) Baldwin, an erstwhile circus acrobat, had toured gainfully in America and England. The year 1889 found him in New Zealand, where he became the first person to make a balloon ascent and a parachute jump. On 21 January he launched from Dunedin, on the southern extremity of the South Island.

In Australia Baldwin was not a success. Twice in 1889 in Sydney he advertised that he would drop from his balloon by parachute; twice he gathered expectant crowds, but on neither occasion did the showjumper actually parachute, nor did he accept William's challenge.

The years 1888 and 1889 were eventful in Australia, as Americans ED Hogan and his partner, 35year old Professor Bartholomew, demonstrated the parachute over Adelaide, Melbourne and Ballarat. Even before Thomas Baldwin arrived, Hogan and Bartholomew had performed their unique jumps in Australia. They were the only parachute-leapers who performed on the trapeze bar while in descent, having made 52 such displays all over America.

Born in County Michigan, Professor Bartholomew had been ballooning since the age of sixteen. By 1877, when only 24, he had commenced parachute jumping. ED Hogan, also from Michigan, was one of a family of aeronauts who had already lost two brothers: Edward, in a ballooning accident over the Atlantic and John on his ballooning and parachuting debut in Detroit, when he went aloft holding the trapeze bar by the hands instead of sitting on it.

These men were among the first of a new generation of aerial showmen, the smoke balloonists, who added dangerous, mid-air trapeze antics to their repertoires, and plummeted down by parachute, often with disastrous results. The smoke balloonists had 'barnstormed' all over the US as freelancers, giving intentionally short exhibitions. (The word 'barnstormer' is said to have originated from the use of barns as hangars.) They relied on quickly and cheaply filling their envelopes with smoke issuing from a fire pit or kerosene burner and then rising high into the sky - harnessed to a trapeze bar attached to the flying wires - before somersaulting down by parachute. The balloon, weighted by a sandbag at the top, would turn upside down, empty through the neck and return to earth deflated, to be reclaimed and used again.

These aerial showmen were the highlight of many fairgrounds and lived mainly by working the country town circuit. Spectators, drawn by the extra element of danger, found themselves in the company of balloons highly decorated with coloured flags or advertising. This then was what the energetic Professor Bartholomew and ED Hogan introduced to Australia.

On 27 December 1888, the two men inflated their balloon over the outlet of a flue containing the fire. They were to ascend from the Adelaide oval after a baseball match and enrolled the players as helpers; however even these burly men could barely hold down the swollen balloon. After a speedy inflation, Bartholomew took hold of the trapeze suspended from the balloon, instead of a basket and ran as the wind caught the machine and whisked him aloft. At a suitable elevation, the Professor grasped the other trapeze attached to the parachute (in turn suspended from the balloon's side) and let go of the balloon,

> "The moment his weight was felt, the parachute became detached, and he dropped down...a couple of hundred feet...before it opened. Then the parachute opened with a graceful movement, caught the air, and was checked in its rapid descent until the Professor floated slowly down, performing perilous feats upon the trapeze as he descended." (13)

The Professor dressed like a dandy, in a close-fitting black dress, trunks and a cap, landed safely. The collapsed envelope "slowly glided downwards, twisting and wriggling in the currents of air, looking like...a great snake or dragon" with smoke issuing from its mouth. (14)

Bartholomew gave repeat performances in Ballarat, where he was injured, and from the Melbourne Cricket Ground in January 1889, where he came down on the roof of a doctor's house in East Melbourne.

Harry Henden's little jewel, the *Gem*, was again borrowed for a performance, this time by former showman Charles Jackson, who wished to use it, partly for experience, partly for the publicity. Like JT Williams the previous year, Jackson took the balloon high above Ashfield Recreation grounds and jumped out, hanging on to his 10' wide silk parachute, made by a Sydney umbrella-maker. He descended fast, swaying violently, to land safely in a garden. The *Gem* fared less well: it shot upwards when relieved of Jackson's weight, was blown out to sea and wrecked. (This is probably the same Professor Jackson who attempted to balloon in New Zealand with a singular lack of success - his balloon escaped at one launching and was retrieved from Lyttelton Harbour; high winds forced cancellation at a Dunedin attempt.)

With the demise of his balloon, Harry Henden retired from ballooning. Instead, he put his extraordinary energy into his family of seven children and his successful jewellery business. This solid respected citizen watched half a century tick by and slip into eternity on timepieces in his shop, in Summer St Orange, the town on the western NSW plains. Aged 89, after fifty years in his jewellery business and 67 years of marriage, Harry Henden died on 6 April 1936 at his Moulder Street house, named 'Dartford' after the village of his birth. The upstanding citizen, "much-loved man", and veteran of 220 ascents, was cremated. (15)

Several obituaries appeared in the papers. He was a keen businessman, but also the epitome of a cultured gentleman; was hospitable and valued family life. An associate wrote, "he has been styled a famous man, an upright man; he was also a much-loved man," and those fortunate to have known him "found the world a better place for knowing Harry Henden." (16)

Surprisingly perhaps, not one of Harry Henden's two sons or five daughters took up ballooning. Of his Australian born children, his son Jack became a jeweller like his father and grandfather before him, residing in country Goulburn; his daughter Violet – who once played in her father's balloon basket as a child - inherited his hand-crafted jewellery and clocks.

Jack's son lives today in NSW, and Violet's daughter Mrs Jill Martin, in Tasmania. She is the custodian of her grandfather's scrapbooks, photos, and ballooning memorabilia. She told me of a favourite family story of how her grandmother, Harry Henden's wife, visited Melbourne as an old lady, and one of her children arranged a helicopter flight. When they lifted off, the pilot turned to her and said, "I suppose this is the first time you've been up?" and she answered, "Oh no, I've been up hundreds of times in balloons." The pilot stared at her and tapped his head for the benefit of other passengers, indicating she must be mad.

Australia's first truly respected, safe and professional aeronaut had gone, and with him the gentle era of ballooning in this country.

(1)   *The Pictorial World*, undated.
(2)   *Sydney Evening News*, date unknown.
(3)   *The Bulletin* 6 December 1884.
(4)   *Sydney Morning Herald* 8 December 1884.
(5)   *Bathurst Times* 2 January 1885.
(6)   *Ballarat Courier* 9 February 1885.
(7)   *Sydney Morning Herald* 6 December 1888.
(8)   Ibid.
(9)   Ibid.
(10)  *Argus* 10 December 1888.
(11)  Stanley Brogden, *History of Australian Aviation*.
(12)  *The Bulletin* 15 December 1888.
(13)  *The Adelaide Observer* 29 December 1888.
(14)  Ibid.
(15)  Obituary, Orange newspaper, undated.
(16)  Ibid.

# Troupes on Tour

By 1890 word had spread that Australia was ripe for aeronautical exploitation and itinerant airmen, at the end of the northern hemisphere's summer season, would flock to countries south of the equator.

The Van Tassel Troupe had toured America with its aerial show, with all employees adopting the distinctive surname. Park Van Tassel and his wife arrived in Australia in 1890. Van Tassel and Thomas Baldwin had both made their first parachute jumps in San Francisco, under the tuition of WE Blanchard, who claimed Jean-Pierre Blanchard as his illustrious ancestor. According to British parachutist Dolly Shepherd, Park Van Tassel, "of Dutch extraction and considerable girth," revolutionised aerial showmanship. He discarded the hoops and discs used in parachutes to hold them partially open, the "cumbersome and artificial opening aids that had so complicated the traditional semi-rigid parachutes." (1)

Van Tassel's chute was of heavy canvas and manilla rope and designed, "to be forced open by the air rushing up into the mouth of the canopy." (2)

Women soon embraced parachuting, despite deaths, and despite condemnation of aerial gymnastics as an unsuitable occupation "for the demure young ladies of good breeding." (3)

Of all the women trapeze daredevils appearing in Australia in the 1890s, not one was native born. The so-called 'Van Tassel Sisters', Val and Gladys, were part of the troupe. It is unlikely that the 'sisters' were related, or even the daughters of the Van Tassels, just employees. As American Val Van Tassel, Valerie Freties became a sensation as the first woman parachutist in the land, as she made her solo ascents, "not in the comparative safety of a basket, but perched on a trapeze bar - at times hanging by her feet, head down." (4)

The shapely American had made balloon ascents before but had not parachuted. Like Dolly Shepherd in England, we can surmise she was given a mere half hour's instruction prior to her first jump. Also, like Miss Shepherd, her immediate predecessor had died as a consequence of the leap before hers, thus making Val's debut parachute jump even more daunting. Being blown out to sea by a sudden change of wind and lost without trace was always a hazard of parachuting and a very real source of fear, especially to a novice.

While waiting nervously for the wind to abate, Val and Gladys performed acrobatics on the ground until almost nightfall, when those in charge decided the wind was favourable and the smoke balloon was made ready. After an emotional embrace by her sister, Val, dressed in circus tights, took up her position. At first the balloon rolled sideways, causing her to run along with it, until suddenly it lifted, and she swung with easy grace into a sitting position on the trapeze bar. The young girl performed above the Newcastle racecourse early in 1890 as the dumbfounded onlookers watched the balloon rise to 5000', estimated as such by an observer with a theodolite. At this height a pistol shot rang out: the pre-arranged signal for her to descend by means of her parachute. A dark form was seen falling; the crowd went wild; the parachute opened, and she came gently to earth in a paddock, a mile from where the balloon floated down.

The older Gladys also made a solo balloon ascent in Newcastle and her first ever parachute drop. From then on, the sisters usually took it in turns to perform. The *Newcastle Herald* wrote of the "daring young lady" and of the "terrible risk" and was quite puzzled that Gladys, having changed into a blue trapeze costume, "seemed very cool and collected, conversing quite joyfully with a crowd of young gentlemen who eagerly pressed her." These same men collected £12 and gave it to her as an expression of their admiration. (5)

Rain caused havoc with plans, for the paper reported that "the family, or rather, company, have had anything but a successful season in Newcastle as they are under the sway of the fickle god, Jupiter Pluvius, and he has been exceedingly cruel to them on 3 occasions." (6)

A large crowd was present at the Sydney performance given on 22 February 1890 by Val. Word of her death-defying feat had spread and the Bondi Aquarium, a pleasure pavilion at Tamarama Beach which specialised in entertainment of the stunt variety, had engaged the girl. An overcast sky threatening rain and a wind off the sea delayed the ascent by two hours, but one paper reported that the suspense had no effect on Val, for she looked "as happy as if she had been going on a pleasure trip." (7)

People were not disappointed: Val kissed her hands to them as she hung upside down in mid-air. The wind blew her along the coast, over Waverley Cemetery to Little Coogee Beach, where her unusual arrival interrupted a cricket match. The cricketers secured a horse cab to return her to the aquarium where she received an appreciative ovation. Interviewed afterwards, Val said she knew the risk she was taking, "because of the exceptionally rough day and the danger of my being blown out to sea." Nor could she swim, she added. Val explained that she and her sister Gladys (described by the interviewer as "a bright, vivacious young lady who was dovetailing in some of her experiences") always "come down feet first" to avoid injury. On this occasion, the girl hailed by the paper as a "heroine", had rolled on the ground, soiling her costume with mud but could still declare, "I wasn't even shaken up." (8)

Although the Bondi Aquarium, later known as the fun park Wonderland City, enjoyed only a short life, Val Van Tassel's career and that of her sister as the daring young girls on the flying trapeze continued. The stoic sisters sailed by steamer to Melbourne to introduce the novelty of a woman parachuting from a balloon.

When the southern winter set in, the Van Tassel camp moved north, chasing the sun to Townsville on the east coast, nestled into the shoulder that extends to form the neck of Cape York Peninsula. Queensland resembled the monarch, Queen Victoria, for whom it was named. Both were strait-laced and god-fearing. The State looked on with disdain as Val Van Tassel took to the skies, innocently believing she could charm the inhabitants with that colony's first balloon ascent.

It was on a Sunday 22 June 1890, with the encamped army's patronage and blessing, that Val ascended above Townsville. The defence force manoeuvres came to a halt at Gulliver's Pleasure Gardens, as 600 men watched Val in her skin-tight outfit complete her gymnastics and parachute down, "cleverly avoiding a bed of pineapples," to be feted on her return to the grounds, by the Defence Force Band playing *See the Conquering Hero Comes*. (9)

The show caused a sensation, but not in the fashion to which Val was accustomed. Instead, an unholy furore broke out and the shock waves resonated around Townsville for many months, and even crossed the ocean to Britain.

A deputation of ministers and laymen presumed the police magistrate and inspector of police would have banned the event, but both refused to interfere. Reverend James Stewart of the Seventh Day Adventists labelled the aerial show a disgrace, particularly as the defence forces had assisted "to desecrate the Sabbath". The Reverend was reportedly hooted by many Townsville residents, but the matter was not allowed to rest there. (10)

After a week, "the Townsville scandal" had not abated. The Member for Ipswich, Mr Macfarlane kept the debate alive in Parliament. He was incensed about the issue, as the extracts show, giving a fascinating insight into the moral and social codes of the times,

"By allowing an exhibition of that sort to take place on Sunday, the good name of Queensland will be spoken of abroad in a very unpleasant manner, but when we find that one of the chief officers of the Defence Force, Major Des Voeux bent down on his knees with a posy of flowers in his hand, with his eyes turned up towards the goddess of the balloon ascent, why, I look upon that as a species of idolatry - downright idolatry. I am sure I don't know what his relations will think about it." (11)

The Premier of Queensland spoke in defence of his Ministry, saying information prior to the ascent was "inaccurate and misleading" and he was not convinced that "the law would have allowed of the prevention of the ascent." He confirmed an inquiry would be effected into the behaviour of the Defence Force. (12)

The *Townsville Bulletin* was in "no doubt that, if the letter of the law was not actually broken, then the spirit in which it was framed was." It expressed outrage at 600 men in uniform paying 1/- each admission, so supporting the event by 600 shillings, when the public purse was paying the troops to be on military exercises.

The *Queenslander* protested at "such a desecration of the day of rest" and the shame they had brought "on the British Empire" no less. It reported that, on the day in question "colonels, majors and captains were as numerous as flowers in May, and twice as gay." (13)

At the inquiry, Colonel French tried to explain the presence and behaviour of his men: the infantry had helped maintain order at the balloon ascent; they had followed their command and completed a route march of six miles. None was forced to enter the gardens. The Commandant told the Legislative Assembly that permission had been granted to watch the preparations on a Sunday, as no officer likes to interfere with the religious principles (or lack thereof) of the men, thus his troops were not deprived of their civil rights, "I have no fault to find with any spontaneous enthusiasm to which they may have given expression at seeing a feat performed by a woman which probably few of them would have dared attempt." (14)

The Lord's Day Observance Society sent a deputation to the Chief Secretary, in the hope that "the Government would do all in their power to preserve the day of rest and concluded by thanking the Government... for stopping the balloon ascent on the Sabbath at Charters Towers." Surely exasperated by now, the Chief Secretary replied diplomatically, neatly dodging the issue of religious beliefs of some being imposed on all. (15)

Incredible as it is to us over a century later, the brouhaha continued fiercely before dying a natural death. It was in Townsville that the trail ran out for the Van Tassel Troupe. Confronted by the power and influence wielded by religious groups throughout Queensland, before which the government had given way, the Van Tassels, after performing again on a Monday at Charters Towers (under the watchful eye of Police Inspector John Islay, sent from Townsville to prevent any further ascents on Sundays), packed their balloons, trapezes, parachutes and costumes and turned their back on Australia. To attract reasonable numbers and earn a satisfactory living, they had to perform on Sundays, for Australians worked on every other day of the week. The troupe shrugged off the losses and treatment in Australia and departed for the Far East, where Gladys fell in love and married a tea planter in India.

The average citizen of Townsville either held no grudge against the Van Tassel troupe - or later felt remorse at their appalling treatment for to this day there is a Van Tassel Road and Van Tassel Creek.

An associate of Park Van Tassel was Professor James W Price, who also claimed to be an associate of Joe Van Tassel, the Joseph Lawrence who had been blown out to sea in Hawaii and whose body was never found. Price declared to a South African newspaper after leaving Australia, that Lawrence "was eaten up by sharks before he could be reached." The man who had a "mortal horror of sharks since then" ascended a few times in Hawaii, on a "spin round the world," and sailed to Australia with "Van Tassel (a brother)...together with Miss Viola, Miss Leila Adair and the Freties Sisters, known as the Van Tassels." (16)

(I think Price was mistaken as there is nothing to suggest Leila Adair performed in Australia before 1896: it was not until 1894 that she toured NZ).

James Price and his assistant, Millie Viola from Texas, not wishing to compete with Van Tassel in the east coast cities, concentrated on performing in outback NSW, South Australia, Tasmania and eventually in Western Australia. The rich mining town of Broken Hill in western NSW produced an admiring crowd in July 1890, to see Price pilot his balloon to 3000', from which Millie, wearing bright red tights parachuted to earth. One can only imagine the wolf whistles the 21year-old, auburn-haired Millie received from the miners.

The slick performance - the quick 'up and down' method that had so irritated Charles Brown - was now the accepted and preferred method. Brown would have argued that short flights gave no pleasure; however, the emphasis had shifted drastically: the actual flight was neither the central focus, nor the esoteric journey it once was. It had been replaced by aerial performance and a more fickle and demanding crowd. The showmen dared not risk the ire of impatient spectators. It was imperative that the balloon be launched after a short inflation; that the gymnastics build tension; be spectacular and culminate in the parachutist leaping into space.

Professor Price and Millie Viola crossed into South Australia. July that year was exceptionally wet and cold; the rivers were swollen, and many burst their banks. The papers informed of floods, drownings, boats lost and postponements of events. Early in August, on the 3rd, the weather cleared, and a crowd of 1000 gathered at the Gawler Recreation Ground. That evening, 'Mademoiselle' Viola, (described exotically as, "the premiere aeronaut of the world") became the first woman balloonist in SA but was thwarted in her attempt to parachute when the ropes tangled, forcing her to land near Willaston cemetery. (17)

In pre-flight advertising local papers credited Millie with seventeen parachute descents in other states, but without supporting evidence, I assume the information was propaganda.

Rain continued to fall over a widespread area, so Price packed and moved on alone to Tasmania, performing in the northern towns of Ulverstone, Latrobe and Launceston. Having introduced the parachute display to Tasmania, James Price bought a steamer ticket and headed for Western Australia. While engaged in these preparations, he was ignorant of another showman who was entertaining Sydneysiders on the east coast 2000 miles away.

Professor Fernandez entertained beachgoers on seven or eight occasions from the Bondi Aquarium in the summer of 1891. They paused as they swam or changed in the bathing boxes to gaze upwards at the Professor hanging from the trapeze by his heels. Children sucking ices let them melt as they pointed excitedly at the balloon going up "with a rush like a rocket." They saw Fernandez tumble through the sky, parachute streaming behind until it opened, as he slowly drifted down. (18)

On one occasion Fernandez made a spectacular night leap from the Aquarium. "The moonlight night was especially beautiful" as the showman "lit a lamp on his parachute and jumped downwards like a falling star." (19)

His fourth jump, on 14 February, was not as auspicious, for Fernandez dropped onto a barbed wire fence at Centennial Park and returned to the aquarium "covered with glory, blood and sand." He was adequately recompensed for his troubles with a purse of gold sovereigns, so was probably not too distressed. (20)

Fernandez made further leaps on 21 February and 7 March but not everyone was smitten with the novelty. After his last display that season, on 4 April, "the nasty, smoky balloon" he had abandoned early in a strong breeze, fell to earth " behind a house on the tennis-lawn, much to the disgust of the players." Fernandez nevertheless had a charmed run in Sydney, for its humidity often caused havoc, when calm skies would suddenly be ruffled by high winds, thunderstorms, lightning and hail. (21)

As autumn turned to winter, he headed north to Queensland, hoping no doubt for a less heated reception than the Van Tassels had received in Townsville. Through no fault of his own Fernandez was exposed to more heat than anticipated, for his balloon caught fire, leaving him with badly burnt limbs after a horror flight and narrow escape from death in rural Harrisville. The manager filled the envelope "with gasoline." The command to let her go was given and the balloon, with Fernandez and parachute attached, shot up to 1500 feet. Suddenly a small jet of smoke issued from the top of 'his balloon and fanned into a blaze. Without "sufficient time to cast his parachute adrift" Fernandez was dragged down by the collapsed balloon until it "caught on the outer branches of a large gum tree," where he was engulfed in flames. The hands which had so often held the weight of his body suspended from the trapeze bar, were the source of his delivery from death. For fully half an hour before his rescue, Fernandez hung to the ropes suspended in mid-air. (22)

Fernandez planned to proceed to Brisbane, to arrange for the making of another balloon but, perhaps unable to afford one, he disappeared from Australian skies as rapidly as his descent that fateful day. He may well have been the Spaniard, Duro Fernandez, who was notable for the major achievement of flying over the Pyrenees Mountains in 1906. (23)

As the expanding Australian colonies moved closer to independence and Federation, its citizens began to enjoy the fruits of their hard labour. An air of progress, affluence and sophistication permeated the capital cities, all originally coastal seaports.

It was not until 1891 that Australia's most isolated capital city Perth, witnessed a balloon ascent. The inhabitants of WA were enthusiastically welcomed James W Price and Millie Viola, with whom he had teamed up again. They set about organising displays, in Perth and also 'off the beaten track' in the rough country towns that clung to the lengthy WA coast.

Price's first attempt on 4 March, a day of rain and wind squalls, resulted in a fiasco when "a small boy assisting in the arrangements, shoved his fist through the material...the climax came with a gust of wind, which split the whole of the material from top to bottom." (24)

Nor was the first WA ascent on 24 March, as debonair as Price had planned. The repaired balloon soared away, with the Professor hanging from a trapeze, but at 150' it slumped earthwards in a leaky condition and became snared in a tree. Until a new balloon was ready, Price had to make do with his damaged one. On Easter Monday 30 March, he was the chief attraction at a fair held at the Albion Grounds; the novelty of WA's first parachute descent delighted the crowd.

By 22 April the new balloon, *Jupiter*, "looking as full as a new moon," stood ready at the Horticultural Society's grounds in Hay Street. Price ascended but, unable to detach the parachute, was forced to land near the tannery. The accommodating onlookers were satisfied with his explanation that the ropes had become entangled.

Millie Viola, Price's assistant, made the first ascent by a female in WA on 25 April that year. A prevailing wind postponed the flight for many hours, but eventually at 9pm, the night now being still, Millie went up to perform and was followed by her devoted fans on foot. Although there was insufficient light for Millie to use the parachute, the crowd watched her land the balloon near Milligan Street.

Not so pleased was James Price, who suffered from the old problem of inducing people to part with their money to watch proceedings. He stated he had made no money yet in WA: one proprietor owed him money; he had lost a balloon and had cashed in his return ticket to England to purchase the *Jupiter*. Sympathisers subscribed small sums of money and several gentlemen guaranteed a handsome purse of sovereigns if Price successfully parachuted. On 5 May the weather was perfect, and all proceeded smoothly, with Price parachuting to earth opposite the Government Printing office.

Millie Viola made a parachute display on 12 May. A total absence of wind augured well for Millie "who looked no bigger than a little child" as she detached herself at 3000'. Price was also happy with the £10 purse and the generous response to a collection afterwards. (25)

Millie took advantage of the calm weather on the 13th to parachute down at nearby Fremantle. The intrepid lady made a farewell descent there on 16 May but sprained her ankle when she hit a chimney at South Beach. She managed to retain her hold of the guttering until a ladder was rushed to the rescue.

At this stage Professor Price and Millie Viola decided to go their separate ways: Price to travel north and Viola to stay in Perth before heading south. The Price/Viola partnership was over.

Millie and her new manager a Mr R Duncan, together supervised the construction of a new, more graceful balloon, officially named the *Westralia* and the first of its size to be made in the colony. On 11 July, in mid-winter, Millie "was attired in a very becoming light silk heliotrope dress, profusely trimmed with white lace." Millie's health was drunk in champagne. Despite repeated requests, spectators persisted in walking over the roof of the furnace, resulting in a section collapsing and the balloon deflating. Disappointed, Miss Viola "cried bitterly for some time". She valiantly tried again later; however, the night proved too cold and frosty, the balloon cooled rapidly, and she descended, landing on the back of a horse. The other horses became frightened by the balloon and "kicked in a terrific manner." (26)

The resultant bruised arm did not prevent a further attempt two days later, but bad luck did: Perth's sandy soil shifted and the trench section of the furnace caved in. Any doubts of her ability were dispelled three days later on 15 July, when she made an ascent from the Guildford Hotel. Although the closeness of a swamp prevented her parachuting down, the onlookers were admiring of her courage and grace and subscribed a liberal sum of money, which became a feature of her appearances.

While the newspapers praised the lady's exploits in Perth, they also reported events far away. Fighting had broken out in the Civil War in Chile, with prisoners tortured and shot; Russia was in the grip of a famine, while Melbourne was under water, from a four day deluge. So severe was the flood, Elizabeth Street in the city was a roaring torrent and the Richmond streets laid down after the demise of the Cremorne Gardens were awash.

Millie Viola remained unaffected by her popularity as she kept up a hectic schedule - often performing three jumps a week - in spite of occasional mishaps and injuries. In the ten days between her Guildford ascents (15 and 25 July) she flew in Perth and Fremantle. On 21 July, a breeze nudged her off course to drift across the Swan River, depositing her in the mud on the opposite bank at South Perth. When asked why she had not parachuted, she replied with typical modesty, "although I am an aeronaut, I am no swimmer." (27)

The following day found her in Fremantle, where an unfortunate accident occurred during inflation, when the fabric of the mouth and neck of the balloon caught fire, due to negligence by the young helpers. Millie eventually ascended at 9pm. The cold night air caused a sudden collapse and the balloon veered over and struck a roof. The plucky Millie suffered only scratches but had to endure the indignity of being rescued from her perilous position. The balloon and parachute had gone through the roof into the hall but were amazingly undamaged.

Undaunted by such hazards, Miss Viola planned a further escapade from the Perth Railway Station for 3 August. Caught up with enthusiasm, one lad employed to work the guy ropes pulled too hard and tipped the envelope over onto the furnace, reducing it to cinders.

Shortly after this catastrophe, Millie left Perth. The flutter of excitement caused by her daring feats and adventures in 1891 were long remembered by residents there. Millie Viola was far from defeated however; she stoically organised a new balloon, wittily named *Phoenix*, and headed for the country towns of the southwest, where entire townships turned out to experience the thrills of barnstorming aeronautics, Millie style.

She appeared at Newcastle WA on 26 August; Northam on the 30 August; Beverley on the 19 September; Katanning on the 23 (where she suffered bruising after a mid-air whirlwind collapsed her parachute) and Albany on the 24th, her final performance in Western Australia.

From there she sailed to India, returning to Australia in April 1892 on what she declared was her farewell world tour. In outback Queensland Miss Viola was accompanied by "a charming young lady of about 17 years of age...prettily dressed" who "of course was immediately the centre of attention." This was reputedly Millie's sister, Essie Viola, (sometimes called Elsie) whom I suspect Millie was training as her replacement. (28)

On the hoop, without basket, Thomas Gale
Sydney 1870

Launceston Tasmania, Gale and Capt. Stourton

Prof. Gale at Sydney Uni with *Young Australian* 1871

Gale at cattleyards, Adelaide SA 1871

Accidental flight across Sydney Harbour
by James Stewart 1877

Rufus Gibbon Wells

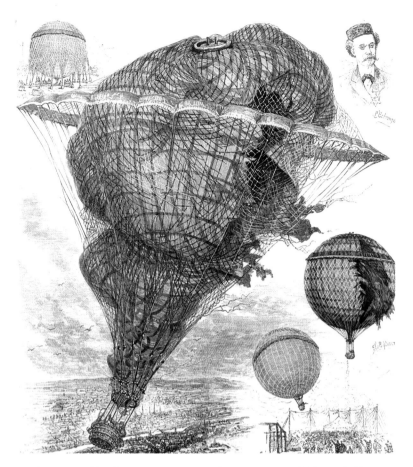

First Australian-born aeronaut, Henri L'Estrange, with burst balloon
Melbourne 1879

The unfortunate L'Estrange's balloon explosion and fire Sydney 1879

Harry Henden in Orange NSW

Henden's UK address

Harry Henden as an older man

# BALLOON ASCENT,

## BATHURST.

FROM THE

## ORDNANCE GROUND,

ON

# NEW YEAR'S DAY,

### JANUARY 1st, 1885.

Under the Patronage of the Mayor and Aldermen of Bathurst.

# MR. H. HENDEN,

From London, who has made such successful ascents in Sydney, under the Patronage of His Excellency the Governor of N.S.W., and Mayor and Aldermen of Sydney, will ascend in his Splendid New Balloon, "GEM," at half-past 4 o'clock, p.m.

There will be a

# SPLENDID BRASS BAND

### IN ATTENDANCE.

Admission to the Ground, 1s.  Reserved Chairs, 2s.
Carriages, 5s.

For the Right to Purchase Cake and Refreshment Stalls, apply to
**Mr. C. F. STRATTON,**
Business Manager,
Oxford-street, Sydney.

Handbill for Henden's Bathurst ascent

Fernandes Bartholomew on trapeze 1889

Roster for the Van Tassel sisters Townsville 1890

Townsville street named after the Van Tassel Sisters

## Extraordinary announcement !!!

### A LADY'S JUMP FROM THE CLOUDS.
### MISS ESSIE VIOLA,
#### The charming young Aeronaut & Paraschutist.

One of the prettiest, most novel, and charming feats ever performed by a lady; who, when at a dizzy height, will jump from the balloon and descend to mother earth by the aid of only a frail parachute.

The Balloon, the largest ever used in Australia, 75ft high, containing 75,000 feet of air being filled by a patent process, the filling of which is most interesting.

Do not fail to witness the grace and courage of the young lady as she takes her place on the trapeze prior to her **Aerial Flight.**

MISS VIOLA Draws special attention to the fact that the prices of admission are within the reach of everyone, and therefore confidently rely on receiving that support that the Towers public always accord to anything worthy of it.

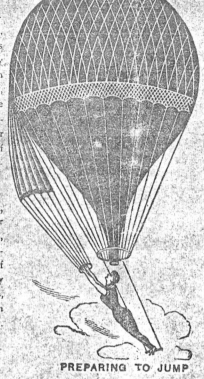

**PREPARING TO JUMP**

### In a Thrilling and Sensational
### ⇒BALLOON ASCENT⇐
### And PARASCHUTE JUMP

J. Brice, Typ.

Essie Viola, balloon and parachute Charters Towers 1891

### —GRAND—
## BALLOON ASCENSION
#### —AND—
## PARACHUTE DESCENT !!!

## THURSDAY, JULY 2, 1891.

Under the Patronage of

### His Worship the Mayor, E. Shenton, Esq.

E. H. WITTENOOM, Esq., & Dr. C. B. ELLIOTT.

## PROF. PRICE

The celebrated Balloonist will ascend with the Monster Balloon JUPITER, and when at a great height will descend to the earth with his frail PARACHUTE, landing very near the starting place.

### THIS WILL POSITIVELY BE
## THE ONLY EXHIBITION GIVEN AT GERALDTON.

Prof. Price and Millie Viola Geraldton WA 1891

Crowd watches Essie Viola

Prof. Fernandez Tamarama Beach Sydney
1891

Wilfrid Burns ballooned around Australia

Charters Towers handbill

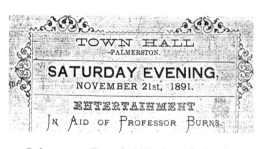

Palmerston (Darwin NT), Benefit for the
injured Burns 1891

Burns as a circus performer

Great grandson Sam Burns and his balloon
cake

# UNITED STATES BALLOON SOCIETY.

Professor JAMES W. PRICE, Chief Aeronaut, on Tour.

20 YEARS PRACTICAL EXPERIENCE.

New York Apr 28th 1902

Dear old Pal

I just received your Welcome letter and was very glad to hear from you, I am still in new york Would like very much to join you but have not got the stuff my trip to Cuba broke me it has cost me more than $800.00 Since Jany 22nd the date I left S africa, I have got the Hemischute Perfected, and have got onto the Human Bomb & Balloon Cannon act these three acts ought to get big Money this Summer, I am also married Wilfred & have a little girl 3½ years old if you Send for me I can leave Mrs Price in new york, I would like very much to be with you old pal and if you want me wire me a ticket and a few dollars and I will come on at once, Every Big Town we Show in is worth at least $1000.00 for the three acts Mentioned if you want me Send at once as there is nothin Doin in n y and you know how I am fixed,

Regards to my old Governor Bert

from your Pal

Jim

106 East 10th St
N. Y. City

Letter from Prof. James Price to friend Wilfrid Burns 1902

Semaphore on tethered military observation
balloon 1870s

Air support for Australian troops, Boer War 1899

Royal Engineers demonstrate militray
usage for Federation Sydney 1901

Antarctica, *Eva* weather balloon 1902

Melvin Vaniman's panorama, taken from balloon Melbourne

Melvin Vaniman's panorama, taken from balloon Sydney

*King Edward VII* ascends, Melbourne Exhibition Building grounds 1908
(courtesy and permission by Linton Lethlean)

Patched balloon Broken Hill NSW 1908

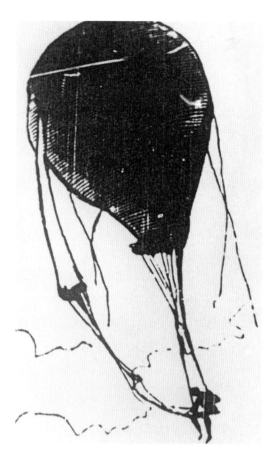

Rinaldo on trapeze Brisbane 1909

Zahn Rinaldo dressed for his performance

Beebee Balloon Troupe with folded parachute L-R Beebee, Sebphe, and Rinaldo (in striped shirt) Brisbane 1909

Inflation 1909 style - over fire pit, Clifton Gardens Sydney

Austral Wheel Race, MCG - Rinaldo and Christopher
Sebphe 1908

Vincent Patrick Taylor (Capt. Penfold) wearing his bravery medal

Taylor instructs his son George, Clontarf Sydney

BALLOON ASCENTS
PARACHUTE DESCENTS

Aeronaut George Taylor
(Australia's Youngest Airman)

BOX 2258 G.P.O.
SYDNEY, AUSTRALIA

Youngest Australian aeronaut, George Taylor

Taylor canvasses airship usage to the Aust. Defence Dept. 1915

Parachuting from the Buffalo Falls View
Bridge USA

In rubberised suit, Taylor paddles over
Niagara Falls 1927

Daring mid air parachute rescue by Dolly
Shepherd UK 1908

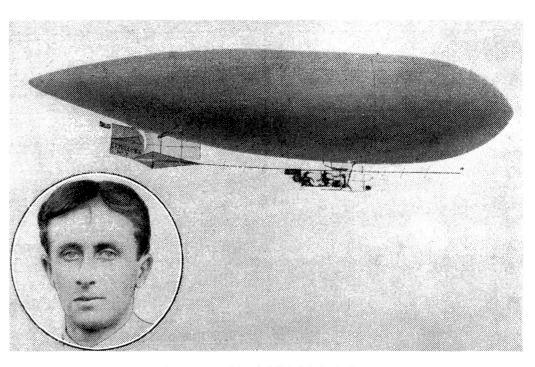

AJ Roberts' *City of Cardiff* dirigible in Sydney 1914

Australian soldiers with air support at Ypres, Western Front 1917
(Reproduced by courtesy of the Australian War Memorial, Collection E01174-1-TIF)

*HMAS Yarra* (79) with kite balloon, Otranto Straits, Adriatic 1918
(Reproduced by courtesy of, AWM, collection EO420 - TIF)

Observation balloon in ship's hold
Mediterranean WWI

Woomera balloon - Caquot Type 1956

Essie's 14 April performance in Gympie, eighty miles north of Brisbane, became a terrifying experience and was probably the most sensational event Gympie ever witnessed. At the precise moment when the stays were let go, a strong gust of wind swayed the fabric onto the flames. Millie grabbed at her 'sister' but it was too late. The balloon shot up and soon became a blazing mass which extended towards the parachute from which Essie dangled, the "frail girl waving her handkerchief in the most fearless manner." Although the parachute failed to detach from the flaming balloon, it operated well enough to steady Essie's descent. "The young lady, on regaining a footing on the solid earth, in the most nonchalant manner requested the bystanders to try and save her parachute." This was done but fire destroyed the balloon. The girl from San Francisco received an ovation from the bystanders, who gave willingly to a collection and organised a concert, to recoup the loss sustained. (29)

The Viola duo moved north to Rockhampton. The *Rockhampton Argus* wrote about Millie, the girl who had first ascended aged fourteen, telling a delightful story: Millie, aware of the certainty of a splashdown in a lake, put on her life belt but incorrectly. Consequently "her head went under and her feet aloft." Fortunately, an old fisherman was on hand to rescue her; from then on male admirers inundated her, not with flowers, but with fish. "Every hour of the day there used to be left at her hotel baskets of fish, attached to which was the sentiment 'If you are too nice for the fish of Chicago to eat, please eat the fish of Chicago.'" (30)

The paper reported Millie's travels through the US, India, China, Japan and South Africa, but proudly stated, "it has been in the Australasian colonies that she has had her most thrilling experiences." (31)

The female troupe went further north, in the steps of the Van Tassel 'sisters' to Charters Towers where on 30 May, Essie Viola took her turn at jumping from the clouds. Millie continued her world tour alone. From Melbourne she sailed across the Tasman Sea to Invercargill in New Zealand, arriving there in June to spend several months on a partially successful tour.

Her former mentor, James Price, had gone north in WA after their split, but his luck was no better than in Perth: only his 28 May 1891 performance in York was successful. July weather was unfavourable and prevented him demonstrating his skills in Geraldton. The paper believed Price had treated the residents in a cavalier fashion, although the display by his assistant Wilfred Burns, "understood to be a novice at the business" was a consolation. (32)

Price accepted such criticism more readily than objections raised on the grounds of safety. He regarded his ways as perfectly safe and defended them. He pointed out that he had made ballooning a study for fourteen years and had ascended over 500 times, "I know I am not endangering my life any more than a railway brakeman or a sailor...thousands are killed annually through accidents on railways, but no one thinks of stopping the operations of a railway. Thousands fall out of windows, but you still build houses with windows in them." (33)

'Professor' Wilfred J Burns made his West Australian debut in Geraldton with a sensational splash: he literally came down, with parachute, three miles out to sea. Not a swimmer, he kept afloat and avoided drowning with the aid of a lifejacket until picked up by a boat. Juveniles in particular, "certainly regarded Mr Burns as the hero of the hour." (34)

Wilfred Burns was not unused to such adulation for, having run away from school at the age of fourteen, he had joined a circus and become proficient in trapeze and acrobatics. At one time he was a World Champion weightlifter for his weight category (he weighed 140lbs and could lift 150lbs with one arm above his head, it is said.)

Over a period of years, I wrote to Wilfred's eighty-year-old son Samuel Burns in America, who regaled me with the fascinating life of his adventurous father; the father he barely saw, and who died when he was only very young. Sam Burns shared with me the contents of his father's scrapbook - the letters, shipping documents, advertising bills and newspaper cuttings, covering the years 1891 (when he was in Australia) through to 1898. His father was born in Quebec Province Canada, and for six years lived in the US, probably in Buffalo,

New York. He was sent to Canada for schooling in Ottawa, where he stayed five years until he joined the circus and was a performer ever after.

Burns came to Australia after four years performing circus in the East Indies, Africa, China and Japan; before that he had toured America for three years. He and James Price had been close friends in America, but, with Wilfred Burns resident in Geraldton, Price quietly disappeared from the Australian scene. Whether he had sent for Burns to join or replace him, or whether Burns arrived of his own accord, is uncertain; however, he was not the novice residents took him to be. Not only had newspaper cuttings described his performances previously in Victoria, NSW and SA, but he is also said to have chalked up in excess of 700 balloon ascents worldwide and 337 parachute jumps.

In the seven months travelling in Australia with balloons, he visited many places principally noted for their acute isolation. Most of the towns had mushroomed during the gold rush era, which peaked between the years 1854-1856, then declined steadily until the mid 1880s witnessed a resurgence. From the goldfields of Victoria and NSW, prospectors forged a trail to Gympie in southern Queensland in 1867, north to Charters Towers and the steamy Palmer River. Pastoralists, Chinese market gardeners and shopkeepers followed. Townsville became the site of a boiling-down works and the port for shipping out gold and agricultural produce.

In the 1870s, Port Darwin came into existence as a repeater station for the new telegraph system linking northern Australia to the south. It was particularly slow to populate, having only 200 Europeans and 700 Chinese residents sixteen years later. Pastoralists seeking grasslands for their cattle populated the hinterland. By 1890 all land in eastern Australia had been taken up but not in the west. This, and the search for new goldfields, prompted the push west after a lull of a decade. Subsequently the northwest of WA was settled in the 1880s, then the Pilbara and Murchison regions; the gold rich towns of Kalgoorlie and Coolgardie in 1892, and the dry interior of WA between 1886 and 1895.

Increased wealth paralleled an increase in money to spend on leisure activities, and the barnstorming balloonists were quick to realise the potential for their form of entertainment. Hours of work were declining for men; consequently, spectator sports enjoyed a surge of interest. In the cities, these replaced the danger and excitement that once accompanied pioneering; in outback regions men leading gruelling, solitary lives were appreciative of the risk, courage and acts of physical daring provided by the men, or even better, the women gymnasts of the skies.

Transport was becoming less difficult for travelling entertainers. Fewer hazards, accurate charts, lighthouses and the advent of more powerful engines in steamships led to safer sea routes; by 1890 fast steamers had halved the time it took to cross the world just forty years before. Small steamships connected coastal towns around Australia; paddle-steamers plied an extensive network of inland rivers in south eastern Australia and fast coaches ran a weekly service to link outback towns to railheads.

Four inland railway routes existed by the late 1880s, two in Queensland and one each in South Australia and NSW. Melbourne and Sydney were connected by rail and travel between the two cities was reduced to 24 hours, where once it took 6½ days by horse, clipper and sailing ship; this often extended up to 16 days if the ships were becalmed. Life was becoming easier in the big cities: electric lighting was installed, the first telephones appeared, and the introduction of sanitation benefitted health. Australia was booming.

This was the country Wilfred Burns discovered for himself. Unlike the miners pursuing rumours of new goldfields, Burns travelled in a clockwise direction, across the Nullarbor Plains, up the coast of WA, across the northern tip of the continent to traverse the inhospitable Cape York Peninsula, before heading down the east coast to inland northern NSW, giving performances along the way. He was the first and only aerial stuntman to undertake such an incredible journey: no balloonist has ever replicated his feat, made all the more remarkable when one considers that many of the towns in the north had been established barely a decade before his arrival and were known for their harsh climates, remoteness and lack of facilities. They were often inhabited by rough characters: men desperate to escape the law, their wives and families, or obsessed with making their fortunes, or drinking themselves to death from a fatal cocktail of failure and loneliness.

Being his own manager, Professor Burns had also to arrange his own publicity and ticket sales along the way; he had to book passages for himself and transport all the trappings of his profession: costumes, balloon envelope and basket, ropes, trapezes and parachutes.

Undaunted by his initiation to the west - his dunking in the Indian Ocean at Geraldton - Burns moved on in August 1891 to Roebourne, situated on the western shoulder of Australia, near its sister town Cossack. Both were tiny ports which served pastoralists and pearlers, only seventeen years old and 1000 miles from Perth. Several hundred residents existed mainly by unloading the pearling luggers or processing the oyster shells in sweltering tin sheds scattered among the mangroves.

These towns had a 'wild west' flavour; numerous hotels did a brisk trade in the shimmering heat, as did the imposing stone Court House at Cossack. The buildings which witnessed the downfall of so many men are among the few still standing in the ghost town that is now Cossack. The winds that now blow eerily through the abandoned buildings and derelict jetty, played havoc with Wilfred Burns' first four attempts to demonstrate his abilities to the locals.

Burns would set up his balloon over the tunnel connected to the wood and kerosene fire pit and inflate his balloon, only to have to keel it over in the stiff breeze. His first attempt was further complicated by the envelope catching fire in several places, extinguished hastily by the man inside, there specifically to regulate filling and to chase sparks. Only the third attempt was comparatively successful. He rose a mere 200-300 feet before slipping the parachute and somersaulting involuntarily several times before landing on his feet near the schoolhouse. The local paper reported that "to descend from so low an elevation was a most dangerous feat...and Professor Burns is greatly to be congratulated on his pluck in attempting it." (35)

Burns busied himself making a new balloon, supposing his persistent failures must be "partly due to the fact that my balloon was almost destroyed on the occasion of my first trial." (36)

In the two weeks that it took to construct the new balloon, Professor Burns entertained "the inhabitants of Roebourne with his other talents. Although he confessed to being out of practice, the audience enjoyed his acrobatic, trapeze, wirewalking and gymnastic performance, finding it a "trying programme involving strength and endurance as well as agility and knack." Burns certainly excelled that night, for he also exhibited his axe-swinging and weight-lifting abilities, "lifting each of the 56lb weights up with his little finger." (37)

At the close of the evening, he announced he would be leaving Roebourne to visit Derby and Port Darwin to the north, but Burns' luck was "out all the way up the coast." In Derby, "the folks rallied him so much for not bringing a calm day along with him that he promised to stay there until he got one, and he did." (38)

News next came of Burns from Port Darwin, where he had disembarked from the *Rob Roy* on 11 October with two balloons. The town, alternatively called Palmerston, was previously part of the colony of North Australia, which from 1863-1911 was known as the Northern Territory of South Australia.

Burns advertised a parachute descent for Monday 19 October, but Darwin's early risers were annoyed on arrival to find Burns packing. He had launched and landed before the stipulated hour, as the breeze had sprung up earlier than usual: consequently, few onlookers saw Burns parachute into Mitchell Street. The balloon was lost out to sea near Point Emery and never recovered. Fortunately Burns had already raised £40-£50 by public subscription - virtually the cost of the envelope material - but it was still no compensation in real terms.

Ten days later, on 28 October, Professor Burns used the new *Sunbeam* balloon and, "in wholesome dread of coming down in the sea," towards which the balloon was heading, he disconnected the parachute at the foolhardy height of eighty feet. He was almost on the ground before the chute opened; the thud with which he struck suggested a fatal accident. The unfortunate Burns, alive but unable to rise, was carried to the Club Hotel, where Dr O'Flaherty sent him to hospital. The report on his health was "quite gloomy," for Burns had "a partial dislocation of the spine, the ultimate effect of which cannot yet be ascertained. It seems certain, however, that his days as an aeronaut are at an end, and it is not at all improbable that he will be a cripple for the remainder of his life." The balloon was indeed plucked from the sea, none the worse for the dip, except for the effects of saltwater. (39)

The *Northwest Times* pleaded for a show of practical and earnest sympathy for the young man who, "up to the time of the mishap possessed unbounded nerves, pluck and energy." The people of Palmerston organised a benefit evening to aid the poorly professor. Printing of the programme was provided gratis, as was the capacity-filled hall. Local amateurs treated fellow citizens to singing, piano performances and an operetta. Even Dr O'Flaherty helped out by singing "a drunken sort of refrain." A respectable £20 cheque was handed to the beneficiary, still recovering in hospital, whose injuries proved less serious than first thought. (40)

The newspaper predicted it would be a long time until the unfortunate showman could balloon again. He was awaiting a vessel to take him to Cooktown on Cape York Peninsula, where he intended to convalesce. Burns was well enough to board the *SS Catterthun* on 24 November and sail east to Thursday Island, off the northernmost tip of the continent, intent not on convalescing, but to ascend there at Christmas in the *Sunbeam* balloon.

Cooktown was Burns' next port of call. It owed its existence to the discovery of the Palmer goldfield in 1873: prospectors arrived at the port then travelled by dray the 210 kilometres to Palmerville, the new township built entirely of canvas and bark. A mere two years later Cooktown boasted 63 hotels, 40 brothels and just 2 churches.

Seventeen years later Burns arrived and distributed handbills espousing him as "the hero of seven hundred Aerial Voyages and 337 Parachute Jumps," (which was stretching the truth), and advertising his one and only exhibition there. He then moved west to sweltering Normanton on the Gulf of Carpentaria. And promising "positively no failure," for his Saturday evening display on 16 January 1892 at Normanton's racecourse.

It is interesting to note the changes to the wording in his advertisements over the next months. They went from the above to, "should the advertised hour not be favourable, Professor Burns will postpone the ascent until suitable weather" and finally to, "should the advertised hour not be perfectly calm, Professor Burns will postpone the Ascension until the first favourable hour following." (41)

Burns, like other travelling showmen, never appeared unduly affected by the heat, flies, mosquitoes or disease of tropical northern Australia. By January, Queensland was baking under the summer sun and the humidity was very high, for it was the wet season, when torrential downpours and cyclones are common, and the rivers of the Gulf country burst their banks and spread far across the plains.

Somehow Burns journeyed the hundred miles to Croydon, taking the advice of locals to head east again before the 'big wet' stranded him. Barely three weeks after leaving Normanton, Burns parachuted on 4 February above the racecourse, from his huge calico and silk *Sunbeam* balloon. From Croydon he crossed the Great Dividing Range to Charters Towers. People there had previously seen the Van Tassel sisters perform but turned out in force to watch the 'celebrated aeronaut' jump from a mile up.

The gifted Professor Burns had joined Messrs Abell and Klaes' circus and had the previous night appeared for the first time in Australia, "in his famous Chinese ladder act, in which he picks the apparatus into fragments while doing some of the most astounding feats of balancing." This circus originated in India and had a strong oriental aspect: not only were there acts by monkeys, dogs, ponies and pigeons, but also contortion, somersaulting and trick riding acts. (42)

Perhaps the circus subsidised Burns' "Only Ascent on the Towers" (Charters), as entry to the Athletic Reserve was a third that charged at Normanton. Special excursion trains left Townsville after lunch on 1 March, to transport spectators to the racecourse to see Professor Burns perform above - now billed as the hero of a diminished number (300) of aerial voyages.

The circus, and Burns, moved down the eastern coast of Queensland and struck inland in NSW, performing at Inverell and Glen Innes. One paper described WJ Burns as the circus' star performer, adding also that the aeronaut was worth two million pounds a minute, but was more likely "to be heir-o-naught in reality, except to six feet of earth." (43)

Wilfred Burns travelled the world for a total of 28 years, as the strong man in Wirth's circus, as manager of others and co owner with Professor Price of their own. They toured the Hawaiian Islands in 1896-1897, with Burns performing in the ring and both of them in the skies. Burns spoke "seven languages and was considered to be an elegant, well-mannered gentleman during his few periods of extended residency in the United States." (44)

Whilst touring the West Coast of America with a vaudeville group, he met and married Elodia Wagner, a pianist for a local theatre in Eureka California. Two sons, Charles Wilfred and Samuel were born in 1904 and 1908 respectively, and they travelled with their parents on various vaudeville and circus tours until 1913, when the Professor felt the urge to do more ballooning. He left behind his family and departed on an extended world tour from which he never returned for, three years later, his luck ran out in Penang, Malaysia when his parachute failed to open, and he crashed through a bamboo roof. In his weakened condition he failed to fight off a bout of dysentery and died a few days later on 12 January,1916.

Charles and Sam Burns were only nine and five years old when they last saw their father. Their mother remarried and the family grew up on a farm near Olympia, Washington. Sam Burns, in his late seventies, corresponded with me on a regular basis. In one letter he told me that, "my father's adventurous life has always been a source of pride to me and I wish I could have known him better." I learnt incredulously that Sam "never had the pleasure of going up in a balloon but would love to experience the thrill my father had so many times. I surely hope to do so some day." (45)

I pledged to find a balloonist in America to take Sam Burns aloft. Meanwhile, a photograph arrived taken of Sam on his eightieth birthday, proudly cutting a cake decorated with a balloon shaped in colourful icing. I redoubled my efforts to get him a balloon flight, to no avail. To my very real regret, Samuel Burns, son of aeronaut Professor Burns, died on 21 December 1989 without ever experiencing the pure magic of 'riding the winds' in a balloon.

His father's epic tour around Australia was a remarkable achievement, which he no doubt shrugged off as being nothing extraordinary. Burns was one of the intrepid, death-defying aeronauts who unknowingly kept ballooning alive, until such time as modern technology could address the problems that made early ballooning such a hazardous occupation.

There were other balloonists who made brief appearances in Australia and then were gone, among them American Professor Bartholomew in Sydney in 1888 and Englishman Arthur Charles Spencer, who was the second son of the renowned Charles Green Spencer and brother of professional balloonists, Percival and Stanley. Arthur left the successful family parachute-making business, ultimately travelling furthest from home; he flew balloons in Brazil, North America and Canada before deciding to prospect for gold in Australia. It was not long however before he reverted to his great love, ballooning, when in Melbourne in 1897. On one attempt a sudden wind gust lifted the gas balloon,12 men and 220 bags of ballast off the ground, resulting in the envelope escaping its net and disappearing. On another ill-fated descent Arthur Spencer broke his leg by landing on a tombstone.

American Leila Adair was another. She had toured extensively in New Zealand in the first half of 1894 (following Millie Viola's lead) with much success, but lost her dignity, and almost her life, when she splashed down in Sydney Harbour on 6 January 1896. Fishermen hauled her out by her parachute, feet first and unconscious. Although she had been under water a considerable time, Miss Adair survived, but took the first ship back to the United States, leaving behind only memories of her embarrassing ducking and a ditty which children sang for many years after her tour,

*"Leila Adair went up in the air,*
*Her balloon came down and left her there."* (46)

The smoke balloonists gave people all over Australia the chance of a lifetime: to see thrilling, aerial events away from the hardship of their everyday lives. Particularly in remote areas, the shearers, stockmen and boundary riders who exulted in their challenges to tame the land were an admiring audience for those who challenged the skies.

The trials and tribulations faced by the late nineteenth century aerobats, "are the stuff of which high adventure is made," wrote one reporter of the exploits of James Price and Millie Viola, but which epitomised the deeds of many, "Like shooting stars they appeared in the West Australian sky, glowed for a brief moment and vanished at opposite ends of the continent."

The barnstorming aerial stuntmen and women retained popularity worldwide until the 1930s, fading away only when the aeroplane wing-walkers and stuntmen encroached on their act.

(1)  Dolly Shepherd, *When the Chute Went Up.*
(2)  Ibid.
(3)  Ibid.
(4)  *Newcastle Herald* 7 February 1957.
(5)  Ibid.
(6)  Ibid.
(7)  *Daily Telegraph* 24 February 1890.
(8)  Ibid.
(9)  *Courier Mail* 24 June 1890.
(10) Ibid.
(11) Parliamentary Debates 26 June 1890.
(12) Ibid.
(13) *The Queenslander* 5 July 1890.
(14) Parliamentary Debates.
(15) *Courier Mail* 6 July 1890.
(16) *The Evening Star*, undated.
(17) *South Australian Chronicle* 9 August 1890.
(18) *The Bulletin* 7 February 1891.
(19) Ibid.
(20) Op cit 21 February 1891.
(21) Op cit 11 April 1891.
(22) *Courier Mail* 11 August 1891.
(23) Robert J Rechs, *Who's Who of Ballooning.*
(24) *The West Australian* 5 March 1891.

(25) Op cit 13 May 1891.
(26) Op cit 13 July 1891.
(27) Op cit 23 July 1891.
(28) *Gympie Times* 17 April 1892.
(29) Ibid.
(30) *Rockhampton Argus*, undated.
(31) Ibid.
(32) *Geraldton Express* 8 July 1891.
(33) Ibid.
(34) Ibid.
(35) Unidentified local paper.
(36) Letter to Editor, Burns, *Roebourne News* 7 August 1891.
(37) Ibid.
(38) Unidentified newspaper.
(39) *Northwest Times*, undated.
(40) Ibid.
(41) Unidentified newspapers Burns collection.
(42) Ibid.
(43) Ibid.
(44) Mike Galvin, *Balloon Life*, Professor Wilfred Burns Early Aeronaut and Smoke Balloonist.
(45) Letter S Burns to author, 16 April 1988.
(46) Ross Ewing and Ross Macpherson, *The History of New Zealand Aviation*.

# Exploration and Military Use

Ballooning did continue in Australia, but in a vastly different form. It became the province of the military, which aimed the spotlight on Africa. For it was in the Sudan War in 1885, and during the Boer War of 1899-1902, that Australians first had air support for their troops, albeit provided by the British.

This period in aeronautic history saw the emergence of the observation or captive balloon in warfare. The military potential of the balloon had been early recognised by Benjamin Franklin who, after witnessing the first ascents in France, wrote to President Washington, "Five thousand balloons, capable of raising two men each...ten thousand men descending from the clouds might...do an infinite deal of mischief before a force could be brought together to repel them." The gentle, impractical balloon was soon to become an integral part of the aggressive and "utilitarian business of war." (1)

Napoleon I was credited with having the world's first air force, when he deployed observation balloons at Mauberge on 2 June 1794 and at the Battle of Fleurus in Belgium 24 days later. The balloons were tethered to the ground and used as observation posts to report the locations of enemy troops and to direct movements of their own.

The use of the captive balloon lapsed in warfare for nigh on half a century. It re-emerged on 15 July 1849, when Austria, with sinister purpose, launched history's first aerial bombing raid in an assault on Venice.

In America, prior to the Civil War, President Lincoln authorised an army balloon corps of five balloons and fifty men. The Unionists corps included balloonists Thaddeus SC Lowe, John Wise, John La Mountain and Ferdinand von Zeppelin. Two years later, after protests of expense, it was reported that, "the employment of balloons has been done away with in the Federal armies." Nine months later the US Federal Government sold all its balloons - military ballooning having proved a failure. (2)

Failure was not how the French described their re-established balloon corps nearly a decade later during the Franco-Prussian war and the siege of Paris, which lasted from September 1870 to January 1871.

Britain had been particularly slow in adopting the idea of military ballooning - the science that Henry Coxwell had advocated and demonstrated for years. His frustration often surfaced: he said the Government was, "...proverbially averse to new-fangled notions, resisted all overtures from an experienced aeronaut for many years, pooh-poohing this kind of feather-brained mode of strategy." It was not until 1878 that the British formed a balloon corps (3)

In 1884 in Sydney, Dr Belgrave delivered a paper to the Royal Geographical Society of Australasia on the subject of sending an exploratory expedition to New Guinea. His idea was to set up camps with a system of signalling between them, using small captive balloons a reasonable distance apart to communicate. Dr Belgrave considered that the use of captive balloons, plus a coded method of signals, "used in conjunction with the instantaneous dry photographic process could be most usefully employed in finding out the lay of surrounding country, and in detecting the presence of an enemy." The only disadvantage Belgrave could foresee was that hostile natives would also know their whereabouts. (4)

The Vice President of the Geographical Society, in addressing members, considered Dr Belgrave's paper an ambitious concept and feared it to be more an invasion than an exploration, "an armed expedition advancing into the interior of the country, fortifying as they went, wore an aggressive appearance, and he was convinced it would never be allowed by the Imperial authorities." (5)

It is pertinent at this point to mention an exploratory expedition using balloons which did eventuate, in Antarctica. There had been talk for years about exploring the region: in 1885 the Hon JG Duffy, proposed an Antarctic Expedition to the Legislative Assembly, but was ridiculed.

Baron Ferdinand von Mueller, an enthusiastic proponent and supporter of polar exploration, addressed the Royal Geographical Society of Australia in January1886. He advocated that no further polar exploring expeditions should be without an experienced aeronaut and a balloon for observation purposes. Six months later he was one of eight to form the first Australian Antarctic Committee, which recommended using the observation balloon, to help establish the new whaling trade venture they envisaged for Antarctica.

His concept was put into practice five years later when Commander Robert Falcon Scott led the National Antarctic Expedition to the frozen southern continent.

In the period between conception and application, came Salomon August Andrée's doomed attempt to reach the North Pole in a free flying gas balloon. His expedition soared away in *The Eagle* on 11 July 1897 from Spitzbergen. A carrier pigeon took back news of their first two days, then there was silence that lasted for 33 years until Norwegian explorers on White Island stumbled across a camp and the bodies of all three men. Andrée's diary and camera revealed their tragic story: they were forced down on the ice on their third day, abandoned the balloon and trekked for three months before perishing.

The disappearance of the North Pole expedition did not deter the British from exploring the Antarctic. A few days before Christmas 1901, the National Antarctic Expedition of 1901-03, led by Commander Robert Falcon Scott, sailed from New Zealand for the Bay of Whales in Antarctica. It was here that the continent's first balloon ascent occurred on 4 February 1902, when Scott rose to the length of the restraining wire rope and scanned the whiteness with binoculars. *Eva* had been inflated with hydrogen from nineteen cylinders, three more than required in England - due to the contraction of gas in the cold atmosphere.

Sub-lieutenant Ernest Shackleton ascended next to conduct experiments and take photos. One other person went up before a rising wind forced them to deflate the balloon. In their study of the great Ross Ice Barrier from aloft, and the clear sighting of Mount Erebus 120 miles away, they had completed procedures first predicted and proposed by von Mueller.

During the long winter months spent iced in at McMurdo Sound, Shackleton edited and printed five issues of a journal, *The South Polar Times*. One contribution for the first volume came from engineer RW Skelton who wrote an informative article, "*Ballooning in the Antarctic*," complete with illustrations, which recorded the unusual circumstances and positive outcome of their Polar ascent.

In 1884 Britain used aeronautics in their expedition to Bechuanaland in the Sudan. The grand British Balloon Detachment consisted of just one balloon, the *Fly*, manned by eight NCOs and sappers under the command of Major Templer. Colonial Australians quickly rallied to join their British brothers. The *Australasian* and the *Iberia* left Sydney's Circular Quay on 3 March 1885 with 750 NSW soldiers bound for the Egyptian Sudan. The war was not going well for 'John Bull' when the Australians disembarked at Suakin on the Red Sea on 29 March. Two months before, General Gordon was murdered by the enemy and his head hung from the gate at Omdurman, across the Nile from Khartoum. The outrage of this barbarism acted as the impetus for Australia to send its first official overseas military force. (6)

It was at Tamai, a three day march from Suakin, that the *Fly* appeared on 1 April above the tiny Australian contingent. Lieutenant William Cope wrote that, "the balloon was taken forward on the march for about a mile and was of great service in determining our course." (6)

The Sudan Balloon Detachment was observed by official historian Sir Walter Raleigh, "the best of the material had been sent to Bechuanaland, and so the equipment was very imperfect," but the balloon operations "at El Teb and Tamai, and elsewhere, proved useful for reconnaissance." (7)

Camels carried the hydrogen gas cylinders from the plant installed at Suakin. The flat nature of the Sudan was ideal for military observations and the balloon was never attacked. The balloon had a terrorising effect on the Arabs, who dispersed at the sight of it bobbing in the air above the troops, carried along by a convoy wagon. This one captive balloon in Africa has significance in Australia's military and aviation history, for it was the first occasion that Australian troops had air support.

The Sudan campaign was short-lived, for the Gladstone government had other problems: colonies were seeking self-government and the Irish were against England's stand, sympathising "with the Sudanese patriots in their endeavour to secure 'Home Rule' for the Sudan." A crisis with Russia in Afghanistan meant British troops were needed elsewhere, so Gladstone called off operations in the Sudan, leaving behind only a garrison. (8)

In Australia there was concern and fear of a Russian invasion. The *Evening News* in April 1885 made dire predictions and spoke in favour of strengthening Sydney Harbour defences. The Australian camel corps was disbanded, and the infantry sailed for Sydney on 17 May in the *SS Arab*. It was an inglorious return home on 19 June, (four short months after first sailing out of the Sydney Heads), for the soldiers carried typhoid fever aboard and the entire contingent and crew were isolated at North Head Quarantine Station.

In the South African War of 1899-1902, 16 175 Australians went into action for the British, against the Dutch South African Republics of Transvaal and the Orange Free State. The war began after quarrels between wealthy capitalists, Afrikaaner farmers (known as Boers) and non-Boer gold miners (including Australians), who resented Britain annexing the Transvaal in 1877. Huge gold deposits had been discovered at Pretoria, and southern Africa was regarded as a wealthy prize. The Republics of South Africa did not wish to belong to England; the Boers saw their independence at stake; the English their supremacy and investments.

At the outbreak of the so-called 'Boer War', British balloon manufacture at Aldershot expanded rapidly. Balloon depots were established at Cape Town and Durban; three British Army Balloon Sections plus one mobile detachment operated in the field. Hydrogen gas was preferred over coal gas for its better lifting ability. It was relatively easy to erect a plant for the purpose of manufacturing hydrogen: the most common method was to dissolve iron and zinc in a mixture of sulphuric acid and water.

There were limits to the war balloon's usefulness: rain, cloud and mist obscured land and strong winds battered the balloon. With varying cloud and sun conditions the gas could expand and the balloon burst. Another drawback was that they could easily be seen by the enemy Boers who, unlike the fearful Mahdis in the Sudan, did not disperse with alacrity but stood and shot holes in several balloons. The balloons then had to be repaired and returned to service. At day's end the inflated balloon was bagged down, anchored and guarded all night. Although kept inflated, the balloon envelopes leaked gas and needed re-inflating. Hydrogen was expensive and required the carting of bulky, heavy equipment on a horse-drawn wagon over difficult terrain, avoiding trees and telegraph wires.

They did have many advantages too: although not entirely steady, balloons could be rapidly raised for observation purposes or to drop a charge on the enemy. The effect on morale was excellent, for a tethered balloon with a dummy figure or sandbags as ballast, might paralyse the enemy, by their believing all movements were under scrutiny. Balloons were best used for short periods for reconnaissance and communication of messages. The air to ground telephone was the quickest way, for a message book in a weighted bag slid down the cable sometimes fell off; a message shouted via a megaphone could be misinterpreted; flag signals proved awkward and slow. The favoured method was to haul down the observer to give a message personally, but that meant a long delay.

Australian troops operated in all theatres of the Boer War. On the Modder River, the 1st Balloon Section remained from December 1889 until June 1900 when Pretoria fell. The Extemporised Balloon Detachment was stationed with the British who had retreated to Ladysmith from the outbreak of the war in October 1889, all through the famous siege until November, when gas supplies were exhausted. The relieving force of mounted infantry arrived in February 1890 and the Boers were finally defeated.

Field Marshall Lord Robert's army incorporated the 3rd Balloon Section on its forward thrust to Pretoria, capital of the Transvaal. Balloons had been in constant use for fifteen days, prior to the relief of Mafeking on 17 May 1890. In September 1900 the Transvaal Republic was annexed to the British Empire and came under the command of Lord Kitchener.

Several books praised the invaluable work undertaken by the balloons and their observers during the Boer War. War correspondent for the Melbourne *Argus*, Donald Macdonald published his book, *How We Kept the Flag Flying* in 1900 and JHM Abbott his *Tommy Cornstalk* in 1902. The name 'Cornstalk' was the name acquired by New South Welshmen who had "acquired a reputation for lankiness and wiriness".

The enemy viewpoint of the observation balloon's successes was delivered during a lecture in March 1902 by an unusual Australian character, Colonel Arthur Lynch, born near Ballarat of a father who had fought with the miners at the Eureka Stockade. He published in 1924, *My Life Story*, in which he related his remarkable tale. He had left Australia after qualifying as a Master of Arts and civil engineer, married and became a *Sun* journalist in London. In this capacity he went to the Boer War and found his sentiments lay with the Boers. Although he had never before commanded troops, he ended up as leader of the Second Irish Brigade; President Kruger of the Transvaal immediately made him a Colonel for the Boers. Lynch had nothing but admiration for the balloon detachments used in South Africa; his assessment being that the British, "possess the best balloon service of all the armies in the world." (9)

Of course, this would not be the last time Australian troops travelled overseas to fight for England, but there would be significant changes in status before they met again in common conquest on the shores of Gallipoli and the fields of France.

For Australia, the twentieth century began auspiciously: not long after death ended Queen Victoria's 55year reign, the first loosening of Britannica's apron strings took place. While Australians were fighting the Boers in South Africa - 250 gave their lives for the British - Australians at home were celebrating that they were no longer a British colony but a self-governing federation of states: the Commonwealth of Australia.

For Australia's Federation celebrations, Britain sent out a detachment of the Royal Engineers Balloon Section which, under Lieutenant THL Spaight's command, demonstrated the abilities of the military balloon and its telegraphic signals. Appearances at Sydney's Agricultural Ground on 7-8 January 1901 were the first in the nation by a military balloon. Spaight thus became the first person in Australia to fly a military aircraft, albeit a lighter-than-air machine made captive by a length of rope attached to a wagon. Newspapers recording the event published photographs taken from the balloon; these are in all probability the first aerial photographs taken in Australia.

(1) Kurt R Sterling, *Skyhooks*.
(2) *Argus*, 22 October 1863.
(3) Coxwell, *On War*.
(4) *Geographical Society of Australasia*, Dr Belgrave: Exploration and Signalling by Captive Balloons.
(5) Ibid.
(6) In New Zealand's Maori Wars of 1863-72, 2500 Australians had fought in a volunteer capacity
(7) Keith Isaacs, *Defence Force Journal*, Australia and the Military Balloon.
(8) *The Bulletin*, 28 March 1885.
(9) Keith Isaacs: *Defence Force Journal*

# Aerial Photography and Barnstormers

Hot on the heels of the first military aerial photographer in Australia, came the first civilian airborne photographer, American Melvin Vaniman. An engineer by profession, he became an inventor, agricultural consultant, opera singer and aeronaut. For years Vaniman sang with opera companies all over the world, performing at night which left his days free to develop his love of photography. His panoramic photos, usually from the rooves of opera houses, were in such demand in tourist agencies that he attracted a commission from a shipping company to tour their ports of call, photographing the local attractions.

Vaniman hit upon the idea of going up in a captive balloon to take his scenic photos. While in Sydney he ordered a balloon from a New York manufacturer, which took ten months to arrive. During this time the inventive genius designed and made a panoramic camera to take 360° photos. He used a circuit system, building a clockwork drive for the revolving camera and for film advancement. This produced large prints 1.2 x 0.4 metres in size which he developed himself and could enlarge further.

In April 1904 Vaniman trialled the balloon in Sydney, taking photos at different altitudes and concluding that 300 metres was the height preferred for visibility and stability. From a vantage point at Crows Nest on the North Shore, Vaniman photographed sailing ships in Sydney Harbour, the city and surrounds. The clarity of the huge photographs is extraordinary: on the two original Vaniman photographs in the Art Gallery of NSW and in a private collection in Melbourne, the signs on shop fronts are easily readable. Although he photographed Sydney and Melbourne by day and sang opera at night, Vaniman took no further photos from balloons in Australia, but his experience did foster a serious interest in aeronautics. (1)

On his return to America, the extraordinary Vaniman became involved with airships. He designed his own semi rigid dirigible, the *Akron*, and attempted an Atlantic Ocean crossing on 2 July 1912, accompanied by his brother and two crew. His experiment proved fatal to all four when the gas caught fire and burst 800 metres above Atlantic City, New Jersey. His wife witnessed the tragedy from the shore as the airship exploded and dropped into the sea.

The forty year old inventive genius took the secrets of his brilliant panoramic camera to the grave, for his camera designs had never been publicly divulged, but some of his innovative wide-angle pictures remain to tell of Vaniman's passion for both photography and aeronautics.

In the early twentieth century, Australians began to recover from the economic losses, the droughts and savage blows brought about by the Recession of the 1890s. By the end of the first decade there was renewed interest in flying. Eyes were beginning to turn skywards again; however, they were directed more towards airships and the newest invention, the aeroplane.

A few optimistic, and perhaps anachronistic, balloonists emerged to keep alive the first manned flying machine, the balloon. The resurgence of the travelling aerial showmen at this time in Australia was to be the last curtain call for the aerial stuntman and his travelling troupe, but it was during this period that the smoke balloonists and parachute jumpers elevated their skills to their highest form and before appreciative audiences.

The first ascent for a decade took place in 1907 at Melbourne's Exhibition Grounds with little publicity. It was made by Canadian Alphonse Stewart, who was probably the unnamed balloonist who entertained the crowds on Saturday afternoons in the summer of 1908 at Sydney's Wonderland City. The newly opened amusement park at Tamarama Beach occupied the old Bondi Aquarium site. Among its many advertised attractions, including balloon races and parachute leaping, was a ride on an airship, the photos of which puzzled me until I realised it was not airborne but, "ran across the beach on a solid steel cable, supported on the cliffs at both ends on massive wooden structures. At high tide it was actually over the sea." There was a landing stage at each end of the 'flight'. According to newspapers, "riding in the airship was quite an experience, and as it had a bad habit of stopping in the middle of the cable, passengers had frequently to be rescued by ladder from the beach, a somewhat hazardous proceeding." The popular ride recouped its outlay; however the entire venture lasted only two seasons and closed with an incurred loss. (2)

One syndicate member blamed Sydney's sub-tropical rainy summers for its demise, "Sydney, as it turned out, had a summer climate spelling disaster for open-air entertainment. Whenever an attraction aimed at drawing a bumper crowd was announced the heavens opened up." (3)

In Melbourne in February 1908, Alphonse Stewart was parachuting. He was the first in Australia to demonstrate a new method of floating to earth using three parachutes for dramatic effect. The *Australasian* described Stewart's colourful triple parachute jump,

"...the tiny object dropped from the balloon. It fell through space for a fraction of a minute, and then a brilliant red canopy spread itself. For another fraction of a minute the aeronaut descended at a moderate rate. The red canopy was cut away, and again there was a swiftly-dropping object in the sky, until a white canopy materialised. Then the aeronaut cast the white parachute adrift, and fell through the air for another instant. Finally a spread of rich blue cloth appeared and filled, to check the descent." (4)

Stewart, still perched on his trapeze, directed his landing towards a patch of green among the South Carlton housetops, by stretching out one arm and trimming the canvas. Six months later Stewart joined forces in Queensland with Vincent Beebe. The Beebe Balloon Company was to dominate Australian and New Zealand skies from 1908-1914, and Beebe himself continued as a smoke balloonist in his native America until 1930.

Beebe and Stewart's balloon, the *President Roosevelt*, rose from the Brisbane Cricket Ground on 4 July 1908, to celebrate American Independence Day. On board with a No 3 postcard Kodak camera was Austrian aeronaut Herr Zahn Rinaldo, who took a series of seven photographs for the *Brisbane Courier* and the *Queenslander* newspapers. His aerial photos of Brisbane were the first taken in Australia from a free-flying balloon. Although operating in difficult circumstances, with the balloon envelope collapsing above him, Rinaldo showed remarkable coolness and courage, holding onto his trapeze with one hand, using the camera in the other, cutting free of the balloon and using Stewart's triple parachute method to land.

Other aerial displays took place from the Woolloongabba Sportsground in Brisbane and in nearby Toowoomba; the latter ascent being undertaken by Christopher Sebphe, the thirty year old Spaniard who had first flown twelve years before in a gas balloon at Calais.

Prior to travelling to Queensland, the visiting ballooning company, known then as that of Messrs O'Donnell and Beebe, had been busy during summer in South Australia. It was here that another Australian first was notched up. Advertising banners appeared, wrapped around the portly girths of balloons, promoting grocery items, tea, soft drinks, flour or soap. The Adelaide agents for Viceroy Tea organised a novel event, using a balloon inflated with hot air generated by burning hundreds of empty tea packets. The parachute landings were off target - one in a tree, another on a bridge and a third splashing down in the Torrens River, but so successful was the advertising gimmick that Viceroy Tea Carnivals, using advertising banners on the balloons, blossomed in many SA towns.

On 21 November 1908, Zahn Rinaldo went up to his highest ever altitude, 7300' above the NSW mining town of Broken Hill. The *Barrier Miner* repeated his claims of thirty Australian ascents and that he was, "the only aeronaut in the world who does trapeze athletics in the air while suspended from a balloon, hanging on by his toes and calves while he operates his Kodak and snapshots the distant earth." (5)

One eyewitness that day was a schoolgirl with the interesting name of May May, who years later recalled the essay she had to write on the event, "Anyway this balloon went down in the dam paddock and in my composition I wrote, 'the balloon went down in the damn', and I got a cane across the hand because I swore in my writing. I put the N on it and that was swearing they said." (6)

The troupe left Broken Hill for Melbourne, where they had been invited to perform at the Melbourne Cricket Ground (MCG) for the annual Austral Wheel Race, an international cycling event. Each year since 1886, the Melbourne Bicycle Club had organised the race which quickly gained glamour and popularity. Hundreds of the best vied for the prize, the richest in the world offered to professional cyclists. The very first race had attracted 28 starters; numbers increased over the years to 187 then declined, along with the sport of cycling, until in 1906 there were only 62 competitors. In 1907 worried organisers offered a prize, "for a novel feature to add to the programme and decided in favour of a suggestion for a flight of many hundreds of pigeons." A more encouraging entry of 96 riders was recorded. (7)

For the 1908 Austral Wheel Race on 5 December the organisers had secured the services of flyers of a different kind, of Zahn Rinaldo and Christopher Sebphe. The various cycling heats and finals attracted 80 riders to face the starter on the MCG track; the crowd attendance was satisfactory, "probably due quite as much to the balloon ascent as anything else." (8)

Vincent Beebe was there making announcements through his megaphone; Alphonse Stewart supervised the fire and inflation. Sebphe and Rinaldo went up together, two tiny figures swinging and swaying beneath the *King Edward VII* balloon; Sebphe perched on the bar, Rinaldo hanging by his feet taking photos until it was time to cut himself adrift and float to earth aided by his scarlet parachute. He landed in a tree in the Fitzroy Gardens "safe, sound and happy." (9)

Sebphe calmly stayed with the balloon until it cooled and touched down on the roof of a North Fitzroy house, startling the woman occupant: the result of a mistake cheerfully explained away by the aeronaut, "I was watching Rinaldo taking some photographs, and I pulled the wrong string." On his return to the MCG, Beebe publicly announced with humour, "neither the balloon, Mr Zebphe (sic) nor the house was injured." (10)

The year 1908 witnessed ballooning peak worldwide. In 1909 when Europe became airship and aeroplane conscious, the balloon began to decline. In nearby New Zealand it ceased with the outbreak of World War I. Australian civilian ballooning and parachuting continued to attract crowds for a few more years before floundering altogether in 1920. Unaware that the end of the smoke balloonist and the barnstorming way of life was approaching, the O'Donnell and Beebe company continued to tour selected regions of Australia. A month after the Austral Wheel Race, the troupe was back in Broken Hill at the behest of the Viceroy Tea Carnival and Two-Mile Wheel Race promoters.

One senses an air of desperation in the advertisements encouraging attendance. In January 1909 there was an extra "thrilling and attractive" feature, a double balloon ascent by Sebphe and Rinaldo and "a parachute race in the air." In addition, "the first 2000 people paying for admission will receive a sixpenny plug of tobacco." A similar flight the following Saturday promised free admission on presentation of an empty Viceroy Tea packet and "a sight to be remembered for a lifetime," which was probably true, for few spectators that day would ever again see a balloon ascent. (11)

In Broken Hill, Christopher Sebphe experienced one of the two accidents in his fourteen year career: he and Rinaldo received severe bruising when the men holding the balloon let go prematurely and unexpectedly, bumping the aeronauts along the ground. (Sebphe's other accident occurred in Switzerland in 1901 but was less trifling. When Sebphe and pilot M Le Braun went up during a storm, the balloon burst; Le Braun's chute failed and he was killed; Sebphe's parachute only partly opened, resulting in severe injuries and permanent scarring.)

The next appearance of the Company was in Riverton, South Australia. A local reporter captured the atmosphere in the small town. People "from all around the district flocked in...in good humour, and keenly interested." When all was ready, "everybody breathed heavily owing to the uncommon excitement" until the pistol shot rang out and away sailed the *City of Adelaide*. Enthralled spectators and satisfied promoters strained to watch the parachutist spinning earthwards at crazy speed until the chute checked his rapid descent. (12)

An integral part of the spectacle was the process of inflation. The envelope was hoisted by pulleys until slung between two upright poles over an outlet downwind from a fire pit. Inside the balloon was a man with buckets of water, whose job was to extinguish any sparks settling on the fabric. This was the worst task of all, for it lacked the glamour of the aeronauts bedecked in resplendent tights and costume. Instead the assistant emerged covered in soot and sweat; indeed, he was lucky if he escaped smoke inhalation or a singeing, for smoke and flames could fill the entire canopy, especially in windy conditions. Young men from the crowd were enlisted to keep the balloon held down so that hot air could enter efficiently and not stray over the flames or take off prematurely. The enthusiastic participation of the public added an element of danger. It must have been quite a sight to see men dressed in suits emerge from their self-appointed tasks, filthy from the soot and smoke that poured from the fire, yet there was never a shortage of volunteers.

Engagements were sparse for Beebe's company that year; the next reported event was not until 27 November 1909, when 11 000 spectators watched at Adelaide's Jubilee Oval. On New Year's Day in 1910, the Viceroy Tea Company sponsored an event in rural Clare. People were enticed by advertisements such as, "these aeronauts are the highest flyers on earth. Life hangs by a thread. If a rope goes wrong death is certain. Do not miss it." Townsfolk were entertained with a warm-up act by Ranjie the snake charmer, and by an alligator. (13)

(Rinaldo's ascent and parachute drop that New Year's Day was re-enacted 69 years later in 1976, when Australian balloonist Roger Meadmore took up parachutist Bernie Keenan in his *Lovely* balloon. Several things had changed over the intervening years: the modern aeronaut used a propane gas burner to fill his envelope with heated air and the event was to promote not tea, but wine from the Clare Valley wineries).

Herr Zahn Rinaldo went on alone to Melbourne with one balloon. The fearless Rinaldo made an unusual landing on 8 February 1910, when he came to rest amongst the tombstones at the Melbourne Cemetery (it would be a nice twist if I could report that it was on pioneer Charles Brown's grave that he landed). Rinaldo appears to have taken this as an omen and began to gravitate away from aeronautics and towards the infant art of aviation. Back in Europe he took flying lessons and entered a race as a fledgling pilot. Falling into a "wind-hole" he came down "topsy-turvy" to crash land in a large tree. Rinaldo abandoned powered flight as too dangerous and revisited his first love, saying, "I reckoned I was not a success at aeroplaning, and came back to ballooning. It is much safer." (14)

On return to Melbourne, he experienced another unusual landing, three years after his descent in the cemetery. On a very windy day on 8 February 1913 at the Exhibition ground the balloon unexpectedly skipped sideways on take-off, banging Rinaldo into an electric light pole. The balloon barely cleared telegraph wires and continued its erratic behaviour, never rising above 200'. Unbeknown to the pilot, the envelope had a 6' rent in it and hot air was escaping. A resident at 56 Faraday Street Carlton received a shock when she looked out of a window on hearing a shout and saw the great Rinaldo swinging on his trapeze, then crash through the windowpane of her upstairs bedroom. She promptly fainted, so missed seeing him swing back out through the broken shards, hit the chimney pots of the house next door and fall to the street, beneath yards of fabric. It appeared Rinaldo had taken several photos during the short ride and could not hack away the parachute in time.

He was taken to St Vincent's Hospital where his severed tendons and compound wrist fracture were operated on. Despite the pain of his injuries, Rinaldo was quick to take advantage of the publicity. Interviewed in hospital, Rinaldo made light of the accident,

> "I have made some hundreds of balloon ascents, and this is the first time I have sustained a broken limb. Of course, I have had many falls - more perhaps than I can remember, you get used to them. It is remarkable, though, that three years ago to the very day of this accident - Saturday - I fell into the Melbourne Cemetery. I did not stay there, though!"
> Rinaldo seemed to wear his various mishaps like badges of honour pinned to his chest, joking that this narrow escape was nothing compared to the "most thrilling fall so far (which) has been out of an aeroplane." (15)

Three months later Rinaldo, the true professional, was back in the air, in country Kerang. One balloon caught fire during inflation, so he went up beneath the second but could not cut away the parachute, "owing to the rope having been wetted while the fire was being extinguished". Rinaldo eventually cleared the balloon at 7800'. Still luck was not with him: as he approached the ground a whirlwind dashed him down, "with considerable force, with the result that the small bone of his left leg was broken." It is said that the plucky, and unlucky, Rinaldo had learnt his lesson and gave away his profession to seek a quieter, safer life in Queensland. (16)

While Rinaldo performed solo in Victoria in 1910, Vincent Beebe and his company went west to Perth. A series of flights at carnivals sponsored by the OT drink manufacturer took place from the cricket ground. Beebe was an impressive figure in his peaked cap strutting around importantly, giving instructions to his aeronauts and keeping the crowd informed of proceedings through his extra long megaphone. On his hip, Buffalo Bill style, he carried a large pistol. The first blank he fired was a signal to the attendant inside the balloon to crawl out to safety. The second shot was to 'let the balloon go', the third for the parachutist to jump.

Christopher Sebphe made a more sensational and daring flight in Perth than he intended. Everything was in readiness: the aneroid (altimeter) was in place, the trapeze and three chutes were securely fastened to the inflated balloon and the automatic knives used to cut away each parachute were fixed in position; however, one of the young men holding down the balloon let it slip from his grasp. The balloon drifted over the furnace, was enveloped in flames and rose, whisking Sebphe aloft hanging onto the trapeze. With great nerve and presence of mind, Sebphe succeeded in wrapping a leg over the trapeze bar and cutting away the top parachute. As he was only 400' above the ground, his fall was not checked to any great extent and he landed heavily behind the scoreboard, just missing a horse, but was unharmed.

In true showbusiness style, Beebe broadcast that Sebphe had purposefully ascended with the fiery balloon so as not to cause spectator disappointment. The *City of Melbourne* balloon was subsequently picked up near the Swan River, almost totally destroyed. Nevertheless, the show continued, using the *King Edward VII* balloon for subsequent Perth flights.

Arthur L Bennett's book, *The Glittering Years*, contains a chapter on balloon ascents in 1910 at the twin gold-mining towns of Kalgoorlie and Boulder. He remembers neither the months of the flights nor names the participating aeronauts, but undoubtedly they were members of the Beebe Balloon Company en route to or from Perth and the eastern states. As Bennett says, "Kalgoorlie's prosperity in the years before World War I was a magnet to fascinated, adventurous entertainers." He was among the youngsters squinting in the fierce sunlight at the balloon turning upside down and coming to rest in the grounds of the hospital.

Onlookers in Boulder packed the oval "and the promoters were using sugar bags to hold the two-shilling coins paid for admission." When the manager called for volunteers, "a hundred kids rushed to offer their services, their taut fingers gripping the cloth and ropes". A local identity was feeding the fire with kerosene but,

"in his excitement, he kicked over a tin of kero. A column of flame shot up, the kids scattered, and in seconds the balloon was afire. Five minutes later all that remained was a heap of ashes. The crowd groaned in disappointment. The promoters were full of apologies and contended that they could not refund the admission money as a percentage had to be paid to the local council for the use of the ground. They would, however, provide the town with a free exhibition when their spare balloon arrived from Perth. They carted away the sugar bags of coins and next day were on their way out of town." The people of Boulder never got their free show. (17)

Mr O'Donnell, Beebe's partner in the business, had disappeared from the scene. In his place as partner came Albert Eastwood, the nonchalant, expert Australian parachute jumper from Brisbane who had parachuted for Vincent Beebe as far back as 1907. The Beebe Balloon Company left for New Zealand in 1910 and toured successfully for many years. Vincent, as company principal, managed the performances of Christopher Sebphe and Albert Eastwood. Their first tour in December 1910 took the triple parachute act to a number of towns between Christchurch in the South Island and Auckland in the North.

Ballooning ended early in New Zealand with the Beebe Company's finale in April 1914. It would be 51 years before a balloon (hydrogen) was again seen in NZ skies and 60 years before a NZ-registered hot air balloon heralded the age of modern aeronautics.

Australian Albert Eastwood retained his interest in parachuting when the aeroplane was well established: he served in World War I then made Australia's first parachute descent from a plane - an Avro 504K - on 22 February 1922. In order for Eastwood to fulfil parachuting engagements in Melbourne, he had to seek permission from the Director of the new Civil Aviation Department. It was no easy task for Eastwood to continue his parachute displays from the wings of powered aircraft. Aviation now had regulations and rules, which had not existed in the years when the aeronauts had toured the countryside arranging their own flights and jumps with no operational restrictions.

The days of true freedom in the air were almost at an end in Australia. Their passing must have caused resentment and regret for those used to flying free. They had two choices open to them: to fade into obscurity along with the dwindling crowds, or to embrace heavier-than-air flight, aviation. Some lovers of flying endeavoured to follow the latter course, despite the frustrations and restraints of the new powered flying machines.

However, it was the activities of the last aerial showmen, the hot air balloonist and the parachute jumper, that kept aeronautics lingering on when interest in the balloon was flagging. They were probably well aware that this was their last hurrah but could not have foreseen that modern technology would resurrect the balloon in the future.

(1) *Sydney Morning Herald*, 23 April 1960.
(2) Ibid.
(3) *The Australasian*, 22 February 1908.
(4) Ibid.
(5) *Barrier Miner*, 21 November 1908.
(6) *The Australian Teacher*, No. 5 September 1983.

(7)   Unidentified newspaper, 1908.

(8)   Ibid.

(9)   Ibid.

(10)  Ibid.

(11) *Barrier Miner*, 19 January 1909.

(12) *Kapunda Herald*, 28 January 1909.

(13) *Northern Argus*, 24 December 1909.

(14) *Argus*, 10 February 1913.

(15) Ibid.

(16) *Argus*, 17 May 1913.

(17) Arthur L Bennett, *The Glittering Years* 1984.

# Changes Aloft

One prominent Australian aeronaut successfully managed to exchange his love of the graceful, if oft wayward balloon in favour of the shiny, new (and also often unpredictable) beast that roared in the skies. 'Captain Penfold', aeronaut, became VP Taylor, pilot.

Vincent Patrick Taylor was an extraordinary character whose personality and stunts ensured that the era of showbusiness ballooning in Australia went out with a bang, not merely a whimper. He instilled in his son a love for aeronautics; his brother and sister-in-law made experimental flights in gliders: all in all, the Taylors were an amazing family.

VP Taylor's parents were proprietors of a shop at 137 King Street, Sydney which sold flowers, fruit and confectionery. It was there in 1874 that Vincent was born. He grew into a bright, restless young man who wanted to taste the adventurous life, rather than devote years to study. He quickly gave up law to enter politics; but, failing to be elected, became a bookmaker's clerk instead.

In 1905 Taylor contracted to undertake aerial advertising by balloon in Sydney and was swamped with requests to drop handbills advertising Heenzo cough medicine, OT cordials and shoe manufacturers. On Christmas Day that year he made an ascent from Balmoral Beach. By 1906, when aviation enthusiasm was beginning to grip Australians, he had experimented extensively with his own models of balloons and parachutes and had attempted several ascents from the harbour suburb of Clontarf.

Realising the dangers associated with a lack of specific knowledge or experience, he gave up his fledgling career and sailed from Darling Harbour, working his passage on a windjammer, arriving in San Francisco shortly after the major earthquake of 1907. He worked variously as an advertising agent, a theatre extra and as a sales representative before walking up to American aeronaut Baldwin, boldly introducing himself as 'Captain Penfold, the well-known balloonist from Australia,' and offering to ascend and parachute down in lieu of Baldwin. To his amazement Baldwin agreed, with the proviso that they do a double parachute jump and share the fee. With the publicity he gained from this, Taylor was soon touring several states with his own balloon and parachute outfit.

In May 1908, he caused a sensation when he decided to prove to the Americans that their warships were vulnerable from the air. From his balloon above the American Fleet, anchored at night in San Francisco Bay, he pioneered aerial warfare by dropping several cane bombs (normally used in fireworks displays) after lighting the fuses. They went off with a resounding boom above the warships. This was the first time the American navy had been bombed from the air and was the precursor to aeroplanes dropping bombs in warfare.

It became Taylor's speciality to stage other night 'battles' before enormous audiences, who watched him ascend with a bag of fireworks hanging from his neck and six dozen large Roman candles strapped to the trapeze. He lit the fuses with a cigar and progressed through the air leaving a trail of red fire behind him.

In America, Taylor dallied only once with airships. He helped prepare JA Morrell's invention and was one of fifteen crew on its maiden flight from Oakland, California on 8 May 1908. This first US built airship had a central gondola, motors of 200 horsepower and was 450' long. The sausage-shaped airship had only covered 500 yards and gained 500 feet in height when it buckled in the centre, collapsed and fell with its motors silent. Although there was no loss of life, fourteen people were admitted to hospital and the airship was written off. Vincent Taylor himself woke in hospital and understood then the meaning of the early aviators' grim jest: 'Once we leave Terra Firma it can easily become a firm terror.'

Late in 1908 Taylor took his balloon and gear and arrived back in his homeland just prior to Christmas. He lost no time in organising displays and had soon signed a contract with Sydney Ferries Ltd, a private company which ran numerous picnic grounds on inlets of Sydney Harbour, such as those at Manly, Clontarf, Clifton Gardens and Parsley Bay. With few cars in use, and no bridge connecting the shores of the Harbour, the ferries were busy on weekends, plying back and forth with families on day outings to their picnic grounds. Long wooden buildings provided shelter and a floor on which to dance. Foot races and wrestling matches were organised for the children; swimming and fishing could be enjoyed by all.

At the Clontarf Picnic Grounds, New Zealand Maoris sang and danced in full costume in a replica of an authentic Maori village. Clifton Gardens had the added, advertised attraction of Captain Penfold's balloon ascent and parachute drop. Penfold had incorporated into his act his bomb-throwing stunt and the sound of the bombs going off never failed to attract attention from the pleasure seekers below.

Taylor often fell into the Harbour and became proficient at diving down and away from the parachute and paddling furiously until a launch picked him up; this of course was an extra thrill for those lining the shore. On his first dramatic rescue from the water, the launch crew told Taylor he was lucky they had been at hand, for they had seen several sharks earlier. From that day on, owners of all boats were informed that there would be a £2 reward - the equivalent of a week's wages - for the rescue of the aeronaut. Thereafter, as soon as Taylor hit the water, fishing boats, humble rowing boats and anything that could float, scrambled to reach him first, to have the distinction of plucking the aeronaut from the water and to claim the reward.

A pound was the reward offered for the general discovery and safeguarding of the balloon envelope until an assistant could collect the costly equipment. Usually the balloon was left to cool on the ground before being packed up and carried away. Recovering the balloon was not always an easy task, for occasionally the material was wrapped around a tree or draped down the side of a building, usually with a perturbed owner dancing around it, having been startled within by the bang, whoosh and slithering sound it made as it hit the roof. All balloonists, including Penfold, wisely paid any damages, pre-empting recourse to the law. Many a house owner later told with pride the story of the day a balloon landed on his roof.

In 1909, at the request of the newly formed Aerial League of Australia (forerunner of the Royal Aero Club), VP Taylor ascended from Prince Alfred Park, behind Sydney's busy Central Railway Station, the city terminus for country trains and the major station for inter-suburban trains. He rose higher and higher, but even at 2000' could find no air movement at all: the rapidly-cooling balloon hung motionless above the steam trains, their drivers oblivious of the pilot's dilemma. Deciding to cut away and drop by parachute, Taylor floated down, preparing himself for the worst as passenger trains swarmed in and out of the station. Providence guided him down beside the tracks, but his parachute spilled out across several railway lines. Moments before an outward bound train thundered by and shredded his parachute, Taylor leapt clear of his chute.

That experience influenced Taylor in his decision to leave the confines of the city and give displays in country towns, such as Gunnedah and Newcastle. It was probably on this tour that he unwittingly shaped the future career of Henry Goya Henry who, as an eight-year-old Grafton boy, attended a hot air ascent at the local showgrounds. Thereafter, the boy destined to become a flamboyant, audacious early aviator made his own balloons from tissue paper. He was forced to cease his experiments when his fire balloon fell on a shingle roof and set it alight. Henry's interest in flight had begun. A decade later, the lad gave away studying Medicine to begin his flying tuition at Mascot aerodrome. Eventually, history listed HG Henry among the gallant band of pioneer Australian aviators; he continued flying after losing a leg in a car accident.

To Taylor, cancellation of a show meant nearly a week's preparation wasted and bills to pay for advertisements, rental of grounds and accommodation. Losses could be substantial and the business a precarious venture; however, Taylor recouped losses by contracting to send down thousands of advertising leaflets.

Occasionally he donated a percentage of his gate takings to the local hospital; at other times municipal councils paid him to appear at festivities.

As part of his entourage, Taylor paid a few trusty regulars a wage, plus travel and hotel expenses. To cut costs, he would employ several strong young men in each town at the launching site. If short of helpers, he would seek out swagmen from under bridges.

Sometimes as a novelty, VP Taylor was called upon to start a football match; as the teams lined up in position, the aeronaut would ascend from the oval and kick off the ball as he swung on his trapeze. One wet and gusty day, determined not to disappoint the patient Manly crowd, Penfold took off but brushed the fire pit's flue, knocking off its lid. The envelope caught fire and turned into a blazing red glow as it ascended. Desperate, Taylor cut away to save himself from a fiery death but plummetted down without time for his parachute to open. An ambulance took him to hospital suffering from a fractured arm and abrasions; the balloon was completely destroyed. Several months later at Clontarf, the exact event re-occurred. On 4 September 1909 Penfold again sustained an arm injury. He rose in his *Empire* balloon to 7000 feet, firing bombs and liberating paper parachutes but drifted out to sea and both he and the balloon required rescuing.

No Australian history of lighter-than-air flight would be complete without mentioning the box-kite and gliding enthusiasts. Lawrence Hargrave was born in 1850 in England and went to Australia with his family at the age of sixteen. He was an engineering draughtsman by profession, but spent time exploring and prospecting in New Guinea and Queensland, before marrying and settling into a position as assistant astronomical observer at Sydney Observatory. It was here his intense interest in air currents and navigable flight began. The man known later as the 'Father of Australian aviation' trialled his box-kites between 1893-95. Hargrave had discovered a basic tenet of aeronautics: that a curved surface provides more lift than a flat one, due to increased airflow. On 12 November 1894, he became famous when he tethered himself to 4 of his box-kites and launched off the cliff face at Stanwell Tops south of Sydney, lifting 16' from the ground in a 21mph wind.

Seventeen years before France produced the Gnome rotary aircraft engine, the brilliant Hargrave invented his rotary engine but failed to interest the Australian government in patenting rights. Within his own country his work was ignored or ridiculed; overseas he was considered an authority on the theory of flight. It is said that Hargrave's research and inspiration influenced the Wright Brothers of the USA, who became the first men to fly a powered, heavier-than-air machine at Kitty Hawk Carolina, on 17 December 1903.

Brazilian Alberto Santos-Dumont adopted Hargrave's box-kite design for the 1906 aircraft which made the first European flight. Farman and Voisin used his design theories in their aircraft and 'Colonel' SF Cody successfully demonstrated military adaptations of Hargrave's box-kites to the Royal Navy in 1903 and at Aldershot the following year.

Blind to the potential of Lawrence Hargrave's inventions, the Australian government offered no support. Consequently, Hargrave gave his original history-making box-kites to museums in France and Germany, where most were destroyed in World War II air raids. It was only in later years that the Australian scientist's contribution to the development of powered flight was appreciated. Hargrave died on 6 July 1915, having lived to see the first two British box-kite aircraft tour Australia in 1911; to see powered flight become a reality.

On 10 November 1960 (almost 66 years to the day since his tethered flight at Stanwell Tops) Qantas flew Hargrave's surviving box-kite models from the museum in Munich for presentation to Sydney's Museum of Applied Arts and Sciences for permanent display.

George Augustine Taylor, Vincent Patrick's elder brother, was not only a close friend of Hargrave, but also built box-kites for him in a factory in Redfern. George tinkered with gliders before becoming the first person in Australia to fly free in a heavier-than-air machine. On 5 December 1909, the 37year old GA Taylor used his biplane to glide 120 yards above the beach sands at Narrabeen at a height of 15'. Although his glider depended on the wind for its lifting power, it was free and untethered, unlike Hargrave's kites.

George's wife Florence, also made a short flight, thus becoming the first woman in Australia to pilot a glider. Several associates of the newly formed Aerial League were present that day to help and observe.

Three months before his historic flight, Sydney-born GA Taylor founded his aircraft factory - the first in the southern hemisphere - in Surry Hills, where he constructed kites and a monoplane and attached a 20 horsepower engine to his glider. His intention was to claim the Commonwealth Government's £5,000 prize money for a flying machine able to be used for military purposes. The money offered proved a major incentive for many pioneer aviators.

Like the rest of his family, GA Taylor was a talented person with an enquiring mind and immense energy. He was a journalist, cartoonist, editor, publisher, architect and inventor. This remarkable man was also proficient at engineering, surveying, town planning, geology, astrology, art and music. Before World War I, GA Taylor was acknowledged to be Australia's leading authority on flight.

Not only was GA Taylor a pioneer of gliding in Australia, he also pioneered the use of the submarine, the machine gun and the wireless for defence purposes. This extraordinary man, who died in 1928 at 56, is honoured by the George Taylor Gold Medal, an annual award of the Royal Aeronautical Society for aircraft design and engineering. Belatedly in 1965, a plaque and the bronze-sculpted face of George Augustine Taylor were erected at Narrabeen to commemorate his historic flight there in 1909. His widow Florence, 86, was too frail to attend the unveiling.

(Becoming Australia's first woman pilot was only one of the outstanding Florence's achievements. Born in Bristol in 1879, she came to Australia aged four. The only woman among 200 men at Sydney Technical College, she eventually ran her own architect's practice. She was editor of building, engineering trade and technical journals; became Australia's first woman structural and civil engineer and a member of the Royal Aero Club of NSW. Florence had 3 children and "worked 60 hours a week for 61 years" (in her own words), retiring aged 82. She was appointed Commander of the British Empire and died in February 1969, aged 90.

While his brother and sister-in-law were flying gliders in 1909, Captain Penfold was in Melbourne ballooning. The organisers of the Austral Wheel Race abandoned Beebe's Balloon team that year in favour of VP Taylor and US lady aeronaut, Mollie Mostyn. The planned double ascent with Miss Mostyn, in her blue and gold drummer's uniform, and Vincent Taylor, mounted on a bicycle beneath his huge new balloon, ended in disaster. The *Austral* (christened by the Mayoress, the aptly named Lady Burston) burst asunder and let loose a dense cloud of black smoke. By December 1910, the Melbourne Bicycle Club had snubbed the balloon and its vaudeville artistes in favour of an aeroplane flight out of the MCG.

In the interim, renowned escapologist, Harry Houdini (born Eric Weiss) had flown his 6 horsepower Voisin aircraft on his 2 mile flight, for 3 minutes 45 seconds, 100' above Diggers Rest Victoria, on 18 March 1910. He had thus made Australia's first powered flight.

Controversy exists over this honour: some credit Fred Custance with being the first. It is said he flew an imported Bleriot monoplane at Bolivar, near Adelaide SA, one day prior to Houdini's flight, however; only a reporter was present, and no photos exist. It is possible that the reporter mistook Custance's series of 'hops' off the ground while taxiing, as flight. Several aviation historians doubt that Custance, not a pilot, could have flown such a difficult machine without training or experience.

GA Taylor, as honorary secretary of the Aerial League, was of the opinion that Houdini's flight, before witnesses and recorded by observers, was the first in Australia to achieve the distinction of flying a controlled, powered plane.

Vincent Patrick Taylor disgraced himself at the first Australian Aviation Carnival in Sydney, which was to feature parachute and balloon races and a flying machine. On the Saturday night, 24 December 1910, Taylor went up in a 'war balloon' and discharged, not fireworks, but cannon bombs. Unfortunately, he damaged telegraph and tram wires around the Royal Agricultural Grounds, with police clamping an immediate ban on further aerial displays.

From the early age of nine, VP Taylor's son, George Augustus, (as distinct from his uncle, George Augustine,) helped prepare balloons and parachutes. It was his job to detach the mouth of the inflated envelope from the flue, seal it, then attach the parachute and trapeze.

On a fine February day in 1914 George, aged eleven, became the youngest Australian to go aloft, an event which emphasised his father's confidence in his own skill. Although Taylor senior preferred to hang head down by his calves from a trapeze, he had attached a basket for his son's first aerial experience. After lifting off from Clifton Gardens, they had a marvellous view of the sandy beaches stretching north to the Hawkesbury River, and south to Cronulla and Botany Bay. East were the Heads and open sea beyond; west he could see up the Harbour, across the flat plains to Parramatta, Penrith and the Blue Mountains.

Below George were the large Manly ferries, looking like toys. He could clearly hear their sirens, dogs barking and Chinese market gardeners talking excitedly. The pair had a lengthy 1½ hour flight across the Harbour and back before landing in Chatswood. They hired a horse and cart to transport themselves and equipment to the Railway Station, where they caught a train to Milson's Point and a ferry to the city.

George became a balloon addict, often performing alongside his esteemed father. It was from Chowder Bay (Clifton Gardens) that the pair made their longest flight, covering 26 miles and drifting west for 3 hours, crossing the Nepean River to land at Blacktown.

VP Taylor purchased cloth for his balloon from Sam Walder (later Sir), Lord Mayor of Sydney and Commodore of the Royal Sydney Yacht Squadron, who hired him a sewing machine. In a warehouse in Castlereagh Street Taylor manufactured parachutes and balloons for his own use. These parachutes were probably the first actually manufactured in Australia.

Mrs Jessie White as a teenager, sewed together Captain Penfold's envelopes. She would catch the Parramatta River ferry to and from work at the city warehouse, where she would sew for ten hours a day. It took just short of a month to stitch a balloon, she reminisced in 1968. Penfold, the "nice, reserved man...used to stand by my machine and watch me as I sewed," she said. Penfold would chat about his Sunday ascents at Clontarf, but Jessie White never asked him any questions about his unusual life for she, "was more interested in skating. The only thing I thought about when I sewed the balloons, was that in every stitch I held his life in my hands." She liked to think that she held the famous balloonist's life by a thread, literally. (1)

Of those days George later wrote, "the work was hard and could be monotonous, but when the balloon was all double sewn and finished with its new cordage in place, lying out white and smelling so fresh, there was a great sense of satisfaction, pride and joy of work well done." (2)

Despite occasional incidents with trees and telegraph wires, the Taylor duo gained popularity and credibility wherever they travelled. Penfold toured country towns along railway lines in NSW and Victoria, accompanied in school holidays by his son George, who was responsible for keeping the cut-away balloon in view and to retrieve it, before the souvenir hunters. George felt proud and important to be helping. "Always there was a crowd of local youngsters looking on, and they made me realise I was regarded as a kind of king of the kids." (3)

They were the first father and son team of professional aeronauts in Australia. Once, the eleven stone VP Taylor parachuted at Coogee, hit the ground hard and fractured both ankles, ensuring weeks of confinement in hospital. During his enforced absence, young George stood in for him and took over his father's flying contracts.

He made many flights dropping advertising pamphlets. At Roseberry Racecourse, he mistimed the drop and let the pamphlets flutter down mid-race, fortunately just after the horses passed. The blurbs on the posters advertised him as "Australia's youngest airman." (4)

His father was renowned for being cavalier about the weather. Only by fulfilling the program was he assured of attaining a reasonable living. VP Taylor often succumbed to sprains and bruises from parachuting, particularly if a drop to the ground in high winds took him onto a factory roof or into a brick wall at speed.

In 1912 VP Taylor journeyed to England, enrolled at Hendon flying school for tuition and gained his private aeroplane pilot's licence. Licence no. 376, issued by England's Royal Aero Club on 3 December, was a first for an Australian.

While in England Taylor gave balloon and parachute displays in Blackpool, Scarborough, Brighton and in London. On 23 December 1912 the effervescent Taylor flew with Harry Spencer from Battersea. They went up on a wintry day with Taylor dressed as Father Christmas, intending to parachute down and distribute sweets to children below. The day was windy and 25 mph winds blew Santa well off course. He crossed the Thames at 1000' but the balloon rapidly ascended to 4000', at which stage Taylor parachuted to earth near Chelmsford. When relieved of its load of Taylor, the parachute and the chocolates, the balloon shot up to 10 000'. Santa Claus was dragged across several fields and ended up rather muddied.

On return to Australia, Taylor tested an emergency chute he had designed to help airmen escape from a plane, and civilians from a high building. On 5 June 1914 V P Taylor trialled a new parachute by leaping from the Cammeray Suspension Bridge to the mudflats of Middle Harbour, 150' below. The canopy opened at 40' and in 7 seconds after the catch was released. He also made the first gas balloon ascent in many years at Clifton Gardens in 1913.

The Royal Melbourne Showgrounds contracted the newly licensed pilot to make a flight in an airship. It was agricultural showtime and Taylor was an added attraction to the more conventional ring events of showjumping, dressage and the Grand Parade of livestock. His ellipsoidal-shaped airship was a poor copy of an early Santos Dumont prototype. It had an 8horsepower petrol engine, sand ballast, wireless transmitter, rigging, rudder and a one pilot payload. On a bright clear day, 26 September 1914, he climbed steadily to 2000' before a huge crowd. It was a dangerous task, for engine failure or a spark from the exhaust igniting 20 000 cubic feet of gas, could be disastrous. Taylor entered a troublesome thermal and the craft pitched and yawed. He held it bow on and clung to the vibrating handrail, thus riding out the thermal and averting disaster. After an hour he landed at Broadmeadows Army Camp by venting gas and throwing out a drag rope, caught by soldiers who broke ranks to do so and who were reprimanded for their breach of discipline.

In a flight over Sydney, Taylor returned the airship to its port at Moore Park festooned with telephone wires. He had had foresight enough to switch off the engine before hitting the wires, thus avoiding an explosion; however, he was unable to dodge the sparks that flew from the Post Master General's office, which issued the aviator with a hefty damages bill. Nor was it the way to win the mail contract he desired, especially as Frenchman Maurice Guillaux had two months previously, demonstrated the practical side of aviation, becoming the first to carry interstate airmail and freight, between Melbourne and Sydney on 16-18 July.

In 1914, Taylor's dirigible was already an anachronism and those two flights were the only ones it ever made. Consequently, father and son resorted again to ballooning for a living. They toured places as varied as Albury, Inverell, Quirindi, Newcastle and the Hunter district of NSW. They visited Mudgee, the birthplace of VP Taylor's friend, renowned poet Henry Lawson. At Goulburn, they arrived amidst a war bond drive and Vincent Patrick spoke publicly, to promote both the sale of the bonds and his coming balloon ascent.

At the outbreak of World War I, the forty year old Taylor joined the Australian Imperial Force and served as an artillery driver in Egypt. He also instructed soldiers in the handling of gas-filled observation balloons.

Wounded at the Somme in July 1916 and shell-shocked in November, he was invalided home and discharged early in 1917, as over age and deaf. George Taylor believed his father's partial deafness was "caused by continually falling into the Harbour, into trees and other severe impediments to a safe landing with his parachute." (5)

VP Taylor and his son embarked on yet another country tour, in the winter of 1917. It took them to Echuca, Rochester, Bendigo, Castlemaine, Ballarat and Maryborough but was fraught with accidents and difficulties.

Echuca, situated on the Murray River, was once a major inland port for paddle-steamers laden with wool from surrounding areas. It was decided that George would fly there, as he needed experience in wooded areas. Many people were drawn to the event, having seen slides at the town's picture house. The last sight that confronted teenager George as he clung to the trapeze, was his debonair father, dressed in the familiar white pants, blue coat and peak cap, generously adorned with gold braid, following his son's flight on foot. George executed a perfect display and landed in open fields. It was 7 pm and dark when father and son returned to the showgrounds.

Rochester was the next venue on the tour. VP Taylor was to ascend late in the day after a football match, by which time it was extremely cold. Taylor took off quickly and, knowing the balloon would cool rapidly in such low temperatures, cut away his parachute early. To everyone's horror, not least his own, it failed to open until 200' above the ground when it billowed out, in time for him to cheat death, though he still hit a high fence with a resounding bang. Those first on the scene carried the unconscious parachutist to the grandstand, from where an ambulance rushed him to hospital. Again he was lucky, suffering only a fractured arm and abrasions and, within hours, was back at the sportsground supervising the packing away of the balloon.

The tour continued on to Bendigo in freezing conditions. Father and son stayed at the impressive Shamrock Hotel and accepted an invitation to venture down the Half Moon gold mine, which had one of the deepest shafts in Australia. At nearby Castlemaine it was so cold the envelope would not inflate. Hours were spent trying to warm the balloon to a temperature where it would be buoyant. Suddenly the erect balloon became a fiery ball and blew up: the result of an excess of Benzine in the filling flue. Weeks of preparation and advertising disappeared in a flash and the Taylors were left with a pile of ashes.

After the end of the Great War, with the balloon in decline, people were again experimenting with aeroplanes. Vincent Patrick Taylor received letters from amateur inventors with no knowledge of aerodynamics, seeking advice. For a fee to cover expenses and the risk involved, Taylor would give his professional opinion on their creations. and would test fly any reasonable machine; this proved more and more a major source of his income.

In 1918 when VP Taylor was attempting to resurrect his pre-war career, his contemporaries were forging ahead in their creative fields. Lionel Lindsay was drawing war cartoons for the *Evening News*; Tom Roberts was painting landscapes; Banjo Patterson was writing poetry and Taylor's great friend Henry Lawson, was penning advertising copy. Another close friend, Charles Kingsford-Smith, like Taylor, turned his attention to the skies, but to the aeroplane.

VP Taylor - he had ceased using 'Captain' as his post-war professional name - tried to ignore the obvious, that ex-wartime aeroplane pilots had killed ballooning as a spectacle. He attempted what was to be the last barnstorming tour in Australia, giving balloon and parachute displays in 1920 in the lush northern districts of NSW.

Coonabarabran treated him well; the locals hoisted him on to their shoulders and carried him to his hotel, to the accompaniment of the town band. It was wintry and almost dark in Lismore when he made the second last Australian ascent.

Casino had the dubious honour of being the last town to witness a balloon ascent and parachute descent. Buggies, sulkies and carts were scattered about the Showground near the Richmond River as their owners jockeyed for the best views. Young George Taylor did not disappoint them but would have been less than happy with his own last performance. Gripping the trapeze bar, the seventeen year old wafted away on a slight breeze. Over the town he lit the bomb fuses and sent them down. A freak thermal lifted the balloon up and turned it around, so that it headed back the way it had come and towards the river. George had two alternatives: to be carried for miles over unknown bush or to cut away to avoid landing in the river where he could become entangled with submerged snags and be dragged under. George decided on the latter course of action. Using all his skills and aware of the narrow safety margin, he manoeuvred his parachute to the riverbank, hitting faster than normal; the severe jolt leaving him with aching muscles for days.

It was an inglorious end for aeronautics. There would not be another balloon ascent in Australia for 44 years, until 1964.

Still VP Taylor would not accept that aerostation had lost its charm for the public. He became a director of Aircraft Ltd at 19 Hunter St, Sydney. The company wished to "carry on business of Aerial Entertainers, Instructors and Advertisers and to acquire...assets including an Airship...and one Passenger Carrying Balloon complete with basket for passengers." (6)

The time was not yet ripe for passenger-carrying balloons to be a paying proposition, which would not be achieved in Australia until the 1970s.

Eventually the Taylors realised they had to look elsewhere for a living. Son George became a bookshop proprietor in Sydney until 1935, then travelled the world and settled in London as a bookseller and librarian, also writing poetry and guidebooks. Returning to live in Australia in 1964, after thirty years overseas, George wrote to his aunt Florence Taylor, hoping to see her again. She wrote in a letter to him that she no longer received visitors, "not even my own nephew...is permitted to come." Presumably, she was either too frail, or vanity prevented her letting even relatives see her, suffering as she was from arthritis and deafness. George went to her funeral five years later and died suddenly himself in 1972. (7)

His flamboyant father was not easily deterred from abandoning the profession he loved. Ever the optimist, he sailed to the USA in 1920 as a passenger on the *RMS Tahiti*. Ever the showman, he amused and alarmed many passengers by hanging by the toes from a rope stretched between two masts while the ship steamed along.

Prior to leaving for the US, VP Taylor's clear head and quick reactions came to the fore, this time at sea. The *Evening News* reported Taylor's rescue of a man overboard, "As the quarter past ten ferry for Mosman was leaving Circular Quay this morning a man was seen to fall from the rail into the water. Captain Penfold the Aviator who was a passenger immediately jumped after him and managed to keep his head above water until both were hauled onto the pontoon." The bedraggled Captain continued his journey to Mosman by the next boat, quite unperturbed by the stares of other passengers and his wet state. The man he rescued "was taken in charge by the police and ultimately taken to the reception house." (8)

Taylor was awarded the Royal Humane Society's medal for bravery but was in America at the time of presentation. On hand to greet him were Major Thomas Baldwin and stuntman Leslie Irvin, who devised the first reliable, folded parachute contained in a pack and harnessed to the body. Irvin's invention - enabling the parachutist to release the canopy in free fall by pulling on a ring - has saved thousands of lives.

Vincent Patrick Taylor soon made the Queens Hotel in San Francisco his home. He revelled in the company of his old aeronaut friends of twelve years earlier. San Francisco was to become the focus of operations for a decade of stunting in and over the cities and towns of America and Canada. Taylor gave aeronautic displays all over the countryside, advertising that he would make flights anywhere, day or night.

He made ascents in 1921 and, in 1922 Taylor accepted an invitation to balloon and parachute in British Columbia, travelling by car on the long road hauls and making as many as three appearances in a week. Using the Americanised name Vin Taylor, he demonstrated the great judgement needed to land at the rate of 11' per second (more in a high wind) hanging on to his wooden trapeze. As soon as he touched down Taylor would let go the bar and allow air to spill from the parachute. On occasion he had to wait patiently for a launch to fish him out of Monterey Bay.

Taylor zig-zagged from one state to another: one week Washington, then Oregon, Idaho, South Dakota in the following ones. Over the border, he would venture to Toronto Ontario, then back to Ohio, Kansas, Colorado, Utah, and Nevada, delighting the crowds wherever he went.

In his prospectus, the aeronaut stated that risk was non-existent, as his thoroughness and care with preparations prevented him having accidents. Taylor's care extended to his own body, for the non-drinker and non-smoker was a physical fitness enthusiast. Although he did fracture many bones, he never became crippled by accident as did many other aeronauts, but lived long as an exponent of his art.

Wearing a rubberised suit and using a paddle to steer, the adventurer went over Niagara Falls in a barrel. He repeated the stunt, to ride mountain cataracts roaring over jagged rocks at Eagle Falls near Index. New York papers reported Taylor's superhuman effort to reach shore, after the 55 year old had leapt from the Falls View Bridge Buffalo, into seething rapids below. Every inch the showman, Taylor made parachute jumps from the Niagara Falls River Bridge and from the (then) world's highest bridge, that of Twin Falls Jerome, which spanned Idaho's Snake River Gorge, 47' above the water. He worked as a stunt man for film makers; the 'Australian Daredevil' featured often on International Film News; movie houses or stores sponsored Taylor to undertake his daring pursuits.

Another of Taylor's interests was the designing and testing of scuba-type equipment. In 1927 after an aquatic display in his rubber suit in Seattle, he quietly slipped away from the admiring crowd. After lengthy and strenuous paddling, he reappeared within hailing distance of the battleships *Mexico* and *Mississippi* without being seen by the watch on board. Once again, Vin Taylor had embarrassed the American navy, demonstrating in a practical way how vulnerable it could be to attack from the water.

It has often been reported, incorrectly, that VP Taylor died in hospital in America following a car accident; however, mystery still surrounds his admission - very ill, in pain and distressed - to the Duval County Hospital in Jacksonville Florida, late in December 1930, where he was treated for failure of the digestive system. The cause of his abdominal illness is unclear but attempts at artificial feeding failed and he died in January 1931. The news reached son George and Sydney relatives via a cable from the British Consulate.

The *Sydney Morning Herald* ran an obituary on 15 January 1931 and reported that he was buried with full military honours in St Mary's Cemetery, his body escorted by the Florida National Guard after a requiem mass at the Church of the Holy Rosary. Members of the American Legion, local dignitaries and diplomats watched as the casket, draped with Australian and American flags, was lowered into the earth. His American aeronautic friend, Captain Ed Allen paid part of Taylor's death and funeral expenses, for he died destitute.

Vincent Patrick Taylor was one of the few successful aerial daredevils who lived to a reasonable age (he was 58 when he died). He had experimented with all aerial forms, but his twin loves were ballooning and parachuting. He expressed his views succinctly in an interview, "Parachuting is the poetry of motion. In an airplane, one is being dragged along. In a free balloon, he is pushed by the wind, but in a parachute he is supported and carried down like a babe in its mother's arms." (9)

Australia was never to see his like again.

(1)   George Taylor, The Challenge of Aviation (Unpublished), Mitchell Library Sydney.
(2)   George Taylor papers, Mitchell Library.
(3)   Ibid.

(4)  Ibid.
(5)  Ibid.
(6)  Ibid.
(7)  Ibid.
(8)  *Evening News*, 12 November 1919.
(9)  *Seattle Post Intelligencer*, 7 August 1928.

# Observation Balloons in World War I

In England in July 1908, a slip of a girl accidentally discovered a vital new use for the parachute. Dolly Shepherd, veteran of one hundred parachute descents, carried out the first mid-air rescue when her friend Louise May, on a second trapeze and making her first parachute descent, could not pull free from the balloon, which continued to rise upwards into cloud. Dolly knew they could not continue to rise indefinitely in the cold, nor could she descend and leave her friend to her fate. She swung over to Louise and clamped the frightened girl's legs around her. With Dolly holding all the weight, and using a single parachute, they descended together. Because of the extra weight, the chute failed to fully open and they thudded to earth, Dolly on her back and Louise on top of her. After the heroic rescue, Dolly was unable to walk for many months but eventually recovered and returned to her work.

Over the years, daring increased with the use of the parachute, but it was not until the parachute harness replaced the bar and freed the hands was it recognised by the military as a practical safety device and became standard issue.

As Dolly Shepherd wrote, the Edwardian years came to be regarded, "as an age of great elegance and serenity, perhaps symbolised by the balloon itself, so majestic." By the second decade of the twentieth century, change was gusting in and the Edwardian era was being ushered out, along with the balloon, which "was being supplanted by an exciting but rather brash and noisy newcomer," the aeroplane. The stranger was also dangerous. Miss Shepherd recorded that as early as 1910 thirty aeroplane pilots were dead, including former balloonist Charles Rolls, co-founder of the Royal Auto Club in Britain and motorcar magnate. (1)

By 1912 there was talk of war, "somehow, some of the fun seemed to be going out of the skies." In the spring, Dolly went up for one last, perfect parachute jump from a balloon, in a sky to herself, with no planes. Never were balloons to have the skies to themselves again; they were destined forever to share with aeroplanes and the occasional airship. (2)

Engineers resolved to find the power and directional control which resulted in the airship. French engineer Henri Giffard, on 24 September 1852, had made the first manned, tentative journey in a powered dirigible. His ship, powered by the world's first aero engine, a 3horsepower steam engine, demonstrated aerial navigation was possible.

The French term 'dirigible' meaning a steerable balloon, became widely used although 'airship' is a more descriptive word; both will be used interchangeably in this text.

Many others experimented with powered airships. Brothers Gaston and Albert Tissandier built a dirigible with a 1.5 hp electric motor and screw propeller but abandoned it after only two flights. It was Gottlieb Daimler's high-speed petrol engine, developed in 1884, that revolutionised propulsion.

On 9 August that same year, lighter-than-aircraft finally succumbed to control by man, when Captain Charles Renard and Lieutenant Arthur Krebs of the French Corps of Engineers, flew a circular course, returning to their point of departure. Their electric powered ship inspired a general in the German army, Count Ferdinand von Zeppelin, to promote the use of military airships in his country.

Many authorities have claimed that Dr Bland's brilliant 1851 design for the '*Atmotic Ship*' was the precursor of the Zeppelin airship. Six years after Bland's death von Zeppelin became interested in dirigible design, but it was not until July 1900, that he flew his first giant prototype rigid airship. He flew 5 passengers for 20 minutes from the airship's hangar in Lake Constance near Friedrichshafen.

Alberto Santos-Dumont gave a demonstration in Europe in September 1900 of his petrol driven cylindrical airship. After several attempts and accidents, Santos-Dumont flew his sixth dirigible from Saint Cloud to the Eiffel Tower. His flying machines became the talk of the age. Governments in France, England, Germany and the US adopted these simple motor balloons. Nine years later France became the first nation to use dirigibles for regular passenger services, but German airships began to rival early French dominance and quickly led the world, travelling distances up to 3165 miles (5093 kms) in a single journey.

The lighter-than-air dirigibles were defined as rigid or semi-rigid. The former had internal bracings which kept the gas bags distended when moored, plus a rudder and engine propeller, mounted on a strong framework, designed to support the weight of the passengers. The semi-rigid dirigible lacked internal bracing.

Eventually the dirigible attained elevational and directional control and could move at a speed of 35 mph. The Zeppelin craft flew successfully for twenty years. In the period between 1910-1914, five 500' long Zeppelins carried 35 000 passengers and flew 17 000 miles without a fatality. Despite such records of safety, it is for the disasters and resulting huge loss of life that airships are mostly remembered today. The rigid Zeppelins had the ability to dip their bows and land in less time than non-rigid dirigibles, which needed to descend in a spiral before landing. The swooping effect of the Zeppelins proved a distinct advantage in battle, for firing small cannon and dodging fire from the newest invention, the anti-aircraft gun.

In Australia the airship was slow to be introduced and never threatened the balloon to any extent. W Jones submitted airship plans to the Australian Defence Department but proceeded no further. In 1908, Sergeant Matthews of the 5th Australian Infantry Regiment also submitted designs for a military airship to the Minister for Defence and was permitted use of workshops at Victoria Barracks in Sydney to work on his invention. His completed model consisted of a flat surface frame, with car and machinery suspended below and two 40' long gas bags. Matthews explained that, "the gas bags are for buoyancy purposes only, in case anything should go wrong with the machinery. The main feature of the airship is the fact that it can be manipulated without loss of gas." His plans never eventuated. (3)

It appears that not only was the Australian military dreaming of flying machines, but also the imaginations of the civilian population were working overtime in the Pacific region.

In July and August 1909, airship speculation was rife throughout neighbouring New Zealand. The *Balclutha Free Press* reported the sighting of an airship in the southern township of Kaitangata on Sunday 11 July. Twelve days later a woman 65 kilometres away, reported seeing a black airship with a bright light and rear propeller. Sightings increased at dusk or night over the next few weeks. Pranksters were exposed releasing light-carrying toy balloons, but sightings continued. One farmer noticed that his horses took fright then he looked up at the sound of a motor and saw an airship with two lights and a flight like that of a seagull.

The unidentified flying object was progressing north over New Zealand and appeared at Oamaru, Christchurch, Riwaka, Nelson, Blenheim, Wellington, Fielding, Napier and Coromandel. Explanations for the sightings ranged from fire balls, flocks of black swans, luminous clouds, to fire balloons, spy Zeppelins from a German warship, an Australian smuggler's airship and a secret NZ construction. Whatever the mystery aircraft was, it ranged far. The final northern sighting took place on 8 August at Kaihu. Witnesses said it flew west over the Tasman Sea towards Australia. There followed a spate of sightings in Victoria and NSW. Day and night sightings were reported early in September, two men being visible on board in one account. From then on, Australia and New Zealand skies were free of such craft except for two sightings four years later, in Dunedin and in Auckland.

While people in the Antipodes in 1909 were dreaming of their skies being filled with fanciful aircraft, other countries, notably Germany, France and America were well to the fore in the unofficial race for airpower supremacy. For they were astute enough to realise that future warfare would be aerial, and that war was approaching. Exponents of military aircraft pressured governments to prepare for war by increasing aircraft experiments. Military advisers in Britain were aware that it lagged behind other nations. Now that aerial attack had placed it within Europe's striking range, Britain suddenly found itself ill-prepared and extremely vulnerable.

The Australian Commonwealth Department of Defence decided it too needed to be involved with the latest aerial developments. It announced a competition on 8 September 1909 for the inventor of suitable 'Flying Machines for Military Purposes.' The government that had long rejected local balloon and airship designs, now entered the area of serious military aviation. Some saw room for both the airship and plane, advocating that, although the plane was swifter, it was incapable of carrying great weight.

The design competition was the brainchild of George Taylor, founder of the Aerial League of Australia but was doomed to fail, due to the lack of finance for most inventors and Australia's small manufacturing base being unable to produce aero engines powerful enough to meet the requirements.

Engineer John Duigan became the first in Australia to fly a powered aircraft of his own construction when he flew his biplane near his farm at Mia Mia Victoria, on 16 July 1910. His invention was several months too late for the competition and the Australian government did not even recognise his efforts. Besides, imported aircraft, such as those of Houdini and JJ Hammond from New Zealand, were already being flown in Australia. Eventually, the country's defence planners saw fit to purchase aircraft overseas and no prize was ever awarded.

Australia was right to face the future, despite the fact that, "operations are at present only fledglings, mostly standing on the edge of the nest, while a few of the venturesome ones are essaying short flights to strengthen their young pinions, others recovering from the sore bruises of falls, and others lying still in death." (4)

Before aeroplanes were accepted in Australia and airships abandoned, there were to be several further flirtations with the outmoded transport form.

In 1911, ET Williams proposed giving military demonstrations in Australia with his airship *City of Cardiff*. The government of the day graciously declined the offer, explaining that the Defence Minister was embarking for Britain and could assess the airship there.

That same year, the Sydney Morning Herald reported the finding of a "stranded airship" in the sandhills at Yamba, New South Wales. It was 30' long and 4' wide with a wing on one side only. In the middle of the strange ship was a platform and seat roughly fixed with fencing wire and padded with bagging. Wires stretched from the platform all over the structure and the "floor was covered with newspapers pasted together to form a thick pad. A deep, narrow track led from the water's edge." Police investigated, but the mystery remained unsolved. (5)

Vincent Patrick Taylor's airship had flown once in Melbourne in September of 1914 and in Sydney. AJ Roberts of Sydney had beaten Taylor, by flying his 'dirigible balloon' on 4 July 1914. At 700' Roberts circled above Centennial Park, but accidentally bumped the cord controlling the petrol lever and shut off the fuel supply. At the mercy of the winds, he drifted towards the Harbour and resolved to land in a vacant paddock at Rushcutters Bay. "In response to his calls, two men seized the anchoring rope, and pulling it tight, enabled Roberts to alight." In his descent, Roberts broke two electric light wires and but avoided injury. (6)

Aviation historians have credited Robert's hydrogen-filled dirigible with only one other flight, in Melbourne on 26 September 1914. As this is the same date as VP Taylor's airship journey above Melbourne and the only one reported by newspapers, I feel this is an error.

Overseas, the small gas balloons that could stay aloft longer than their hot-air counterparts, were again in use for military purposes. The Germans used tethered spherical balloons, but found their tendency to rotate made observation difficult, so they introduced elongated balloons which lessened air resistance. These were the 'Drachen' or 'Dragon' type, referred to by the Allies as 'sausages.'

It is ironic that France, the first country to use manned balloons (1783), the first to employ military observation balloons (1794), and the first to disband its balloon corps (1812), now readapted the clumsy aircraft to vastly improve its stability. Early in World War I the French captured a Drachen balloon. Engineer Capitaine Albert Cacquot streamlined its shape by adding three stabilising tail fins, designed to keep the more aerodynamic 'Cacquots' as they became known, nose into the wind and able to operate in strong gusts.

The amusingly shaped blimp, with its tiny tail, protruding nose, distended abdomen and cauliflower ears, may have looked an oddity, but was in fact the first stable observation platform. It is estimated that 26 000 - 35 000 of these hydrogen-filled blimps were used by all the major armies: the German, the Russian, the French, the British and Americans used squadrons of observation balloons after their introduction in January 1915.

Germany's early use of the Drachen to keep watch over the North Sea and to bombard the British, struck terror in England, brought industry and transport to a standstill, caused blackouts and a lowering of British morale. The balloon, once regarded as capricious and beautiful, was now seen as menacing, however; the French Cacquots reversed this trend and caused Germany ultimately to lose hold of its world supremacy in airships.

Goderic Hodges in his book *Memoirs of An Old Balloonatic*, told of a shortage of balloon officers during the War. (They were trained by balloonists, fresh from competition in Gordon Bennett races.) Observation balloons were used on the Western Front on both sides, but the Germans were the first to supply the front line with hydrogen in high-pressure cylinders.

Operational difficulties were encountered, not the least the mud on the Somme battlefield. When the sun shone the hydrogen tended to overheat and had to be valved to avoid exploding. This "rate of spillage meant that the supply depots, starved of both gas and transport, never quite caught up with demands. Fabric and cordage were scorched and frayed by desert dust, rotted by humidity, and eaten by insects." (7)

However, with the stable observation platforms, the balloon played an important role, for the observer was linked by telephone and cable. He could report the location, progress and intensity of artillery fire; position of enemy tanks, troops and balloons; areas occupied by Germans and the dropping of ammunition by their own planes. The observer's commander and headquarters could contact him directly. Telescopes and cameras were taken aloft for reconnaissance purposes. A tethered balloon was now capable of remaining aloft in all weathers and often went as high as 5000', depending on visibility.

The Germans discovered how vulnerable to anti-aircraft fire and incendiary bullets were the Zeppelins. As casualties and losses rose, raids over Britain were discontinued in 1917.

Remarkably, the parachute had never been regarded as a safety device until World War I (130 years after its first use). British balloon observers carried them, but not their plane crews or pilots until 1920, when they became standard air force safety equipment. Germany began to outfit their observation balloon crews with parachutes in 1915 but they were rarely used. The heavy parachutes hung free from the balloon, but improvements saw compact parachutes being harnessed to German balloonists and aircraft crews alike; this safety equipment was timely, for the Allies began a campaign soon after to destroy all enemy balloons.

The No 4 Squadron of the Australian Flying Corps (AFC) was to shoot down 33 enemy balloons during the war years and in a period from 1 July to 11 November 1918, destroyed 22 balloons. One account of balloon operations was given by Lieutenant-Colonel Strange who wrote that the Australians, "continually laid traps in the air; you could depend on it that the simplest looking Australian patrol was part of some scheme or other...They used to take it in turns to attack balloons and when you sent one down in flames you earned an extra turn, but they never made a habit of indulging in balloon hunts every day for that would have given the Hun time to get a surprise packet ready for them...they had plenty of variations to keep themselves amused and the enemy annoyed." (8)

Some Australians were members of the Royal Flying Corps; others manned balloons or flew fighter planes for the RAF. However Captain AH Cobby of the AFC has been acknowledged as Australia's greatest 'balloon buster' with the destruction of 13 balloons, plus 29 enemy aircraft, which established him as the leading Australian air ace. He wrote,

"Every German balloon had all suitable artillery ranged round them, and machine-gun nests were placed so that they could cover the balloon. As soon as anyone poked his nose in the direction of a balloon everything would open up - anti-aircraft, field guns, 'flaming onions', machine-guns... Sometimes a balloon basket would be filled with explosives and several...fell into the error of thinking that the lonely-looking bag of gas was easy money, and they went right in and blew themselves up. That happened once or twice to my knowledge. The job was always looked upon as being particularly dangerous and on one occasion two of our experienced chaps collided in one attack and were lost." (9)

Not only were observation balloons utilised by armies on the Western Front and by various air forces; they also served with naval units. Previously, the British Army had sent its Cacquot Type M kite balloons to the Dardanelles in October 1914, where 26 ships were employed to assist the Australian and New Zealand Army Corps (Anzacs) and British troops.

Six days before the Anzac landing at Gallipoli, the specially equipped balloon ship, *HMS Manica* stood off the coast, experimenting with its tethered balloon. An Australian, Lieutenant P Roach-Pierson, Royal Naval Air Service, helped ascertain the feasibility of operating balloons from warships in action. On the first day of the infamous landing on 19 April 1917, three balloons were raised off the coast of Anzac Cove. So successful were the balloons' surveillance, gun spotting and ranging operations, that two more warships and their Goodyear-manufactured airships were called in. *HMS Hector* joined the Dardanelles campaign in July and the *HMS Canning* relieved *HMS Manica* in October.

As there were few press photographers with the Australians during the Dardanelles Campaign, the only visual records that have survived came from soldiers with smuggled Box Brownies. Although amateurish and poor in quality, the photographs are important records. Sapper Horace Moore-Jones, a New Zealander, painted several watercolour scenes of the coast from his precarious perch in one of the tethered balloons.

Originally the naval balloons were used for stationary observation work, above drifting ships or at speeds not above 10 knots but rapidly the balloon carriers became mobilised. Two further balloon ships joined the Grand Fleet in early 1916: Roach-Pierson was a balloon observer on the *HMS Menelaus*, who was transferred on 8 June that year to a Drachen type balloon on board the battleship *HMS Benbow* to undertake an experiment. The Australian and another naval man were winched aloft once the warship was underway - the first time a balloon was towed at height from a ship at full speed. After an hour and "a great deal of swinging and diving the balloon was safely bagged down on deck, much to the relief of the occupants of the car, who had received a thorough shaking up." (10)

Back in the hold the balloon was examined and found to be considerably stretched, but the experiment was deemed successful. Not long afterwards, the naval observation balloon, with adjustments, was given the freedom to undertake patrol work and to direct naval gunfire and "at least one vessel in every flotilla carried a kite balloon." (11)

Naval observation balloons began operating in the Adriatic against German anti-submarine patrols, towed at speed from the aft decks of the destroyers. Trained observers sought underwater shadows indicating possible mines or enemy submarines, then directed an accompanying destroyer to drop depth charges. Balloons were particularly useful in convoy work, as Roach-Pierson wrote,

> "The German submarine commander who dared to attack a convoy whilst one of the escorting destroyers was flying a balloon, was simply asking for trouble, for once the locality of a submarine is known to the navigator of a fast destroyer he is able to drop his depth charges with almost never-failing results." (12)

It was a vigorous, effective campaign, in which the Royal Australian Navy (RAN) played its part. It is seldom acknowledged in Australia's military history that RAN destroyers used dirigibles on anti-submarine patrols in the Adriatic and Mediterranean, because they operated under the auspices of the 5th British Destroyer Flotilla.

Several RAN destroyers had Cacquot balloons aboard: the *HMAS Huon, Parramatta* and *Yarra* - identified by pennant numbers 50, 55, and 79 respectively - were all used to protect ships in convoys or on search and destroy missions. The balloons were usually sent to heights up to 305 metres (1000') but could go four times as high.

Diary entries written by men on *HMAS Parramatta* make interesting reading:

> "3 May 1918 Balloon *Edith* alongside...we went to sea with balloon at 10, but by noon it was seen that the *Edith* needed more gas. We brought her down and gassed her and sent up observers, but they soon came down owing to a leak in the balloon.
> 19 May This morning we got our balloon (*Madge*) on the winch, and by 9am were well clear of the outer boom.
> 20 May At daybreak we placed observers in balloon and sent them up...about 2.30 we sighted an enemy submarine on the surface...Went for her at full speed and fired three rounds 4-inch at extreme range but no good...at 8 we tried to pull down balloon but winch jammed and balloon ripped herself and fell into the sea. So ended *Madge*.
> 2 June The (new) balloon is doing well - There are about eight other destroyers with us on patrol, but we are alone all day." (13)

It became quite common during the war to see a battleship, cruiser or destroyer steaming into harbour with a kite balloon in tow. Eventually, Spanish flu raged through the crew of the *Huon*, resulting in the death of sailors and depletion of its manpower resources. As a consequence, the *Huon* never returned to sea before the war ended.

In Australia during the war there had been relatively little airborne activity: a balloon unit was formed at Point Cook RAAF base in Victoria and parachutists were encouraged to enlist. Ultimately the Great War came to an end. On the last day of fighting, 11 November 1918, a British Army communique was dispersed, stating "all along the Front, the balloons are down."

Australia, with a population of only 4 million, had sent overseas 325 000 of the 400 000 men enlisted; 59 000 of those never returned and many more were injured.

After the cessation of hostilities, the British government put 273 balloons up for tender, to be sold for cart covers and tarpaulins. Both dirigibles and balloonists were suddenly redundant. It was an ignominious end for the gallant observation balloon and its trained personnel, and the close of a colourful chapter in early military aviation. War balloons would be seen again in future conflicts, but never again manned.

Between the World Wars, manned balloons virtually disappeared, but airships limped along with mixed success. In June 1919 an airship successfully traversed the Atlantic Ocean. The British airship *R34*, transported large numbers of paying passengers over long distances but broke up over Hull, killing all Americans on board and 27 British. For many years after the war, disaster followed disaster, mostly due to the use of the inflammable hydrogen. Britain's commercial airship era came to an abrupt halt in 1930 with the crash in France of the *R101*, while en route to Egypt and India: 48 of its 54 passengers died. Prior to this, several committee members had visited Australia and discussed the possibility of flying airships, the infamous *R101* in fact, to this country.

America's first helium-filled airship, the *Shenandoah*, flew for only two years before being destroyed with heavy loss of life in an Ohio storm in 1925. The world's largest airship, the German *Hindenburg* became the first to supply a regular transatlantic service between Germany and New York. It made 56 flights and carried 2656 passengers in safety and luxury before exploding on 4 May 1937, as it approached its mooring in New Jersey, after a flight from Frankfurt: 33 of its 97 occupants died.

The explosion of the giant airship was attributed to the substitution of hydrogen for the preferred helium. Some said static electricity was the cause, but the real reason was political sabotage: just two years before the outbreak of World War II, both the US and Russia - the only two countries where helium was available - refused to supply Germany with the gas in commercial quantities. The *Hindenburg* catastrophe sealed the fate of large airships.

By 1940 the airship had virtually been abandoned. Like the balloon, airships were most vulnerable during landing and taking off, especially in blustery conditions. Engines provided the necessary thrust to take off and to descend, as only a percentage of their lift was gained from gas. With the rapid growth of technology, the slow, unwieldy and unstable large airships were doomed. Only a few small, non-rigid dirigibles remained, earning a much less gracious living sporting advertising banners: this being the birth of the advertising blimp.

However, the airship was responsible for reigniting public interest in aerial transportation and the excitement was just as intense as it had been for the first balloon ascents.

With war declared again in Europe, unmanned barrage balloons saw service, acting as protective barriers over British and French cities against low flying enemy fighter planes. The defence consisted of 10 balloon 'aprons' of 5 Cacquots each, suspended by strong connecting vertical cables. The aprons were winched aloft and hung in the sky 7000-10 000' above factories, ports, power plants, strategic sites: the tethered cables fouled propellers, entangling the planes, to be caught like flies in giant spider webs. As many as 102 unwary planes collided with these 'apron strings' and others were forced to drop their bombs ineffectively. This strategy helped save Britain. Again, Australia had provided its countrymen and women to fight overseas. Out of 7 million citizens, 1 million served in Australia's defence forces; fortunately, casualties were far less than in World War I, but 27 000 paid the ultimate price.

After the war years, the versatile and invincible balloon took a well-earned rest, selflessly allowing the aeroplane to dominate the skies, while it patiently awaited the advancement of technology until it could again ride the winds; not as an instrument of science or of military aggression; not to be exploited by the showmen, but to participate in the sport of ballooning purely for pleasure's sake.

(1)   D Shepherd, *When the Chute Went Up*.
(2)   Ibid.
(3)   *The Australasian*, August 1908.
(4)   Major Henry Hersey, *Early Flight* 1909.
(5)   *Sydney Morning Herald*, 15 May 1911.
(6)   *Argus*, 6 July 1914.
(7)   Alan Morris, *The Balloonatics*.
(8)   LA Strange, *Recollections of an Airman* 1935.
(9)   Cobby, *High Adventures*.
(10)  Roach-Pierson, *Sea, Land and Air* Nov 1919.
(11)  Ibid.
(12)  Ibid.
(13)  AW Jose, *The Official History of Australia in the War of 1914-18*.

# PART THREE

# THE BALLOON AS SPORT

# Disaster Strikes

After the Wars, the pleasure balloonists became apathetic, finding the sky filled with obstacles, and fuel either too expensive (helium), too explosive (hydrogen), or in short supply (coal gas). The balloon seemed to have gone the way of the dinosaur, but it proved only to be endangered not extinct.

The technological advances that all but killed the balloon paradoxically helped it awaken from its moribund state. A young American on a posting in Europe, Ed Yost, was instrumental in reviving the dormant beast. During the Cold War of the 1950s, the US Navy gave Yost a brief to produce an inexpensive, high altitude research balloon capable of travelling long distances, ostensibly for espionage purposes. Yost designed and built hydrogen balloons, which were used to distribute propaganda leaflets behind the Iron Curtain from bases in West Germany.

Smitten with the desire to pursue ballooning, Yost endeavoured to solve the old problems of generating and storing hot air in an envelope. In 1953 he flew a lightweight polythene envelope heated by a plumber's blowtorch. Within years he had added a burner connected to propane gas bottled under pressure, and a valve enabling the flame to be switched on or off at will. In 1960 Yost demonstrated his ability to regulate a balloon's rate of ascent and descent - for the first time the pilot of a hot air balloon had directional control, albeit only vertical.

The new envelopes of nylon or polyester and the use of the low-cost propane burner ensured a new lease of life for aerostation. Without the millions of British Thermal Units (BTUs) per hour generated by burners (which heat the crown of a balloon above 100 C) there would have been no revival. As no more than two to three hours fuel could be carried on board, the new method was obviously unsuited to long distances, but perfect for pleasure flights.

Sport ballooning itself was not new, for it had emerged in France in January 1899 with the foundation of the Aero Club, which arranged competitions for gas balloons, which control vertical movement by discharging ballast to ascend or valving off gas to descend. The first race, held in Paris on 17 June 1900, attracted contestants keen to test their pilot accuracy and flying skills. The combination of endurance, altitude, horizontal distance covered and of descent close to a target, remains the basis for modern competition.

Charles Rolls, a fanatical competitor, devised the ever popular aerial pursuit task, 'Hare and Hounds', in which the 'hare' balloon launches before the 'hounds' who try to locate the beast, which has descended after a pre-determined time, placed a target cross on the ground and hidden. The pursuit pilot who drops his marker closest to the centre of the cross is declared the winner. Gas ballooning however, was inherently a wealthy person's sport.

News of Yost's successful experiments reverberated around the world, registering in the minds of men and women who, post-war, had leisure time and money to spend on their sport or the ability to access corporate sponsorship money.

In Sydney in 1962 Terry McCormack, a science and engineering graduate, made a tiny balloon just 12' in diameter which he released from a paddock in Albury, watching it soar to 2000' before it cooled and fell. So began a passionate interest in balloons. A year later, on 21 September 1963, Terry and five friends experimented with a red, white and blue sailcloth balloon named *de Rozier*, inside the University of New South Wales' Round House. Other tests followed on the football oval of St John's College Sydney University, where Terry had been a student and later, a tutor. They were days of eager activity. In May 1964, nine enthusiasts, (mainly scientists, engineers and teachers), brothers Terry and Laurie McCormack, Brian and Peter McGee, Terry Golding, Mopsy Mauragis, Zenon Kociumbas, Don Melley and Stan Grincevicius, formed the Aerostat Society of Australia, the first such club in the country and the first affiliated with the FAI.

The Society (later the Aerostat Balloon Society of Australia) with Terry McCormack as President, expressed its formal aims: to design and build LTA craft; undertake scientific work with balloons; train pilots; further sport ballooning, and promote safety standards. It was to be a non-profit organisation, seeking financial support from sponsors and at shows and air pageant appearances.

Less than two years after Terry McCormack's first experiments, and only a month after the Society's formation, members publicly christened the balloon they had constructed, *Archimedes I* (35' in diameter, 45' high and made of nylon and industrial sellotape) at Parkes NSW. Terry arrived at the launch site with the glistening silver balloon folded in a cardboard box in the boot of his car. He assured the press and onlookers that there was no risk of fire but acknowledged that there were definite dangers in this flight and was reported as visiting a local church prior to the historic flight.

With the help of fellow members, Terry inflated the envelope with air heated from a propane/butane cylinder; strapped an altimeter, 2 way radio and parachute (later discarded as too weighty) to his body and boarded. He took off at noon and shot up at an alarming 40' per second before levelling at 2000' and descending near Parkes airport. The date was 5 July 1964. One newspaper claimed the 15 minute, 3 mile manned flight to be the first in Australia for 50 years; in fact, 44 years had elapsed since VP Taylor signed off in Casino in 1920.

Although the flight itself had been stable, it was back to the drawing board to iron out difficulties with the take-off, and the bumpy, drag landing. Two weeks after its first flight, *Archimedes I* appeared at a Cowra air pageant, followed by a tether at Quirindi. Further free flights at Parkes and Trangie were aborted due to winds and insufficient burner power.

In early 1965 the Japanese Teijin Company donated a huge roll of cloth, enough material for a 60' diameter balloon. The Aerostat Society members considered the possibility of an epic flight across the Australian continent and decided to make *Teijin I*, a 100 000 cubic foot balloon, consisting of an outer polyester envelope with an inner of plastic, for the attempt. At the time, this was the world's largest balloon. Five of the Aerostat Society's members - Terry McCormack and his brother Laurie, Ken Bath, Terry Golding and Brian McGee spent over 200 hours cutting out and sewing together the 68 panels, each 3' wide and 94' long.

For their planned non-stop flight from the west to east coast of Australia, using the jet stream that John Wise had first outlined, they decided to abandon the traditional ballast method to offset rise and fall, in favour of 3 compensatory, 20' pressure balloons attached to the sides. A compressor in the balloon was to pump up the small balloons with air, to be released as desired. This pioneer super-pressure balloon was tested on the night of 12 October 1965, in ideal conditions at Sydney University. Terry Golding and several crew members went aloft on a tether. A serious accident occurred when a bystander interfered by pulling the zipper cord, causing the envelope to collapse on to the burner. Terry Golding was dragged from the basket and suffered burns and Terry McCormack, on the ground directing the landing, was trapped by his legs beneath the aluminium gondola. When the flames were extinguished it was revealed that much of the fabric had been destroyed.

It was not until February 1966 that the repaired balloon was again inflated, with better equipment and perfected safety devices. Two months later at Cargo, *Teijin I* made its first free flight with brothers Brian and Peter McGee and Mrs Cherry McCormack. In July, an eighty-minute flight at Canowindra was fully controlled and successful: on completion of the flight the balloon was tethered but broke away. Without a balloon or the hope of replacement (for the Society was in debt), it seemed the Aerostats were no longer viable; however, eight weeks after its loss, news of the balloon came in and it was recovered from thick forest, rather the worse for its taste of freedom. After feasibility studies the trans Australian venture was abandoned, despite overseas interest and local contributions of money.

In 1967 Terry McCormack and his family moved to Melbourne where Terry worked as a systems analyst, leaving vacant his position as President of the Aerostat Society. In his absence, Graham Wilson became the guiding force of the Aerostats until fate struck him a hefty blow: in 1970 he became a semi-quadriplegic in a hang gliding accident. Before his ballooning days ended, Graham was responsible for introducing fellow teacher, Peter Vizzard to ballooning. When he joined the Aerostats in 1967, Peter was unaware that he would make his future livelihood from balloons, by co-founding the first modern ballooning company in Australia, Balloon Aloft. Even in those early days of involvement he espoused the promotional and commercial qualities of aerostation.

In Victoria, around the same time as Terry McCormack and Aerostat members were dabbling with balloons, so too were Tony Norton and Peter Hodges. Tony Norton, born in Norwich England, came to Australia with his parents and was early influenced by matters aerial when his father took up work in an aircraft factory. His son became an industrial chemist and chemical engineer. In 1963 while working at a Melbourne laboratory, Tony realised the company had to rent an entire cylinder of hydrogen, although only requiring a cupful. "Like a flash," said Tony, "I decided on a balloon." For his first experiments he used condoms, then dry-cleaning film. Intrigued, he calculated the dimensions needed to lift a person's weight. (1)

Impulsively, Tony decided that if he was going to construct a balloon he may as well fly it across Australia, in an attempt on the world distance record of 1897 miles, made 50 years earlier in 1914, by German Herr Berliner, and the endurance record of 87 hours aloft, held by his compatriot H Haulen. Tony wrote to Don Picard in the US and the Goodyear Company in England, seeking information. Peter Hodges, along with other friends and relatives helped construct several balloons in the three years prior to the attempt. With the trans Australia flight in mind, Tony formed the Australian Balloon Club in 1966.

The *Cadbury* gas balloon was the result of donated material and sponsorship from the chocolate company. When first inflated, the hydrogen balloon dissolved into holes but was hastily patched with Sellotape and tethered long enough for a TV commercial to be filmed. Another balloon Tony Norton inflated from the gas pipeline at Warragul, where a loop valve was sited. He flew this on tether before it escaped. Although retrieved in a badly torn state, the balloon was repaired and flown several weeks later, on 19 June 1967, the first flight of a gas balloon in modern Australia.

Letters flew back and forth to the Department of Civil Aviation (DCA) for 18 months prior to the proposed transcontinental flight, with the DCA taking notes for a future operations' manual. The DCA had a dilemma for it had not dealt with balloons, and the existing rules and regulations were geared to powered aircraft, not for balloon flying. The Department granted Tony design clearance but required operational and airworthiness approval from the Regional Director, who requested his headquarters forward airworthiness data for balloons. The reply came: "Regret NO DATA AVAILABLE your query on balloons." (2)

In a warehouse lent by his boss, Tony began work on one large and one smaller gas balloon, named the *Kolotex* balloons for their sponsor, and specifically designed to cross Australia. A successful trial inflation took place at Williamstown Town Hall in September 1967, but a pressure test inside Melbourne's Exhibition Building resulted in a seam bursting with a loud explosion. After the failure of this test, stress reinforcements were carried out and passed by the DCA, which inspected the net rope construction (80 year old netmaker, Eric Taylor, made all Tony's nets) rip panel, instrument installation and insisted on a basket drop test.

Meanwhile, three RAAF pilots also had their sights on the world long distance balloon record and set in motion a plan more organised and detailed than that of Norton and Hodges. However they had no experience with flying balloons. They dreamed up the plan one steamy night at Butterworth Air Base in Malaya. They considered all the great challenges had been achieved: Everest climbed, the South Pole trekked to, solo yachtsmen had circumnavigated the world and astronauts the heavens. David Robson suggested the epic adventure.

The three Mirage jet pilots discovered their idea was feasible for, in July and August each year, the prevailing westerly winds across southern Australia could whisk a balloon across the continent in five or six days. Australia is one of the few places in the world where long distance attempts can be made safely over land, due to its unique combination of weather, low altitude terrain and far less international air traffic than in Europe or America. While stationed at Williamtown Base NSW, Flight Officer Robson, Flight Lt. John Ellis and Flight Lt. Jack Hayden planned their journey. DCA granted them permission for the attempt on the strength of their documented proposal, RAAF experience and an interview. Although involving RAAF personnel, the flight was not officially an RAAF undertaking, with the men taking annual leave for the project. Newspaper publisher John Fairfax sponsored the event; Ford provided retrieve trucks and CIG provided and shipped the 31 tons of hydrogen gas in cylinders as deck cargo from Sydney to Fremantle, WA.

The balloon *Nancy* was purchased in the UK from MA Brighton and Co in Camberley Surrey. Although in the midst of constructing a balloon for the film "*Chitty Chitty Bang Bang*", the company rushed through the Australian order in half the normal time so as to catch a Qantas flight. The balloon was of silver rubberised cotton and held 58 000 cubic feet of gas with a rot-proofed net covering; weavers from the Royal Blind Society in Sydney provided the wicker basket, which was fitted with a single bunk, a table and chairs.

Newspapers interviewed the three men, trying to understand their sudden 'madness' when each had "had his share of thrills in the sky," pulling out of a dive just before hitting the sea, landing with jammed nose-wheel or parachuting out of a burning jet as it ditched. Why choose a balloon when you could fly a Mirage between Sydney and Newcastle in three minutes, they asked? Robson's answer was totally plausible to balloonists, "Jets travel so fast that much of the romance of flying is lost. In the balloon we will be going right back to man's first attempts at flight." (3)

At Perth's Pearce RAAF base the team waited, straining to be airborne but thwarted for three long weeks by fickle winds. During this time an ex air force navigator and member of the opposition Labor party, Gough Whitlam (later Prime Minister of Australia), visited the base, climbed into the basket and studied the maps for the intended journey. The critical decision to fly came and the 'Westwind Endeavour' expedition was ready to set off. On 16 August 1968, volunteers and sixty sandbags were assembled to hold down *Nancy* during inflation, but the envelope refused to fill. With the balloon faulty, and only sufficient gas for one inflation, the attempt was abandoned, the balloons stored, and the crew dispersed to various postings.

Just six weeks later the Norton/Hodges team arrived in Perth, intent on their trans Australia attempt, named 'Project Long Hop.' They described the main anticipated problems as keeping warm and staying over land and not sea. At Cunderdin, 100 miles north of Perth, the pair made a few practice flights in the smaller balloon. One trial flight of 70 miles was hailed by the *West Australian* of 8 October 1968 as the "first successful flight in WA and the longest distance flown in a balloon in Australia."

Four days later the wind pattern was favourable, however; after using 34 cylinders of gas to inflate, the balloonists discovered with horror that they were four short. While awaiting transportation of a further fifty tons of gas from Perth, Tony and Peter tried to distract themselves by watching televised events of the Olympic Games being held in Mexico. On 14 October, the WA town of Meckering felt the full force of an earthquake, which reduced three quarters of the town to rubble, fortunately without loss of life. For several days, Tony and Peter helped the townspeople move to safety and clean up, while experiencing the unnerving after shocks that rumbled beneath their feet.

Just as half a world away, Jacqui Kennedy was in the midst of preparations for her marriage to Aristotle Onassis, so too were the modern-day 'Phileas Foggs' and their ground crew frantically preparing the balloon and equipment, working throughout the night as suitable pressure systems were emerging over the continent. On 16 October, stocked with ten days supply of dehydrated food, radios, fire extinguisher, parachutes, crash helmets, blankets, first aid kit, chemical toilet and emergency raft, *Miss Kolotex II* launched successfully. Shortly afterwards she ran into a rainstorm. The sandbag ballast soaked up the rain, causing them to become heavier and heavier. "No matter how much ballast we jettisoned, we couldn't keep up with the rate we took on water," Tony said later. Following the golden rule of gas ballooning, that a flight must end when the amount of ballast remaining is reduced to the minimum required to land safely, Tony put down the aircraft in heavy scrub at Bommie Rock,180 miles south west of the launching site. Due to faulty radio communications, pilot Tony and radio technician Peter remained stranded in the scrub for several days before being picked up, leaving the balloon and basket for collection later. (4)

The DCA complimented the team "on its presentation and scope of report on Project Long Hop " and stated that the "engineering basis of [the] balloon [was] very sound" but stipulated that there could be no further free flights for twelve months. Bitterly disappointed, the men had to be content knowing that they had broken their record set two weeks earlier. Although the cost of the venture, excluding Peter and Tony's own labour over the two years of preparation, totalled $30 000, the sponsors were reportedly satisfied. (5)

A year after the first attempt by RAAF personnel, a second team tried in 1969 to cross Australia by balloon. Neither Flight Lieutenant Christopher Furze, nor Flight Lieutenant Lee Jones (a formation member of the RAAF aerobatic display team, the Red Arrows) had flown a balloon, but between them had 29 years flying experience. They formed the RAAF Pearce Balloon Club, "to facilitate the administration and technical backing for the attempt." (6)

Lee Jones flew to the US to attend a balloon school, but it failed to eventuate. He returned to Perth with a 70 000 cubic foot dacron and plastic, pear-shaped envelope, especially constructed by Raven Industries at Sioux Falls South Dakota. Perth's Lord Mayor and supermarket chain owner, Tom Wardle, announced his intention to sponsor the epic journey, and to follow *Spirit of the West* balloon in his private plane. In July 1969, as they waited for a low pressure system to form off the southwest coast of WA and a high pressure off Queensland - the essential weather pattern that occurs just five or six times a year - they suffered a setback: Chris Furze was transferred interstate. His replacement, Flight Officer Peter Dickens, was quickly briefed on the flight expectations and hazards. He learnt about the realities of static electricity and ensuing fire (for which reason flash bulbs and battery-operated cameras were banned); that a bird's beak could puncture the balloon's skin; that in sub zero temperatures at night over a desert and above 4000', ice could form and its extra weight force them down.

Preparations were thorough and intense. Food would be a special low residue diet of chocolate, fruit, soups, honey and concentrates, to provide all food requirements. Coyly, they stated that "Medical action will have been taken on the Balloon crew before take off to preclude any requirement for toilet facilities in the basket other than (sic) H2O carrying plastic bags." These bags were to be disposed of as ballast (7).

The land party of nine was to be self-supporting for a possible fourteen days of Search and Rescue work. Under the leadership of Bill Hector who doubled as navigator, were drivers, fitters, a radio officer, photographer, even a quartermaster. With true military precision, a contingency plan was drawn up and submitted to the DCA.

Among other balance and stability tests, the basket - fitted with 300 lbs of sandbags - passed a DCA test, which encompassed lifting the basket by crane and dropping it onto concrete from the not-so-great height of 3 feet! The DCA thoroughly examined envelope material, ropes, cables, sealants, lubricants, valves, the rip panel and associated line which was to achieve a discharge of gas when landing in winds in excess of a few knots. The men launched *Spirit of the West* at dawn on 23 August 1969. Navigating by a mixture of dead reckoning, radio bearings, map reading, use of sextant and prismatic compass, and with escort aircraft, the fliers passed an uneventful night, averaging a speed of 8 knots and varying in altitude between 5000 - 10 000', always seeking the southwest wind. By morning the SW wind had died, to be replaced by a northerly which would carry them into arid, inhospitable country, so at 10am they landed, 30 miles east of Salmon Gums, still within WA. Nevertheless, Lee Jones and Peter Dickens' time aloft (28½ hours) and distance covered (378 miles), had broken the Australian endurance and distance records set the previous year by Norton and Hodges.

The following year, Lee Jones and Flight Officer Michael Greentree launched *Spirit of the West* in yet another attempt to cross Australia by balloon. Again, it was winter in the Southern Hemisphere when they took off on 18 June 1970 from the Pearce RAAF base. It was an all-out effort as they struggled against sub-zero temperatures at 15 500' and 35 mph winds which threatened to sweep them out to sea. Due to incorrect channels being set on the two-way radio, ground crew were unable to contact them directly, so could only relay messages through the DCA at Kalgoorlie airport. After the third night, as the wind was pushing the balloon towards Bass Strait, the men landed in a paddock near Naracoorte SA, a mere 15 miles west of the Victorian border and 400 miles short of the world record. In all they had flown 1500 miles in 55 hours aloft, an amazing achievement, but Jones and Greentree felt disappointed, curled up in their sleeping bags beside the basket to await the ground crew.

The two air force officers made one last bid just two months later, on 27 August 1970, but were forced off course in fickle winds and landed 60 miles north of Meekatharra in WA. No further RAAF attempts were made, as Michael Greentree transferred to a new posting and Lee Jones left the air force to set up an aviation academy in Jordan. With their departure, the Pearce Balloon Club disintegrated and gas record attempts in Australia ceased.

By 1970 Terry McCormack, licensed by DCA as a Flight Examiner, was back in Sydney and the Aerostats had constructed several more balloons. The balloon *Ego* ('nothing inflates or deflates faster than') had several free flights, its most famous passenger being 'Skippy' the kangaroo of the TV series.

The Aerostats computer designed a super pressure balloon specifically for tether, a balloon that would keep a rigid shape and not distort in wind. The *Spirit of Endeavour* was sponsored to participate in the Captain Cook Bicentenary celebrations at the Sydney Showground on 8 February that year, with a large ground-blower used for rapid inflation. The *James Cook* balloon followed, helped in its construction by Phil Kavanagh, another person destined to make ballooning his livelihood, as well as his sport. In 1968, newlyweds Wendy and Phil (a former television cameraman and boat builder), were introduced to the Aerostats by brother Steve Kavanagh, then sharing a house with Peter Vizzard. Later, Phil became Australia's only hot air balloon manufacturer but credits his initial interest to a trip to the countryside. As Phil had a strong car and a towbar (for a boat) he was prevailed upon to drive balloonists and their aircraft, "otherwise I may never have become involved." (8)

In 1970 Phil and Wendy Kavanagh, (having left the Aerostats Society the year before), brother Steven and architect Keith Willcox constructed the transparent *Little Bear* balloon, so called as it was held together with 'Bear tape', an industrial strength, fibreglass/polyester film tape, developed in America as part of its space program. The nylon balloon was built only after the group deciphered US Air Force books of complex, computer calculations. They cut out the 34 segments of material on the floor of a local basketball court, being the only flat, non-abrasive surface available. *Little Bear* retired early, its place taken in 1973 by Phil's next effort, a red and black balloon named *Ulinga*, from the Aboriginal word 'to fly'. Decades later, this balloon was still flying under the guiding hands of Joe Blitz.

Phil Kavanagh gave away boat building to produce balloons professionally. His first commercial balloon - a green one with 12 silk-screened signs of the Zodiac and named *Destiny*, was featured in the zany Australian film "*Young Einstein*". Brother Steve, ironically, remained involved for only a year.

Wives and friends of the men actively involved with ballooning sometimes flew as passengers, but it appears likely that the first woman in Australia since the Van Tassell sisters to pilot a balloon, was Jenny Keats (Mrs Dale Martinson), who had her first experience in Berwick, Victoria in 1971. Later, she and her husband belonged to a syndicate that owned the balloon *Puff*, which Jenny flew under instruction. By early 1972 Joy Norton, Tony's first wife, had logged 2½ hours in control of a free-flying balloon.

Although balloon club members in different states had been lobbying for the flying of manned free balloons to be recognised as a sport, there was still no official licensing or operational code in Australia. The long-awaited UK examiner of balloonists, Wing Commander Gerry Turnbull, arrived in Australia in 1972 and tested and passed Tony Norton and Peter Vizzard for their British Balloon Licences. They became the first pilots to gain licences in Australia but were not the first licensed Australians to pilot balloons.

This honour went to a woman Kathryn Tracy, who had been awarded her licence when on a working holiday in the UK, having first gone aloft in 1968 with a boyfriend. Kay (as she is known) joined the British Balloon and Airship Club which at the time boasted 350 members, 25 hot air balloons and 5 gas balloons. After 7 months of crewing, flying and studying in her spare time Kay became only the 3rd female pilot to pass the tough British test and only the 15th female balloonist in the world. Her examiner was Gerry Turnbull, whom she married in Australia in 1972. Kay had logged 60 hours flying time in Europe, but had flown her red, white and blue balloon *Goonawalla* only once, on its maiden test flight in England. (Its name, an aboriginal word meaning 'haven of peace' was named after the Bathurst property of her childhood). She flew it first at Canowindra, before leaving for the UK with Gerry Turnbull and selling it to Peter Vizzard.

Although several professionally made balloons called Australia home, there were still numerous problems to solve: grass burns, holes appearing near the chimney top, retaining tapes breaking, basket wires of unequal length, the instrument panel lid regularly popping out of its groove and chimney rings needing strengthening.

In September 1972, Terry McCormack attempted a tether at the Royal Show in Adelaide. When 15' off the ground the balloon tilted in the NW breeze and "his red and white checkered pressure balloon (one with a burner inside the closed mouth of the envelope) caught alight at one of his performances but was not badly damaged." (9)

Between tethered flights at showgrounds, Australia's twelve balloon pilots flew privately. In those days of learning by experimentation, methods were often fairly primitive. Several people were employed on the mouth of an envelope to flap it up and down to facilitate air entry. Launching required four men to stand the basket up and run with it in the same direction as the wind, in order to prevent cooling or toppling of the envelope. During those comic capers - the burner was on at the same time - it was hoped the balloon lifted off before it collapsed or hit a barbed wire fence. Landing also had its difficulties for the 'trial and error' pilots. The pilot had to choose a landing site from a considerable distance and let down by adjusting the amount of flame from the burner: not an easy task with two tons of balloon and a slow reaction time. Balloons overseas had valves for letting out hot air to control the rate of descent, but Australian balloons did not boast such a refinement until a side vent was added to the *James Cook* balloon.

It was in 1972 that Crawford Productions approached several balloonists, proposing to film a balloon and ground safari across Australia for a TV series and travel book. Tony Norton in *Zeus* and Peter Vizzard in *Hamlyn* joined the expedition as pilots; among the ground crew were Ed Selman and Dale Allan. They spent nine weeks filming and travelling from Perth to Kalgoorlie, Laverton, Ayers Rock, Birdsville, Mt Isa, Cloncurry, the Gulf of Carpentaria, then southeast to Bourke, Canowindra, Albury and finally Bairnsdale. There were some memorable moments during the safari: the arrival of the party at Ayers Rock coincided with one of the rare storms that bleach the rock of the entrancing colours for which it is renowned. Cameramen in the balloons shot footage of waterfalls cascading down the sheer slopes of the Rock and the lake which formed at its base. They recorded the first flight of a balloon over Ayers Rock and the setting of new Australian endurance, height and distance records for a hot air balloon - 2¼ hours flying time, 1000' and 24 miles, but the footage was never released.

Balloons have featured in many films and advertisements, their allure attracting producers and endearing them to millions of viewers. Advertisers who had earlier deserted the balloon for other media, flooded back as sponsors in the 1970s. The captive balloon that never flew free or felt the warmth of hot air, has proven invaluable for advertising purposes. Moored at a fixed location and attracting attention from passers-by, such balloons need to be resistant to atmospheric factors and have a low (gas) diffusion rate. In some countries, the cold inflatables have an underlying scientific purpose: to mark oil exploration sites.

The other type of captive balloon, the Kytoon or kite balloon, developed for stability in high winds, still finds a niche as an advertising platform or as a scientific tool. In civil engineering it serves as a survey target in rough terrain; in military circles as an artillery target. The kite balloon can be a marker for crop dusting and photographic flights. Although familiar with the balloon as a site for advertisers' signage at fetes and shows, pioneer Charles Henry Brown could never have foreseen to what extent the balloon would be adapted.

NSW and Victoria continued to monopolise the newly discovered sport of ballooning and attracted a small, but dedicated, band of participants. Canowindra in NSW had become the unofficial headquarters of Australian ballooning. Originally Cherry McCormack selected this location as being "perfect for the sport in the mid-sixties." Her words, essentially about a place, inadvertently distill the essence of sport ballooning as it was then and as it remains,

> "I have some very happy memories of ballooning weekends, mainly in the small western town of Canowindra...Frosty mornings stamping down the frozen thistles so that they would not damage the balloon; chasing after the balloon in cars...the exhilaration of the flight; the frustration if conditions were not right for flying; and the evenings of camaraderie in the Canowindra pubs, golf-club or other borrowed accommodation." (10)

Learning was still mainly ad hoc; still there was no official set of rules and regulations written specifically for balloons; still no licensing system. This freedom for fliers and 'laissez faire' attitude by officials could not last; incidents began to occur.

One pleasant Sydney Sunday afternoon, on 17 August 1975, a publicity stunt for the opening of a pancake parlour went astray. Roger Meadmore from Adelaide had set up a chain of such restaurants in Australia and had tethered his balloon *Lovely! Lady* (featuring an old fashioned girl holding her knife and fork in the air in a less than genteel fashion) to promote his newest parlour at the Rocks in Sydney. Just past noon, the 41 year old pilot apparently fired the burner too long and the *Lovely! Lady*, resistant to being tied down, impetuously broke her bindings and soared past a clutter of old buildings and narrow laneways jammed in beside the Sydney Harbour Bridge.

Away she sailed, literally taking Roger Meadmore for a ride, which ended 3 hours and 40 kilometres later, after a "comic chase by police, reporters, curious members of the public and the balloonist's friends." Meadmore drifted over numerous Sydney suburbs to the bushy fringe and low hills of the Hawkesbury River. "Then - with a lot of skill and a little luck - he landed the balloon in the back of a small launch cruising near Milsons Island," no doubt to the astonishment of its occupants. (11)

The incident was reported in a jovial fashion and the flamboyant Meadmore was suspected of plotting the whole event for publicity. The accidental flight had its more serious side: the control tower at Sydney airport had to divert planes from the runaway's flight path and a helicopter was scrambled to search for the balloon. Aviation regulations had been broken and authorities were quick to ask for a detailed report. Meadmore continued to fly as a commercial pilot and instructor, described by fellow balloonists variously as romantic, mad, wild and indestructible.

Regrettably, it took a double tragedy to shake balloonists and aviation officials from their complacency, innocence or naivety - call it what you will.

On a hot November day in 1975, Terry McCormack and friends Tony and Jillian Hayes, Michael Small and his girlfriend (later wife) Cheryl Chilcott, went away for a weekend of ballooning. (Terry's pregnant wife Cherry stayed at home with their two sons). They had chosen Wagga to practise flying to a target in readiness for competing at the forthcoming World Championships.

Michael Small had first become fascinated with ballooning when he saw David Niven in the film "*Around the World in 80 Days*" and joined the Aerostats in 1971. As a maintenance engineer for QANTAS for six years, Michael had always been interested in flight but had not flown until he went up in the *James Cook*, the balloon Terry McCormack made in a garage. The *James Cook* balloon was an attractive green and silver balloon, made from heavy aluminised acrylic coated nylon with a scalloped mouth, a chimney at the top and a side vent. It had one burner; cables ran from the wicker basket to the burner frame (unlike the rigid support poles used today), which meant, on landing, the burner fell on the occupants' heads. For this reason, they used crash helmets; parachutes were also worn as a safety measure.

Terry's flying skills were such that he had once landed a balloon on his car trailer in order to quieten detractors, who scoffed at how useless and uncontrollable, was the balloon. The group had chosen Wagga because gas was available and, "because of better forecasts with respect to wind conditions." The Mayor had welcomed them and given them official permission to fly in the district. (12)

That morning Michael flew with Terry at Brucedale, 50 kilometres from Wagga to a stated altitude of 9000'. After lunch Terry took Tony Hayes up in the balloon to practise low level flying. Michael Small helped with the launch and left the site 15 minutes later in the retrieve vehicle with his girlfriend Cheryl and Jillian Hayes. Cheryl intended to go on the fateful flight but felt ill, so withdrew.

The balloon climbed to about 1000' and tracked to SE on a 2-3 knot wind. Several times Michael unsuccessfully tried to contact the balloon by two-way radio. (It was later discovered the other radio was not on board). He caught sight of the balloon 500' up in an area north of Bomen and headed towards it. Coming over a small hill on the Oura Road, 8 kilometres NE of Wagga, he saw smoke and people standing in a paddock. A passing motorist informed him that the balloon had crashed, and that police and ambulance had been notified.

Half an hour previously, the Brown family had been photographing the *James Cook* and talking to Terry and Tony. They witnessed the balloon get into difficulties in a willy-willy and watched helplessly as it collapsed and plummeted to the ground, forced down by the strong wind gust that caused the mouth to twist closed, and the top vent to be forced open, with resultant sudden loss of hot air. The family said that, at an altitude of 400' the balloon began to fall, out of control and spinning wildly on its axis, "then one side collapsed and it tilted over 45 degrees...then it turned over the other side as more hot air escaped and began to fall sharply. Then I saw one man dive out of the basket...his parachute didn't open, he just went straight into a paddock from about 100 metres up...the balloon hit and a sheet of flame shot up right away," said Mr Brown, who dashed to where Anthony Hayes lay after jumping. He was dead. Terry McCormack had been thrown clear of the blazing balloon, which had set alight the surrounding grass: he was on fire, but also dead. (13)

At that stage Michael Small and Jill Hayes arrived at the scene; she became hysterical at the sight of her husband's body and was taken to hospital. Local farmers and police gathered and beat out the grass fires; the balloon was a charred mass. It was Michael Small who had the grisly task that afternoon of identifying the bodies for police. Following his friends' funerals Michael gave up flying balloons, not taking to the air again until 1982.

Local and daily papers wrote of the balloon fatalities on front spreads and inside pages. Other aerial accidents occurred in NSW on that same day but, paradoxically, only one sentence recorded the 1 death and 1 critically injured person from a glider crash at Bungendore; a further sentence briefly mentioned a plane crash at Armidale in which 3 people were injured, 1 critically. Undoubtedly, editors would defend this imbalance, justifying the sensational coverage by dint of it being the first balloon tragedy in modern Australia. Over ensuing years, the media were to have a love relationship with balloons, depicting magical romantic flights at dawn all over the country, but that ended in 1989 when balloons were again involved in loss of life. Suddenly, the media labelled balloons dangerous, and exaggerated the slightest of incidents thereafter.

Thirty-year-old Anthony Hayes and his pilot friend Terry McCormack, 36 - pioneer of modern Australian ballooning with nine years experience - died at 1.45pm on that 30° summer day at the whim of a thermal. Today balloonists are fully aware of the devastating effect of a thermal: it sweeps up a balloon and pummels it down to the ground as if a mere plaything. For that reason, sport balloonists avoid summer, and even commercial balloon companies that operate year round, fly only in the stable conditions at dawn and never in the middle of the day when thermals are at their strongest and deadliest.

In his statement to police, Michael Small admitted, "we encountered thermal effects when we landed at Brucedale (earlier that day) but we were able to fly out of the affected area and land safely." When questioned about the Aerostat Society's recommendations of action to be taken when turbulent conditions prevail, Michael responded, "we are all aware of the necessity to ascend out of the area of influence of the thermal and prepare again for landing." (14)

Michael Small has since stated that in 1975 they had no documentation on, or experience with, the effects of thermals on balloons and he loyally defended Terry's decision to fly on a hot summer day. Previously Terry McCormack, in answer to a letter of enquiry from Brian Smith in Scotland, regarding restrictions on flying hours wrote, "we fly at any time and thermals have been very rare." (15)

Other contemporary balloonists whom I interviewed disagree, and claim that Terry was aware of the danger associated with thermals and had previously and deliberately flown in them, regarding them as a challenge against which to pit himself. One person wrote to me, describing Terry as "foolhardy, an accident waiting to happen." It is true that Terry had had a series of accidents - he was pilot of the *Teijin I* balloon when it burnt at Canowindra and twice had almost severed his hand by holding onto the rip wire after landing and being dragged along the ground behind the basket. Hindsight was no consolation to Cherry McCormack coping with the death of her husband. Her two boys had flown in balloons with their father but their third son, born after his death, had his first flight only on his tenth birthday. It was an offer quietly extended by Peter Vizzard, that brought the joy of flight to the boy who never knew his father or his great love for balloons.

Cherry, of necessity, became the breadwinner for the young family and rose to the position of Charge Nurse at Camperdown's Hospital for Children. To my letter requesting information, she wrote a reply that stands as an epitaph to her husband,

"Terry was so passionately involved with the whole concept of lighter-than-air-craft that I am sure he would not be surprised at how popular the sport is now.
Terry made an extremely significant contribution to the sport and I wonder at what stage ballooning would be at in Australia had he not initiated it in the sixties. He was very generous in the time he spent instructing others and his enthusiasm was infective. As to the man himself, he had a deep spiritual faith and great compassion for the underdogs of this world. He was a wonderful husband and father, his joy in living was contagious and the only fear he had of dying was the fact that his

family would be left alone. I have wonderful memories of him and count it a privelege (sic) to have known him for 13 years."

She ended her letter on a positive note that balloonists everywhere understand without explanation, "In spite of everything I still think one of the most beautiful sights in the very early morning is to look up and see a balloon drifting through the mists." (16)

(1)   Interview, Tony Norton.
(2)   DCA Archives.
(3)   *The Sun*, (Melbourne) 27 July 1968.
(4)   *The Age*, 24 October 1968.
(5)   DCA Archives.
(6)   Ibid.
(7)   Ibid.
(8)   Interview, Phil Kavanagh.
(9)   Marion J Mitchell, Julie L Smith, *Ballooning in South Australia* 1983.
(10)  Letter C McCormack to H Rogers.
(11)  *Sydney Morning Herald*, 18 August 1975.
(12)  Michael Small, statement to police 23 November 1975.
(13)  *Sunday Telegraph*, 23 November 1975.
(14)  Michael Small, statement to police.
(15)  Letter B Smith, 17 May 1972.
(16)  Letter Cherry McCormack 1988.

First modern balloon - *de Rozier*, Round House, University of NSW

Terry McCormack's second balloon - *Archimedes I*, held together
with adhesive tape 1963

Police at Agricultural Show watch *Teijin I*
1964

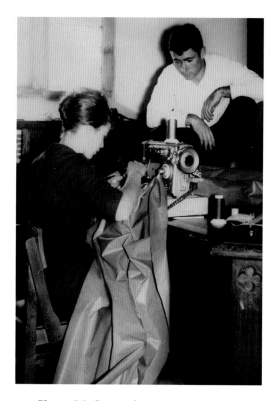

Cherry McCormack sews *Teijin I* under
Terry's guidance

Burnt envelope *Teijin I*

# THE AEROSTATS BALLOON SOCIETY OF AUSTRALIA

Logo for The Aerostats

Members at Yeovil Show L-R, P Vizzard, P Kavanagh, G Smith,
the Mayor, K Wilcox, S Kavanagh, A Welsh

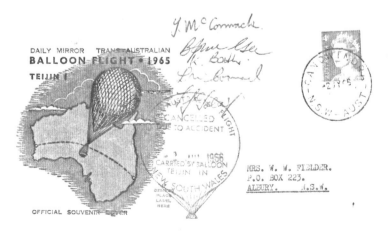

Cancelled 1964 airmail flight, due to burnt balloon

Expedition Westwind - RAAF attempts to fly across Australia

Cylinders used to inflate *Nancy* 1968

Gough (later Prime Minister) and Margaret
Whitlam with FO Dave Robson

All courtesy of Dave Robson

Crew check *Nancy's* crown
(courtesy of Dave Robson)

The attempt is over, the crew flee
(courtesy of Dave Robson)

Queensland premier, Joh Bjelke Peterson
with Roger and Ruth Meadmore

Kay Turnbull, the first Australian to hold a balloon licence (UK)

# The Sun-Herald

Incorporating "The Sunday Sun and Guardian"
(No. 3780) and "The Sunday Herald" (No. 1393)

SUNDAY, NOVEMBER 23, 1975

152 Pages

FIFTEEN CENTS†

# BALLOON CRASHES —2 KILLED

*By PHIL SCOTT*

### Two men were killed in a horrifying hot air balloon tragedy near Wagga yesterday.

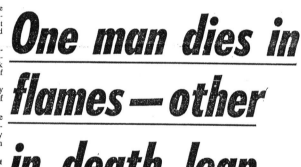

## One man dies in flames — other in death leap

One man died after he leapt from the stricken balloon seconds before it hit the ground and exploded in a ball of flame.

The other man was killed when the balloon erupted in flames in a paddock five miles north-west of Wagga.

Police late yesterday released the names of the two men.

They were Terrence McCormack, 36, of Beecroft, and Anthony Hayes, 30, of Longworth Avenue, Point Piper.

In another air tragedy at Bungendore, near Canberra, yesterday a man was killed and another injured when a glider crashed (see story, Page 5).

And at Ebor, near Armidale, three people were injured, one critically, when the wings of their Cessna plane clipped a tree and crashed (see story, Page 4).

The man who leapt from the balloon plummeted 160ft to the ground after his parachute failed to open.

### Wife's horror

Police said the balloon was caught in a willy willy and spun out of control.

Mrs Hayes was following the balloon in a car and arrived at the scene of the tragedy seconds after it plunged to the ground.

Police, ambulance and fire brigade units were on the scene at 2.30 pm — 20 minutes after the accident.

One of the first on the scene was Senior Constable Les Miller. He said:

"The bloke who jumped out of the balloon didn't have a chance.

"He landed about 45 metres from the balloon.

"His mate was badly burnt — the balloon was just a charred pile sitting in the middle of the paddock," he said.

The balloonists were in radio contact with their support car but did not have time to relay a distress message.

The balloon crashed 300 metres off the Oura road in a vacant paddock.

Reports from Wagga said the two men were from the Sydney Ballooning Society. Both were married.

Mr Michael Small, who identified the bodies for police, is now in a state of shock and staying with his fiancee in a caravan park in Wagga.

He was following the balloon in a car with Mrs Hayes.

Police said the people in the car heard an explosion as they were mounting a rise in the road and found the blazing balloon in front of them.

### Spun around

Mrs Annette Brown, an eye witness of the tragedy, said the balloon collapsed inwards as the willy willy spun the basket around.

"My husband Bob and I had pulled up to talk to the balloonists only 10 minutes before the accident.

"They were just hanging in the air about 200ft up. We could hear them quite plainly.

"They told us they'd left near Ganmain early in the

"We hopped in the car and followed along the Oura road.

"The balloon stopped again and just hung there motionless. It was about three paddocks away when the willy willy got hold of it.

"It seemed to get up inside the balloon and it just collapsed. One chap jumped out. He had a parachute on, but it didn't open.

"The other man seemed to hesitate, as if waiting for the balloon to get closer to the ground.

"He jumped out about

**Continued P 4**

1970s pilots wore parachutes - Brian McGee and Terry McCormack 1975

*James Cook* crashed with fatal consequences

Newspaper report of the tragedy 1975

Payload attached
(Courtesy of CSIRO)

Project Hibal Mildura Victoria 1960s-1974
(Courtesy of CSIRO)

Parachute falls to earth with the payload
(Courtesy of CSIRO)

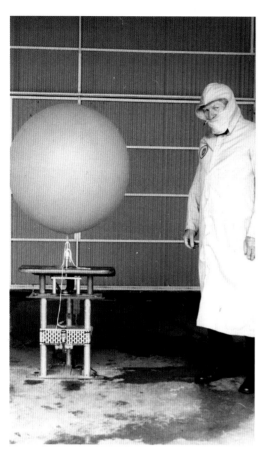

Protective clothing needed to inflate
weather balloon 1980s

Attached payload, tracker ready, Bureau of Meteorology

Early special shapes *Golly I* and *Golly III*

Fire-fighting airship Forests' Commission of Victoria 1976
(Courtesy of Tony Norton)

A tetrahedron

Inventor Tony Norton

*Ardath* airship 1976

*Snoopy* airship pedalled by Brian McGee
(Courtesy B Smith)

Tim Woodbridge's *Marie Antoinette* 1975

*Cascade* over historic Richmond Bridge
Tasmania

Dewhirst and Wicke's first attempt to
overfly Mt Everest 1985
(Photo by Leo Dickinson,
Courtesy of C Dewhirst)

Balloon near Everst

Everest success with second attempt 1991 - *Star Flyer*

Star Flyer lands
(Photo by Eric Jones,
courtesy C Dewhirst)

Jenny Houghton, Shirley Adkins,
Chris Dewhirst at his Oswald Watt
medal presentation

Joanne Delesantro with her 1975 bronze
Worlds Championship medal

Vizzard's World Championship trophy

Peter Vizzard with his World Hot Air
Balloon Championship Trophy 1983

Attempt to circumnavigate the globe, Julian Nott and 'Spider'
Anderson with Mike Willesee 1984

Gren Putland lands in nudist colony Battle Creek 1985

Bass Strait crossing in *Bassoon* 1981
(Courtesy of John Casamento)

Transferring people to Police launch, Port Phillip Bay Victoria

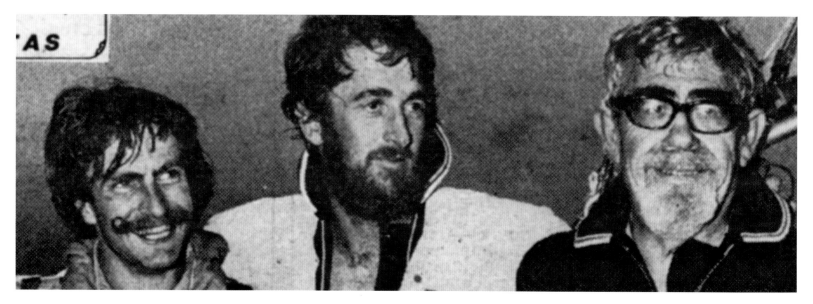

Pilot Gary Geier, Phil White, and adventurous instigator Arnold Himson

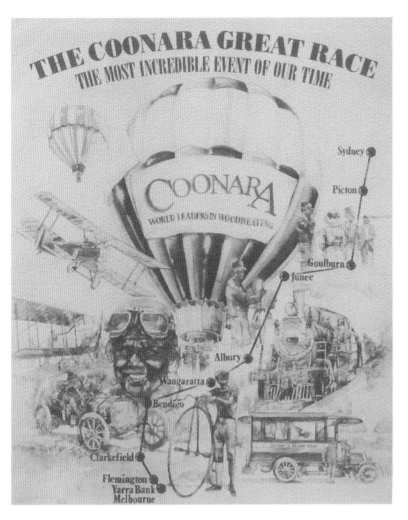

Poster for Coonara Great Race 1986

Start of race Sydney

Good farmer relations are paramount

Nurses, Firemen and bushrangers participated

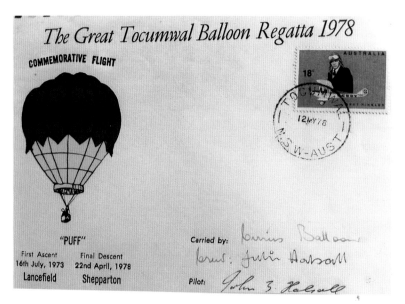

The Great Tocumwal Balloon Regatta 1978

COMMEMORATIVE FLIGHT

"PUFF"

First Ascent
16th July, 1973
Lancefield

Final Descent
22nd April, 1978
Shepparton

Carried by:

Pilot:

1978

BAROSSA BALLOON REGATTA, SEPPELTSFIELD
Brian Smith's Balloon "CAPTAIN STARLIGHT"

Bay Stamps "Silk" Cachet

Queen's Birthday holiday weekend saw many
hundreds of interested spectators witness a
magnificent spectacle when up to five balloons
simultaneously soared to cloud level in a matter
of seconds.

1979

First Day Covers and their respective dates

1988

HOT AIR BALLOON MAIL

MARCH 19-21 1988 CANBERRA
BICENTENNIAL PHILATELIC CONVENTION

Australia Post Issue

*Skippy* stars in Northern Territory film

*Destiny* featured in *Young Einstein* movie

Ruth Wilson, Chief Organiser of the Trans Australia Balloon Challenge 1988, for Australia's Bicentennial

*Sydney Opera House* (piloted by and photo courtesy of Chris Dewhirst, Australia)

Joe Kittinger Snr. (USA) Above Mt Isa Queensland

*Richard Branson's Virgin Jumbo* piloted by Carolina Witt (UK, Courtesy of Chris Dewhirst)

Winner David Levin (USA) with the youngest competitor 20 year old Mark Wilson (Aust) (Courtesy of Ruth Wilson)

Balloon that crashed at Alice Springs 1987 - 13 killed

Michael Sanby

David Bowers died when he hit a power pole 1989

Crossing Australia non stop 1983
(Courtesy of Dick Smith)

Ross Spicer (d. 1989 in balloon accident) and Anne Blaxland attempt
to cross the Blue Mountains

Successful - John Wallingron and Dick Smith
(Courtesy of Dick Smith)

# The CSIRO and Meteorological Balloons

In the early sixties, when the first modern sport balloonists were tentatively flying, Australian scientists were employing unmanned balloons as vehicles for research. On 17 December 1960 the Atmospheric Research Division of the Commonwealth Scientific and Industrial Research Organisation (CSIRO) and sponsor, the then US Atomic Energy Commission (AEC), launched Project Hibal (literally meaning 'high altitude balloon') in Mildura in north western Victoria. The town's airport was chosen as an official Balloon Launching Station (BLS) - one of five monitoring stations worldwide - because Mildura was free from pollution, was accessible to capital cities yet away from major air routes and was surrounded by accessible country. Importantly for the United States, Mildura lay at 34 degrees of latitude, matching perfectly the same latitude in the Northern Hemisphere where tests were undertaken in the US.

For the next fourteen years Hibal balloons were sent up to take samples of the stratosphere as part of a cosmic radiation survey. Chemical analyses of nitrogen and ozone were undertaken, and solar radiation measured. Hibal was part of a global program to collate data on the long-term effects of atomic explosions in the upper atmosphere, in the interests of health and safety. The *Canberra Times* reported one such event: a huge balloon was released at the BLS at 6.40 am and went up to a height of 22 miles (119 000'), the highest to date for a scientific balloon, "The balloon climbed steadily for 2½ hours and drifted further west. At 11.45am, the payload of scientific instruments...cut away from the balloon and hit the ground almost an hour later." (1)

Facilities supplied at the BLS included an office, workshop and storeroom; equipment supplied included heavy trucks (each fitted with a gantry to support the payload and a winch to unwind the balloon), and trailers to transport helium cylinders to the various launch sites. A 4WD recovery vehicle and spotters' aircraft fitted with direction finders to receive the balloon's beacon were available. A resident Project Leader and a team of permanent Mildura residents manned the BLS; other staff travelled from Melbourne as required.

Set up specifically to launch about 30 medium sized balloons annually, the facility and team of 10, additionally catered for around 10 large, independent flights a year. In comparison, the Texas USA facility had 50 staff for 100 flights per year, with equipment able to support extremely sophisticated experiments. The Australian facility lacked the best technology and was criticised for its minimal service but had an excellent reputation for reliability.

Seven Frenchmen and one woman spent 4 weeks at the Mildura centre in December 1967, using the facility to launch a series of 30 balloons as part of a world-wide project, designed to track previously unexplored ocean air currents and to gauge the angle of the sun above the horizon. Each 8' balloon was expected to circle the world at an altitude of 30 000', taking from 12-16 days to reappear over Mildura.

In October 1969 scientists from NASA, the American space agency, used the BLS whilst "searching for sources of gamma radiation from suspected exploding stars in the galaxy...part of a continuous NASA study into the conditions astronauts will face in future journeys to the planets." The payload, a gamma ray telescope, camera and other equipment, was taken to 128 000' and cut loose by a radio command and drifted to earth at the end of a parachute, landing 250 miles from the launch site near Hillston NSW. The data was taken back to America for analysis. (2)

The following month, the world's largest balloon - 30 million cubic feet and carrying almost a ton of instruments - was to be sent 30 miles above the earth into the stratosphere, to study invisible rays from the

Milky Way. Even deflated the envelope alone weighed nearly a ton. It was filled with helium imported from Texas. When extended vertically above the payload, the balloon was released, and the entire flight train became airborne. Launching occurred at dawn, to ensure winds at their lightest, and maximum daylight hours in which to track and recover the payload, returned to earth with their heavy scientific equipment and data by parachute. Imported also from the US were the Hibal balloons, from the Winzen International Company. The balloons were designed to be used once and to burst at a certain altitude.

Scientific balloons were used at higher altitudes than previously and subjected to longer ultraviolet light exposure, ozone gas and lower temperatures. Envelopes needed to be larger in size to enable high speed ascents and day and night use, and of extra tensile strength for strong wind release. With advances in technology it became possible to build balloons with very thin walls, yet resistant to extreme changes in temperatures. The 'zero pressure' space balloon was designed so only a fraction of the envelope filled with helium. In the thinner stratospheric air, the gas expanded to fill the entire envelope. Such balloons were able to go up into the jetstreams and stay aloft for several weeks of data gathering.

Observations from outside the earth's atmosphere were possible then via satellites, unmanned rockets and balloons. Satellites, being expensive vehicles, were limited to use only by top scientists. With rockets, observational time was very brief, but the balloon was able to achieve a satisfactory operating altitude of 50 kilometres. This ability, plus the relatively low cost of high altitude balloon flights, led to widespread scientific use.

Operation Hibal was the largest special project undertaken at BLS Mildura. Although the AEC in the USA funded the project, it agreeably flew Australian CSIRO payloads 'piggyback.' The agreement terminated in 1974, but not before Hibal had achieved in excess of 600 successful launchings. Four to five balloons a month had been followed over an unmapped maze of saltbush, spinifex and mallee scrub with only bush tracks to guide the recovery teams. The AEC transferred the assets of the station to Australia free of charge on the basis that it would continue as an international facility. The Commonwealth Government thus assumed responsibility for the BLS, funding it on a non-recurrent basis for one year.

The CSIRO's Division of Atmospheric Physics and Cloud Physics, being dependent in the 1970s on large balloons for its studies of atmospheric and stratospheric particles, regularly used the BLS Mildura facility. The CSIRO's interest in the build up and dispersion of radiation, gases, aerosols and particles (such as ash from erupting volcanoes) injected into the stratosphere, led it to collect southern hemisphere data of global significance. These suspended atmospheric materials are now recognised as pollutants, altering air climate and significantly affecting our environment and human health.

Although Mildura was the main BLS, balloons were occasionally launched from Parkes to the east, Waikerie to the west and Longreach and Alice Springs to the north; however, these sites proved more expensive in travel and transport costs. Alice Springs was favoured, and a modest facility developed there, but expeditions to the centre were limited to two per year, with a doubling-up of participating experimenter groups.

One of the few incidents in Mildura occurred on Flight 736, where an infra-red telescope was smashed when it crashed to earth after free falling without its parachute. Investigations discovered an incorrect connection that caused half of the parachute shroud lines to cut away. Despite the BLS conducting hundreds of flights without serious incident or damage to property, and despite its good working arrangements with weather stations, aviation authorities and farmers, the Australian Government determined to close down the facility in 1975 after a year's trial period, ostensibly because it could not recover full operational costs.

A reprieve came in August that year, with joint funding between the (then) Department of Science and the US National Science Foundation, in order to keep the BLS Mildura operational for use by independent scientists. One such was Professor VF Hopper, Reader in Physics at Melbourne University. His proposal, to use radioactive isotopes in the balloon payloads, caused a flurry of concern with the Departments of Health, Civil Aviation and Foreign Affairs. Professor Hopper had been one of the first to use the balloon facility in 1960-61, sending cameras with unmanned balloons to photograph cloud formations. Later he preferred to launch at Longreach in Queensland, where more certain winds gave the best conditions in the Southern Hemisphere for long-range tracking. During the course of his studies of gamma, infra-red and x-rays in the atmosphere, Professor Hopper developed a valve technique to enable standard meteorology balloons to reach and maintain high altitudes. The neck valve in the expandable balloon released gas when the balloon reached a certain diameter, so increasing the rate of rise to a predetermined height, where the valve closed, and the balloon levelled.

In the typical year of 1975-76, the facility was used by the Universities of Tasmania, New Hampshire, the Imperial College London and the Massachusetts Institute of Technology. Astronomers from Australia and overseas universities used high flying balloons at Mildura to carry telescopes to observe stars and celestial objects, denied them by earth bound telescopes: the bodies lay in the infra-red part of the electromagnetic spectrum, thus being obscured by the earth's atmosphere. Many gains were made in the infant discipline of infra-red astronomy by virtue of the scientific balloon. Together, the various researchers provided a wealth of new information on naturally occurring, energy-exchanging processes, particularly relevant in recent recognition of resource limitation and atmospheric side effects.

Despite scientists' attempts to promote the cost-effective advantages of research by balloon, Australia's BLS was shut down in June 1981. The success of its balloon flights remains as a tribute to the combined efforts of manufacturers, launch crew and research teams.

Balloons after all have made significant contributions to science. In Australia, the results of the atmospheric studies slowly filtered through to the general public, but not until the late eighties, did people become focussed on issues such as high altitude pollution and depletion of the ozone layer.

Far from the flat, dry landscape of Australia's interior, cheaper hydrogen balloons were launched regularly in former British Antarctica, controlled by Australia since 1936. Meteorological (Met) balloons were sent aloft with radiosondes on board to monitor air movements at the Antarctic bases. Gale force winds at times made launches difficult and could bring about the loss of expensive equipment and hours of work.

The humble Met balloon was used in Australia from 1959. Meteorologists assessed temperature, humidity, wind movements and air pressure at various altitudes in the lower atmosphere. Numerous Bureaux of Meteorology tracking stations throughout Australia sent up small expandable balloons at synchronised intervals, every day and night of the year. A weather observer, dressed from head to foot in anti-flash clothing, would fill the highly inflammable hydrogen balloon and spray it with water, to reduce static and fire risk, then attach an aluminium, pyramid-shaped radar reflecting panel, a parachute and an electronic package (radiosonde) to record and transmit to a receiver on the ground.

Released to fly free, like a carrier pigeon sent aloft to relay a message back to earth, the balloon train was tracked by the observer, who continually adjusted gun sights, range rings, strobe rings, spinners and range wheels, in order to estimate wind speed and direction. Data from the balloon's radiosonde was processed and translated from computer to charts then transferred to city headquarters. By this time the balloon, instruments, radar target, and torch if a night flight, had risen to 70 000' in altitude and travelled over 15 miles. Its work done, the balloon expanded from 3 to 20' in diameter, burst and returned to earth via its parachute.

Eventually outdated, this system has been taken over by Automatic Weather Stations (AWS), which can be programmed to collect and transmit at three-hourly intervals. Increasingly more sophisticated, the AWS are more cost effective than maintaining staff and stations for balloon flights.

Experiments were made in 1976 to discover further uses for balloons. The Forests Commission of Victoria ordered two Kytoon-type balloons from Tony Norton, who trialled his solar-charged blimps near Dimboola in the desert terrain of north western Victoria, on 16 February 1977. The purpose was to increase the transmission range of VHF radio, useful in issuing early fire warnings.

The year 1976 saw the maiden flight of Tony Norton's remarkable, pedal-powered airship *Snoopy*, the world's smallest airship, that took just six weeks to build and cost a mere $1000. Noted Melbourne journalist Keith Dunstan launched the aircraft by sitting on the bicycle frame of the fun machine and pedalling furiously to turn the balsa-wood propeller, to get the shiny plastic airship moving.

A more serious attempt at airship construction was made by Tony Norton and Tim Woodbridge. They were the recipients of a government grant and commissioned by a cigarette company to build a non-rigid, powered airship capable of carrying freight. *Ardath* was constructed at Tony's factory which specialised in the design and manufacture of PVC products. A team of five worked on the project: Tony and his brother Alan Norton, Brian Smith, parachute rigger Joe Chitty and aircraft maintenance engineer Bruce Blake. They used Egyptian cotton in its construction and attached two 45 hp engines capable of pushing it along at 55 kmh (35 knots).

In the US and USSR, airships were used for pollution monitoring, search and rescue, aerial photography, transportation of logs, traffic reports, coastal surveillance and for mining companies to service remote areas and carry cargo.

Nothing so grand awaited the *Ardath* airship in Australia. After six years and $60 000, the helium filled airship was tested in the ignominious surrounds of the dog pavilion at the Melbourne Showgrounds. Having passed its inflation test the airship, filled with $6000 worth of helium, made its test flight at Tocumwal, but Norton's airship dream disappeared, along with his livelihood. According to Tony, the promised government grant arrived only at the completion of the airship and the sponsoring company paid just one $20 000 instalment. New directors took Tony to court for failure to honour the contract: his factory was sold, and Tony turned to chauffeuring and teaching science for a living; the airship was sold to America.

Tony Norton was not the only Australian dreaming of airships. In 1971 a Bruce McNally of Tasmania had written to the Department of Aviation and included sketches of a proposed balloon tug-barge, to be used at sea to overcome the problems associated with shipping cargo between Tasmania and the mainland. His idea was to use a 'Siamese' twins' approach: two helium-filled horizontal balloons with a long rack suspended underneath for cargo. The tow and the power were to be provided by a helicopter operating at low altitude. The Department of Aviation was not enthusiastic and wrote Mr McNally that his idea was not a practicable alternate means of transporting cargo by sea. Thus, McNally's vision dissipated and his plans gathered dust on a shelf in the DOA's archives, alongside other such 'good ideas'.

Having established Balloon Aloft as the largest company in Australia providing passenger rides and pilot training, Peter Vizzard turned his attention to airships, purchasing a Thunder and Colt AS 105 thermal airship. As there was no licence structure in Australia for airships, Peters Vizzard and Evans obtained UK licences and began aerial advertising and photography. The Department of Aviation allowed them to use public government property, for unlike balloons, the airship required air traffic control clearance. After a day's work, the thermal dirigible had to be deflated and packed away, unlike the helium airship introduced in the 1980's by the Bond Corporation, which returned to hangar and mooring mast and required its $60 000 load of helium to be filtered every six to eight weeks when the gas became too heavy.

Perth millionaire and entrepreneur Alan Bond, had purchased troubled British Airship Industries in 1984, rescuing the newly developed *Skyship 500*, designed for use in military surveillance and advertising markets. He ordered two airships to cover yachting's America's Cup defence in Fremantle in 1987; however, his airborne activities gave rise again to speculation on the potential for lighter-than-air defence of Australia.

Air Vice-Marshall FW Barnes wrote in *Pacific Defence Reporter* about dirigibles. Since 1975 the RAAF, he said, had been researching the development of free-flying airships in relation to Australia's coastal and surveillance needs, especially in the vast unmonitored northern regions. He acknowledged Airship Industries Ltd as the forerunner in producing small dirigibles, the Skyships, for military roles. Barnes wrote of moored balloon-borne surveillance radars and of the US Customs use of towed balloons for detection of drug runners. He believed the major advantages of the dirigible were its low altitude coverage and "being able to remain on station for very long periods." (3)

The Air Marshall warned Australia's military not to consider "the problems involved in their operation and support," which included "limited speed, altitude and height change capabilities" and a "vulnerability to adverse weather conditions." Barnes concluded that the RAAF studies "indicated that there may well be a role for dirigibles in the National Air Defence and Air Space Control System (NADACS) towards which the RAAF was moving." (4)

The general public was unconcerned re possible military usage, but initially protested about invasion of privacy and were disgusted by the floating advertisements for beer and cigarettes. Australians eventually became so blasé about the airship floating above them, that they paid for flights, and barely noticed when the bulky airship disappeared, a victim of Alan Bond's crumbling financial empire.

Pioneer advocate for scientific balloon use, Charles Brown, would have been delighted to know that his loyalties to scientific balloons were upheld; how astonished he would have been to discover that a balloon could be sent deep into the galaxy and bring back data for cosmologists, or that it would play such an important role in ozone sounding, weather forecasting and myriads of other scientific uses.

(1) *Canberra Times*, 26 February 1966.
(2) *The Australian*, 25 October 1969.
(3) *Pacific Defence Reporter*, "Dirigibles may have role in Australia's defences." February 1986.
(4) Ibid.

# Clubs and Syndicates

With the demise of the *James Cook* balloon, and with the super-pressure balloon *Archimedes I* being suited only to tethering, the Aerostat Society had no flyable balloon and consequently disbanded. Prior to this there had been a split in the ranks of members: Terry McCormack and his friends wished to fly for pleasure; whereas Peter Vizzard was interested in the commercial prospects the balloon offered.

There had been talk for years in Australia of establishing a national balloon federation to give all pilots and balloon owners equal representation and a united voice. In 1972 several men gathered in Victoria for this express purpose. Present were Tony Norton, Dale Allen, Peter Vizzard, Dale Martinson, Ivor Davies and Ross Smith. However, it was not until October 1975 that the Australian Balloon Federation (ABF) was formalised, with Peter Vizzard as inaugural President, and it became the representative body for Australian balloonists with the Fédération Aéronautique Internationale.

The ABF's immediate objective was to initiate and set down written balloon regulations. Envisaged was a standardised pilot licensing and balloon registration system, ratified by the federal government's aviation department.

Balloonists were frustrated by rules and regulations suited to aeroplanes but ludicrous when applied to balloons. To fly free, a balloon pilot had to apply in writing fourteen days in advance, stating details of flying experience, the balloon to be used, its equipment and the area desired to fly in. Such restrictions presented numerous difficulties, not the least being that the day chosen to fly might be either too wet, windy or misty and therefore unflyable.

Phil Kavanagh was among those concerned about the safety of equipment used, saying it "was abysmal, almost comical. There was no pilot light on the burners, the pilot simply stood in the basket with a cigarette lighter in one hand." (1)

Nine months before the double balloon fatality at Wagga, Peter Vizzard had written to the federal ruling body, expressing his dissatisfaction with the lack of operational standards for manned balloons,

"...it can be noted that most European countries, the UK and the USA - all license pilots and certificate balloons...We would appreciate not haveing (sic) to fly under regulations that are ten years out of date with the rest of the world and feel that both the commercial and sporting potential of ballooning are presently being prejudiced by your department." (2)

As a science and maths teacher, Peter Vizzard had first learned to fly in the home-made *Ego* in 1966 - a basic balloon held together with industrial tape, a lawn chair instead of a basket, and a weed-burner for heat. In 1973 Peter, accompanied by a Mr W Weallans and two aviation officials, flew from Canterbury Plains Christchurch to make the first flight of a modern hot-air balloon in New Zealand.

Desiring to pursue ballooning as his chosen livelihood, Peter Vizzard moved to the USA where he became production and quality control manager of The Balloon Works, which taught flying. There he obtained his balloon pilot's licence and became an instructor and examiner. He constructed and repaired balloons and worked on a solar balloon project in 1973; that same year he was placed sixth in the World Championships in

Albuquerque. The following year Peter returned to Australia with American Joanne Delesantro, (whom he later married, naturally in a balloon) and set up his commercial balloon operation and school, Montgolfier Balloons.

Early in 1976 Tim Woodbridge brought the *Marie Antoinette* to Australia from England. One Melbourne newspaper claimed it to be "the world's first painted balloon since 1783" and "the Sistine Chapel of balloons", even though her owner spent only 6 months painting her, "admittedly not as long as Michelangelo took for his masterpiece." (3)

During an English winter, beneath a stage, Tim Woodbridge and friends worked on the limp canvas. As they painted the gold and crimson panels, the dye emitted poisonous fumes. "There we were", said Tim, "painting away in gas masks and overcoats while upstairs a very bad orchestra played the William Tell overture, often out of tune. It was not very romantic." One panel depicted the first manned ascent in 1783, another showed suspicious peasants attacking the balloon with pitchforks. When completed, the overall effect was likened to "a delicate, stained glass translucence," according to the newspaper. This balloon was the first since VP Taylor had toured, to travel all around Australia on a lengthy promotional tour. (4)

It was not until the Presidencies of Eddy Selman and Susan Kurosawa that the ABF achieved any major success in forging a set of operational rules and regulations specifically for balloons. Problems became compounded when pilots began taking paying passengers on champagne balloon flights. Aviation officials became concerned for the safety of passengers but were powerless to outlaw the practice. The operators of such flights skirted legalities by insisting their passengers were paying for the champagne, not the flight itself. After balloonists themselves lobbied for the removal of such a ridiculous loophole, the Department of Aviation decided ballooning matters would have to be made legal. The DOA established regulations for private balloon pilots first; others keen to set up commercial enterprises had to wait until all balloons, by law, were registered and met airworthy standards.

There were grey areas in the regulations; neither the private nor the commercial categories encompassed balloons operating with corporate sponsorship, nor the taking up of passengers on tether. Commercial operations could only be established by a Chief Pilot approved by the DOA; each pilot had to hold a commercial licence; standards were set for balloon maintenance. Balloon accidents involving injury had to be reported to the Department.

The drafting of official, complex documents took hours of consultation and liaison. In 1984, the specific requisites essential for safe balloon conditions: Regulations, Air Navigation Orders and an Operations Manual were in place. The ABF had to take on the task of self-administration in the same fashion as other sports aviation clubs in Australia. This left it with responsibility for balloon registration, pilot training, licensing and flight operations, whereas the DOA issued certificates of airworthiness.

Until 1984, virtually the only financial assistance for sport aviation bodies was through private sponsorship or subscriptions: that year Aviation Minister Kim Beazley agreed to provide an annual government administration subsidy. The aim was to assist, but not totally fund, sports aviation clubs: members were to bear some of the costs.

During that slow, painful process, balloonists must have wondered why they pursued such a daunting task. Peter Vizzard had spent virtually a decade haggling with authorities; later Phil Hanson devoted more than his paid time, as part-time ABF Administrator, to the onerous job. The days of learning by trial and error were mercifully over in Australia, yet among pilots there were mixed feelings: some felt cheated of their freedom to fly without regulations; others argued that they had more freedom once specific regulations were enforced.

Resistance to the regulations gradually subsided: indeed, the main side effect of the regulations was an increase in aeronauts and their aircraft. Over the years, amendments were made, eventually sport balloonists became regulated, examined and certificated by the ABF in conjunction with the DOA; whereas commercial balloonists came under the direct jurisdiction of the Department. The divisiveness that had earlier separated commercial and private pilots continued in the new affiliation. Sport balloonists objected to paying high insurance premiums when it was demonstrated that their claims were statistically fewer than those of commercial balloon companies, which logged more hours.

By 1985 all state clubs were operated under the auspices of the ABF constitution. Representation on the ABF committee by each state also included a Safety and Technical Officer; henceforth all participants would benefit from the safe and orderly development of the sport of ballooning.

By this time most states had formed their own clubs. Bendigo was the setting for the formation of the Balloon Association of Victoria (BAV) by Ray Smith and Bob Ross which also encompassed Tasmania; followed by the establishment of the Balloon Club of NSW and ACT. The Queensland Balloon and Airship Club was formed in 1982, specifically to run the National Balloon Championships, held at Gatton.

As elsewhere, balloonists flew in SA before the formation of any club: Bill Lynas, with previous experience in WA, had flown his *Golly I* balloon in Adelaide in 1976. The golliwog-shaped, black balloon with white collar, red bow tie and mouth drew crowds whenever inflated. Imported from England, it was the first modern 'special-shape' balloon worldwide. Later *Golly III* appeared in Adelaide as a promotion by West Indian Neil Robertson, for its sponsor, Robertson's Jam. (5)

In 1984 Rob Robertson, Simon Fisher, Gordon Cowley and Phil Hanson founded the SA Balloon and Airship Club (SABAC) with three balloons: *Kingfisher*, *Rainbow Connection* and *Sultan*. Brothers Roland and Robert Shepherd managed to get sponsorship from Solomons Carpets for an airship and two *Sultan* balloons, and from Coca-Cola for another balloon. Neighbour Steve Aldrich gave up farming to form a commercial balloon company in SA. Simon Fisher, having flown passengers over the Masai-Mara National Park in Kenya for six years, returned to Australia in 1980. In 1984 he encouraged South African Balloon Champion Alan Shore, to work for his Clare Valley commercial balloon company.

Country SABAC members privately flew John Pickup, (renowned as one of the five 'Brushmen of the Bush' artists in Broken Hill), in his balloon *Don Quixote* (which appeared as his trademark in subsequent paintings); Mike Sanby launched a large commercial balloon, *Big Joey*, in Alice Springs in the Northern Territory.

The Western Australian Balloon and Airship Club (WABAC) was the only club formed by Australians living overseas. Several Cathay Pacific airline employees, who had learnt ballooning in the UK and owned balloons, found pursuing their sport in densely populated, mountainous terrain difficult in the extreme. On stopovers in Perth they chose Northam as a suitable base and introduced ballooning to the locals. This unique club was formed in complete ignorance of events in the eastern states. Pilot Paul Gianniotis, a Greek born, was one of those foundation members.

Because the cost of owning, operating and maintaining a private balloon was so high, several interested people formed syndicates to share payments, work and flying time. Brian and Garry Smith were the first to form their own balloon group, which was based in the Blue Mountains in NSW.

Dale Allen, Ross Smith, Jenny and Dave Martinson formed the Victorian Puff Balloon Group in 1972, with Dave Martinson making successful altitude, distance and endurance records before *Puff* - true to its name - disappeared in smoke after hitting 25 000 voltage power lines on 21 April 1978. Fortunately, Dave Martinson and former motorcycle ace Jack Halsall, leapt from the basket before it struck and before the gas bottles exploded.

The Shepparton Hot Air Group (SHAG) was formed in October 1975 by Jack Halsall and ten businessmen. Excluding the late John Abell, introduced to the sport by Dale Allen and who eventually left to work in Darwin radio, most of the members were 'cocktail balloonists.' They shared a Cameron-built balloon and had initial training sessions from the *Puff* crew.

The Pegasus Balloon Group, consisting of Tony Norton, Peter Bennett, Noel and Margaret Canning, Allan and Julia Moore, imported an English balloon and used the Point Cook/Laverton airforce base to launch. This group flew in Maldon in October 1976 to commemorate a purported pioneer flight the previous century. Within months the syndicate, like others before it, began to disintegrate and eventually folded in 1981.

There will always be people enthusiastic about a sport, whose eagerness wanes when confronted with maintenance involvement. A balloon syndicate is one of those ideas that is good in theory, but which rarely works in practice.

While ballooning as a sport was developing rapidly on the mainland, the island state of Tasmania missed out on the excitement. Jack Buzelin became interested in ballooning after answering an advertisement for crew for the 1982 National Championships in Queensland. He moved to Tasmania to become a park ranger and was that state's sole balloonist; he flew a porous envelope rather irregularly near Launceston. For a short time Buzelin shared the Tasmanian sky with Mark Stevens and his landlord John Henry, who purchased a worn envelope in Sydney in 1985. En route to Tasmania the balloon became wet and mildewed in the ship's hold and the basket was wrecked. Undaunted, the self-taught aeronauts dried the envelope and built a new basket, which they used to fly over the Midlands. When John Medlock, a visiting British balloon pilot requested a flight, he quickly appraised the situation and informed the men that they should not be flying unlicensed. Even in later years, when commercial balloon companies mushroomed on the mainland, Tasmania was overlooked, with only occasional tours visiting the state for short periods.

The 1980s witnessed a surge of interest in ballooning in Australia. Paying passengers enjoyed drifting silently over the countryside but by 1984, balloonist/farmer relationships were deteriorating, with prohibited zones and sensitive areas such as poultry farms, piggeries and stables marked as 'no fly' regions. There were complaints of crop damage, gates left open, noise pollution and invasion of privacy. At Canowindra, a balloon landed near stockyards, scaring cattle which stampeded through fences. An irate farmer spent the rest of the day rounding up cattle; he was angry that the balloon had just flown on. In another incident, a child's first pony took fright at the balloon, fell down a riverbank and broke its neck.

Such unfortunate incidents have led to one of the biggest problems facing balloonists - farmer relations. To dampen fears of grass fires, burners are shut off prior to landing; as an extra safety precaution balloonists refrain from flying on days of total fire bans. Nevertheless, it is probably only a matter of time before a 'trespass by balloon' action is pressed in Australia.

Ed Selman, a Sydney real estate agent, was one of the earliest of the commercial pilots, flying for Flights of Fancy, a venture set up in 1982 with Australian Himalayan Expeditions. Canowindra, 326 kms from Sydney, became his flying base. Previously Ed had piloted the *Winfield* balloon on a promotional tour of Australia in 1977-78 and had flown a balloon for the Australian film *Let the Balloon Go*. With an impeccable safety record, Ed Selman went on to compete in the third World Hot Air Balloon Championships.

Judy Lynne became involved in commercial ballooning in an unusual fashion. An American born in Indiana, she came to Australia to work in radio and television production. Judy loved Australia and wanted to stay; her husband didn't, so they separated and Judy became an Australian national TV personality. In 1973 as a reporter for *A Current Affair*, she was sent to cover a balloon meet and her 'affair' with balloons began. The story goes that Roger Meadmore, owner of the Pancake Parlour chain, enticed Judy to become his publicity officer and co-pilot, with the gift of her own balloon *Little Lovely*.

Judy became a commercial balloon pilot, an instructor and co-owner with Peter Vizzard, of Balloon Aloft. Formed in 1982, it started out modestly, being conducted from the front room of Judy's house in Rozelle Sydney and with just two balloons. Peter recognised Judy's talent for publicity, so she flew promotions while Peter flew passengers.

Peter Vizzard is one of a select band of Australian balloonists - amongst them Tony Norton, Phil Kavanagh, Joe Blitz and Kiff Saunders - who have attained the rare accomplishment of flying gas balloons. Peter participated in the World Gas Balloon Championships in 1976, 1980 and, in 1986 in Phoenix Arizona, he won a Bronze Medal in a borrowed balloon. Peter has also competed against the world's best in at least seven World Hot Air Balloon Championships.

As Australian champion and having been amongst the first six place getters in four previous Worlds attempts, Peter Vizzard arrived in Nantes France, determined to win. Competition was fierce, with 73 teams representing 22 countries vying for victory. Peter piloted the *Lovely! Lady* balloon; Roger Meadmore acted as navigator. The ground crew, consisting of the late Michael Conran, Judy Lynne, and Roger's daughter Samantha, had great difficulty retrieving. Visibility proved a problem "in the misty pre-dawn and dusk takeoffs in front of the majestic castle of La Pervenchere" and there appeared to be perpetual smog. The balloon disappeared into the haze and the chase crew kept losing its way and losing sight of the balloon. (6)

Seven events tested participants in navigation, manoeuvrability and wind control. The tasks were described as "an exercise in skill, speed and efficiency in balloons that use jet-age materials and controls." (7)

Two other Australian teams competed. Gren Putland took eighth place and Ruth Wilson was one of only two women pilots, but Peter Vizzard's team emerged triumphant. He thus became the first Australian to hold the title of World Champion, Hot Air Balloons. It was the pinnacle of a lofty career as a professional balloonist, begun just a decade earlier. For Peter the real satisfaction came from winning the event on the 200th anniversary of man taking to the sky. A descendant of the Montgolfier Brothers attended the celebrations, where the balloonists and their crews wined and dined on the finest local reds, on 1000 bottles of champagne, 200 bottles of whisky and mountains of lobster, salmon and cheese.

They were heady days for the new champion. Indeed, Peter Vizzard shared World Champion Title for aerial pursuits that year with two other Australians: Steve Moyes became the world's best in his sport of hang-gliding and Ingo Remner became the top glider pilot.

(1)   Interview Phil Kavanagh, 8 January 1988.
(2)   Letter Peter Vizzard to Director General, Department of Transport, Air Transport Group 22 January 1974.
(3)   *The Age*, 24 February 1976.
(4)   Ibid.
(5)   Ibid.
(6)   *People*, 7 November 1983.
(7)   Ibid.

# Balloons Further Afield

In any generation individuals appear who enrich our world by pushing accepted boundaries to new levels. One such person is Gren Putland. On 30 April 1981, Gren sat amongst the quokkas - those unique marsupials found only on Rottnest Island - awaiting favourable weather to enable him to fly his hot air balloon *Rainbow Lady* solo across to mainland WA. He achieved this Australian first, crossing a large body of water by balloon, when he opted to land in strengthening winds, not at the Swanbourne Rifle Range as intended, but at the nearby beach, a haven for Perth nudists. Naked beachgoers, in events best described by Gren Putland himself, "provided plenty of hands for the critical landing at the surf's edge, bouncing along the beach, but few were available for the full stop in the prickly scrub beyond!" (1)

Having achieved notoriety with this touchdown, Gren consolidated his position as a balloonist voyeur in 1985 during the World Championships at Battle Creek USA, when he accepted responsibility as navigator, for their balloon *High Rise* landing unscheduled at the Sunnyside Nudist Camp, where a lapse of concentration delayed the Australian team's takeoff. The distraction of their surroundings caused the team to fumble the rigging of the envelope and they were placed only 59th in the competition overall. It is said that Gren was unperturbed at the lowly result; nor were there complaints from the nudist colony of invasion of privacy.

Gren Putland's trans-sea crossing from Rottnest Island to Perth in 1981 beat by a day an attempt by Arnold Himson and his companions to tackle the notorious Bass Strait in a balloon. People with more conservative perceptions often describe those who undertake such challenges as mad or foolhardy and dismiss their achievements as due to chance. Such were the labels given the Australian adventurers who dared fly a balloon across the treacherous waters of Bass Strait, from Winchelsea in Victoria to Tasmania.

Those who knew Arnold Himson described him as an eccentric with a difficult personality; some called him obnoxious. What is certain is that the 62-year-old German-born Himson, a retired postmaster, spent all his superannuation on the trip. Those who helped him prepare were of the opinion that his motive was to go down in history, dead or alive, but those who flew with him believed that Himson (nicknamed 'Himmler') would rather live to tell his tale. Whatever his reason or influence, Arnold Himson had contacted Tony Norton requesting he design and build a silver hydrogen-filled balloon, named the *Bassoon*, a shortening of 'Bass Strait balloon'. When completed Himson pressured Tony to fly with him without the benefit of a test flight. The experienced, safety-conscious Norton was unhappy with this arrangement. He came to regard Himson, who had never been in a balloon, as underhand.

The balloon was duly launched at Warragul with Himson, Tony Norton, Tim Woodbridge and Gary Geier on board. Himson was convinced they were commencing their historic flight, but the devious Tony Norton always intended it to be a trial flight. One can imagine Arnold Himson's reaction when they flew in a NW direction and landed at Bendigo, and it is no surprise that he and Norton severed their relationship.

The Department of Aviation's archives contain the correspondence which flew between them and Himson. The Department tried to persuade Himson that he would have a greater chance of success by flying from Tasmania to the larger land mass of the mainland, than the reverse as planned. Himson rejected their advice in caustic tones and insisted on his original plan.

Gary Geier aged 27, a doctor at Royal Melbourne Hospital, took over as pilot of the *Bassoon*. In the days before regulations he was perceived to be a pilot with flying experience, having logged a total of 10 hours flying instruction time. Phil White aged 30, an aviation engineer who had never been in a balloon, became their navigator and radio operator. The three men launched from Winchelsea near Geelong, after dawn on 1 May 1981. There was no "noise of hot air balloon burners nor the roar of a straining aircraft engine" as the hydrogen balloon rose and cleared the Otway Ranges. Near perfect conditions of 25-30 knot winds pushed their balloon over Bass Strait; however, the wind changed direction, forcing them west. They contemplated ditching into the sea but cruised on between 650 - 2400' in altitude, past King Island and over the tip of Three Hummock Island. (2)

They carried life jackets, a raft, radios, emergency beacons and night lights; the men themselves wore wetsuits beneath flame proof overalls and parachutes strapped to their backs. Before their journey's end, they almost required the use of all three, but eventually escaped having tested only the flame-proof clothing; the only liquid to dampen their wetsuits was celebratory champagne.

After two years of obstacles and frustrations, including lack of support from sponsors and government departments, Himson's dream came true, but only just. They were lucky to dodge disaster. Late in the day, the men saw the coast of Tasmania looming ahead. They crossed the shore at Smithton on the north-west extremity at dusk and landed dramatically; hitting and bringing down high voltage powerlines; blacking out the small township and surrounding farms. The balloon, renamed *Son of Hindenburg*, "almost met the same disastrous end as its famous namesake." As they hit, sparks erupted, and flames licked at the remaining sandbags and at the basket but miraculously failed to ignite the 1000 cubic metres of hydrogen. (3)

The men had, nevertheless, succeeded in the first and only crossing by balloon of the 400 km-wide Bass Strait. Despite the terrifying landing Arnold Himson wrote that he had no regrets, because "for 10 hours we lived a little." (4)

When writing of the eventful journey for a magazine, Himson admitted his 'raison d'être': "after 15 years of humdrum existence I needed to do *something*! The last country telephone exchange in Tasmania, which my wife and I ran, was now automated." (5)

Although Geier and White realised the flight was a once in a lifetime adventure, Arnold Himson was keen to push his luck with a solo crossing in 1987. He contacted Phil Hanson, National Administrator of the ABF, with a view to gaining the requisite balloon licence. Himson requested a 'one off' licence be granted him for the planned flight. As Himson had no qualifications, the ABF refused his request, explaining that, "you do not reach a reasonable standard and to issue a certificate to a person who has participated in two flights would be a gross abuse of authority delegated to the ABF." (6)

Himson wrote that crossing Bass Strait in a balloon was less risky than in a yacht. He complained that "Mr Hanson lives in a cuckoo-cloud land" and that the ABF executive committee had made a "draconian decision." (7)

Eventually Himson lost interest, some would say fortunately. All three participants in the historic Bass Strait crossing had a reunion at Winchelsea on 1 May 1991, ten years after their amazing flight. Gary Geier continued to fly balloons; in 1986 he was to attempt a round-the-world flight in a stratospheric balloon, but Project Capricorn never got off the ground.

When Tim Woodbridge and John Abell trained Chris Dewhirst as a pilot, they never thought he would push the boundaries of ballooning, literally, to new heights. In November 1985 Chris Dewhirst, British film maker Leo Dickinson, Qantas pilot Aden Wickes (in the *J&B* balloon), American photojournalist Jan Reynolds and Australian balloon manufacturers, Brian Smith and Phil Kavanagh (in *Zanuzzi*), celebrated two hundred years of manned flight - albeit two years late.

Mountaineer Chris Dewhirst had always been drawn to outdoor pursuits, working for Adventure Travel and successfully combining business with pleasure. While leading a trek in Nepal five years earlier he decided to balloon over the Himalaya. It took crew members three years to raise the $500 000 sponsorship money. Eventually, Italian company Zanuzzi, and British distiller Justerini and Brooks, (J&B) backed the expedition; Brits and Australians invested in a film of the flights, entitled, "*Flight of the Windhorse*". In his Sydney factory Phil Kavanagh made the two 200 000 cubic feet hot air balloons for the expedition and two smaller trial balloons. All six team members learned to parachute in case of severe turbulence; equipment was pretested up to 31 000' and to the expected temperatures of -40ºC.

British Meteorologist Martin Harris advised that November was the month of choice, following the monsoon and before the bitter cold and jet streams of winter. At any time of year, the balloonists could expect hazardous conditions: winds up to 60 knots and turbulence and wind shear generated by the gargantuan mountains.

Brian Smith volunteered to drive overland the expedition's old Bedford van containing their equipment. In India port authorities impounded the van and, considering the tonne of propane tanks to be dangerous, ordered they be dropped into the harbour. Brian needed all his powers of persuasion to convince the Indian officials to let himself and the laden truck float precariously on a raft in the port, while the paperwork was attended to.

Brian Smith is someone who thrives on such challenges. While at an English University in 1969 he joined a ballooning group and obtained a UK pilot's licence. By 1972 he was corresponding with Terry McCormack on ballooning and by Christmas, he had settled in Adelaide, the city his great-great-grandfather had flown over in a balloon. Brian relishes storytelling; he has regaled many with tales of his balloon exploits, recalling landing in a smelly pigsty and descending in the middle of a funeral. For the second Tocumwal regatta, Brian was persuaded to take up a reporter; one suspects that he engineered their subsequent splash down in the fast-flowing Murray River. At gumboot height, they bobbed like a cork with the river, winding around the bends among the huge trees. When he blew the trumpet that always accompanied him, it was full of water and only emitted gurgles.

Essentially a fun-flyer, Brian disliked the commercial character of Australian ballooning, preferring to fly privately. Nevertheless, he commercially manufactured cold air advertising inflatables that stood tethered above buildings. Brian was refused permission to fly his double-burner balloon in Australia but, on his own admission, he flew it anyway, considering that if the balloon had a British Airworthy Certificate and Registration, it was good enough for him. He claims to have been SA's first modern balloonist, albeit it unofficially. It is typical of Brian Smith that he named his balloon *Captain Starlight*, after a character based on infamous Bogong Jack, a mysterious English aristocrat turned eclectic Australian bushranger. The balloon was as flighty and colourful as its namesake, flaunting stripes of blue and purple. There are obvious parallels between the legendary Captain Starlight and Brian Smith: both were regarded as eccentrics and rebels against authority.

In 1983 Brian met Chris Dewhirst in Melbourne and together they planned to fly in Nepal. Having overcome a gamut of Nepalese bureaucratic, diplomatic and political hurdles, the 25 strong contingent converged on Kathmandu and met Brian Smith and the battered van containing their equipment. A period of high altitude acclimatisation ensued in Lukla and a test flight which took them close to the summit of Annapurna. After last minute negotiations with the Nepalese military to avoid incidents with neighbouring Chinese rulers in Tibet, they were cleared to fly.

Despite low altitude cloud on the 10 November 1985, the two balloon crews gathered in pre-dawn darkness in the city square at Bhaktapur. The forecast wind pattern should see them on course for Everest. At 6.40 am they were airborne. The balloons, flying Nepalese prayer flags, were an arresting sight as they floated from Bhaktapur, the mediaeval city and seat of Nepalese kings; soared over the 5000 onlookers and past the temple, seemingly close enough to reach out and touch it to gain a final blessing. Once through the cloud cover, they were in dazzling sunshine over Machapuchare and Lamchung and climbing at 230 metres per minute in order to catch the high winds that would sweep them towards their goal.

The flight became a logistics nightmare with possible dire consequences: their fuel calculations had been made for temperatures of - 40ºC, with expected 40 knot wind conditions. It soon became apparent that the triple burners (required in the thinner atmosphere) were guzzling fuel at twice the expected rate as the temperature hovered around zero, and they were advancing at half the anticipated wind speed.

Chris Dewhirst as navigator in *J&B* quickly calculated that fuel supplies would not permit flying above Everest. Pilot Aden Wickes took the balloon higher to 8540m, increasing the speed by 10 knots, causing them to swing off course for Everest. With 85 per cent of fuel gone and having covered 120kms and in sight of Everest but 24kms short of it, "a large, squat, black pyramid beginning to dominate the horizon," Chris and Aden sought a possible landing site amongst the steep mountainsides and valleys. On their descent to a less rarefied altitude, the oxygen became enriched, causing the burners to surge and blow out all three pilot lights. *J&B* began an uncontrolled descent; Leo Dickinson kept filming as Aden and Chris struck match after match, only to find "each one snuffed out by the lack of oxygen the moment it was lit." After free falling at 1000' per minute, they managed to rekindle the burners and drop out two empty cylinders to add buoyancy, finally correcting the potentially fatal plunge just 300 metres above an icy crag. All later admitted they were close to bailing by parachute. Cross currents tossed *J&B* about at the edge of the tree line and rhododendron forests loomed up but fortunately, the only possible landing site revealed itself: a snow-covered slope ending in a tiny ice plateau. *J&B* landed safely after a momentous 2½ hour flight amongst the most dangerous peaks in the world. (8)

*Zanuzzi* was still in the air, with pilot Phil Kavanagh battling "a witch's cauldron of thermals and cross-currents" created by the hours of sun heating the valley below. To land Phil had to choose between an icy, rocky crag or the rhododendron forest. Choosing the forest, he vented and landed in a large tree, which ripped the envelope to shreds. Within seconds the basket tipped, entangling Brian Smith in the ripcord and throwing Phil onto the burners, which flicked on, shooting out a 6' flame that rapidly set alight the undergrowth. Jan Reynolds, who had been thrown clear, beat at the flames with her hands, burning them before the fire was extinguished. (9)

Radio contact was all that could be made between the two crews as thick fog swirled in, forcing the men to spend the night on opposite sides of the ridge. The following morning, realising that a village was nearly a day and a half's walk away and the terrain possibly impassable, Chris summoned a helicopter and spent days airlifting out crew and equipment before all could be reunited and celebrate their achievement in Kathmandu - the first ever flight over the Himalaya. This remarkable flight achieved two records: - the world's first Himalayan balloon flight and the highest-ever alpine flight, at an altitude of 27 750' (8000 metres), just 2000' short of the Mount Everest summit.

A year earlier, two men and manager Tim Woodbridge set up a project in Perth, to attempt the first around-the-world manned balloon flight and the first unaided, nonstop circumnavigation by any aircraft. One of the men, Julian Nott, was a physicist; head of his own aeronautical engineering firm in the UK and a veteran balloonist of eighteen years. Julian had participated in Nazca flight experiments in Peru, had crossed the Sahara by balloon in 1972 and was the current world altitude record holder for hot air balloons, having reached 55 134' in 1980.

Perth company, Western Continental, had underwritten the first $1 million; notable patrons were Sir Edmund Hilary, America's Cup skipper John Bertrand and Thor Heyerdahl of *Kon-Tiki* fame. In March 1984 they announced the joint British/Australian plan simultaneously in Melbourne, Tokyo, San Francisco, New York and London, with November the planned departure date. They publicly sought a lightweight Australian who could pass rigorous physical and psychological endurance tests, to accompany Nott without payment on the sixteen-day adventure. The successful applicant was Peter 'Spider' Anderson, a non-balloonist but a qualified long distance yachtsman and artist.

Don Cameron, of Cameron Balloons in Britain, cut out the fabric for the revolutionary concept. The white, pumpkin-shaped *Endeavour* was filled with helium. Attached to it was a pressurised cabin able to withstand winds up to 180 kph and temperatures below minus 80°C in jet stream conditions. On board was sophisticated long-range communication equipment and oxygen and food for 40 days. The super-pressure craft was a giant leap forward, operating at five times the pressure of Alan Bond's *Skyship*. It is said that Don Cameron at the balloon's first test hid behind a 'DANGER, MEN WORKING OVERHEAD' sign in case it blew.

In Australia, Brian Smith made a hangar for the balloon whilst the team waited for suitable weather. On 20 November 1984, the prototype undertook a trans-Australia attempt. Nott and Anderson's flight went as planned, from takeoff at Pearce RAAF Base until the next afternoon, when they encountered a very cold air mass moving north from southern latitudes, which caused the gas to contract. Anderson and Nott jettisoned oxygen, food and reading material to stabilise the craft which then flew onwards over the Great Australian Bight.

The following morning found the balloon over the NSW state boundary. Inexplicably they landed, gently, north of Broken Hill. *Endeavour*'s flight created new Australian endurance and distance records, having been in the air 34½ hours over a straight-line distance measuring 2700 kms. The reasons for cutting short the journey remain unclear: contemporaries stated that Julian Nott was too tired to continue; others say the lack of food and magazines was a contributing factor. Anderson himself said he and Nott had a clash of personalities and that the balloon, although technically successful, was too heavy to maintain flight. Julian Nott returned to England; 'Spider' Anderson gave away aeronautics and went north, back to his first love, sailing.

When the prototype balloon landed short of its trans-Australian destination, dreams for an around-the-world flight dissipated for another 18 years, as there were no forthcoming funds or sponsors. It was no disgrace to abandon plans to circumnavigate the world non-stop. For obvious reasons, insurance companies would not underwrite balloonists flying over large bodies of water and only the wealthy or the rebellious persisted, for the sake of freedom and adventure. (This ultimate challenge tempted balloonists for years until achieved in June/July 2002 by late billionaire adventurer Steve Fossett, who flew his Rozière balloon *The Spirit of Freedom* from Northam WA around the globe, to land almost 15 days later in Queensland.)

In 1985 the Chinese government issued a joint invitation to Balloon Aloft and Weldon Publishing to fly two balloons in China and carry photographers aboard. The result was a book commemorating the fiftieth anniversary of the 'Long March', the episode in history which placed Mao Tse-Tung at the head of the Communist Party.

As aerial photographs from helicopters or planes were not permitted, balloons were chosen to take photographers up in China's interior. This experience was not without difficulties: propane cylinders needed to be trucked in; maps were basic, written in Chinese and held by the police who accompanied each flight. Weather forecasts were haphazard, launch and landing sites were non-existent, as every square inch was given to agriculture. Peter Vizzard and Judy Lynne launched from schoolyards or truck depots and took pride in landing between rows of crops without damage; however, crops were demolished by hundreds of people running to reach the balloon. Peter and Judy found it impossible to keep people from trampling the balloons, with feet wet and muddy from the rice fields. After ten flights, the balloons had visibly deteriorated due to a combination of travel, humidity, dust and mud.

The following year Balloon Aloft received an enquiry about supplying New Guinea with a dirigible for crop dusting, with the specific requirement that it "would need to be resistant to piercing by spears and arrows." (10)

In 1987 members of the HKBAC were also invited to take balloons to China to act as photographic platforms for a book, Over China. Paul Gianniotis took his *Cathay Pacific* and the *DHL* balloon to the Guilin region of Guangxi Province. The team was restricted to landing in mountain country, often necessitating retrieval by riverboat. In ten days, they flew free on twelve occasions; the misty mountains, rivers and ethereal balloons made stunning subjects.

Stardom aside, Australians forged ahead with newly whetted appetites to fly in far-flung spheres. Peter Vizzard and Judy Lynne took their *J&B* balloon on a promotional tour to New Caledonia in 1987 and made that country's first balloon flight, despite initial reluctance from aviation officials, who had never before seen a balloon. The island features a central mountainous spine flanked by narrow coastal strips; little land is cleared and there are few roads. Fortunately, the balloon drifted along parallel to the coastline, tracking straight for a slow 1½ hours. As Judy wrote, "the wind was gentle, the sky was blue, Noumea and the ocean were laid out at our feet. It was beautiful." (11)

Judy and Peter were invited, the following year, to celebrate the tenth anniversary of the Solomon Island's independence and had the honour of being the first to fly there. As a symbol of the country's history, they tethered *Justine* before flying free.

(1) Letter Gren Putland 20 June 1988.
(2) *Prime Time*, June 1983.
(3) *The Sun*, 2 May 1981.
(4) *Prime Time*, op cit.
(5) Ibid.
(6) Letter ABF to Himson.
(7) Letter Himson to ABF 4 March 1987.
(8) *Australian Geographic*, "Hot Air over the Himalayas" Vol 1 No 4 Oct/Nov 1986.
(9) Ibid.
(10) Interview Judy Lynne.
(11) Judy Lynne, *Aeronotes* "The First Balloon Flight in New Caledonia." July/August 1987.

# Races, Philately, Films and Records

Following the achievements of Australians at the 1983 World Hot Air Balloon Championships, the DOA, government bodies and international ballooning movements held Australian balloonists in high esteem. The general community accepted ballooning as a skilled sport and its popularity increased dramatically, with passengers eager to experience its delights. Public interest and enthusiasm were further aroused by media coverage given to several balloon races.

The DOA proved amenable to the idea of a hot-air balloon race across Port Phillip Bay to celebrate Victoria's 150th birthday celebrations in 1984. Air space was organised so that the ten qualifying pilots (each requiring a minimum 100 hours pilot experience) could contest the honour of being the first to cross the Bay by balloon and claim the $15 000 prize money. Sunday 19 November was as close to Montgolfier day (21 November) as possible, thus making a double celebration. Contenders Joe Blitz, Barry Bristow-Stagg, Adrian Clements, Ed Michell, Tony Norton, Simon Potochnik, Gren Putland, Bob Ross, Ian Tooth and Chris Tuttle planned to fly from St Leonards to Carrum. Such intentions became unstuck in November's heat and unfavourable winds; however, spectators, sponsors, participants and surf rescue teams were not entirely disappointed as nine balloons eventually crossed the smaller Corio Bay on a course across Bellarine Peninsula, landing an hour later at Ocean Grove. (1)

In 1986, members from Victorian and NSW balloon clubs participated in another fun venture, the Coonara Great Race. Promoter and organiser Les Jabara, advertised the event as "an epic and intrepid adventure in which 25 teams of pioneering peregrinators will be endeavouring to traverse the trackless and forbidding wastes between Sydney and Melbourne in the astounding time of 6 days, travelling by balloon, horseless carriage, steam locomotion and flying machines." (2)

John Woodhouse founder of the Coonara heaters firm, was the sponsor. Entrants were to dress in Victorian and Edwardian period costumes and use outdated modes of transport to reach the finishing line. It was to be a mini Australian version of Phileas Fogg's heroic attempts, using a variety of vehicles to circumnavigate the world in a set time. The spectacular, 'olde worlde' event was to take place from 28 February - 5 March, timed to coincide with Queen Elizabeth and Prince Philip's visit and to end in Melbourne during their Moomba Festival.

Jabara chose teams from the hundreds of entries on the basis that they were genuine adventurers or represented a town, charity or the media. Former sportsmen, Members of Parliament and the army, thrill seekers and TV personalities jockeyed to be members of the 25 teams competing for the $50 000 prize money. The Association for the Blind's team included 73-year-old, blind woman Doris Nothling.

A month before the event, the Lord Mayors of Melbourne and Sydney jointly announced the details of the contest. There were to be different stages in the race - from Sydney to Camden, Picton to Goulburn, on to Junee, Albury, Wangaratta, Bendigo, Clarkefield then Melbourne's City Square and a torchlight procession to the banks of the Yarra River. Organisers worked feverishly. Balloon Aloft was responsible for organising the balloons in NSW and Ray Smith those in Victoria: the intention was for balloons to fly the first and last legs. The DOA was adamant that no balloons were to fly out of Sydney but allowed balloons to use Camden Aerodrome.

The bizarre race commenced with fanfare, a kaleidoscope of colour and anticipation on 28 February 1986. World Champion Town Crier, Graham Keating declaimed the rules to the teams dressed as nurses and firemen of the period. Phileas Fogg, the Keystone Cops, Ned Kelly and a team of Funnel Web spiders were there. Spectators in costume and in horse-drawn vehicles arrived at the starting point, Hyde Park Barracks; old cameras recorded the scene.

The pilots who gathered in Camden were Asbjorn Damhus, Bruno Dupuis, Paul Gianniotis, Phil Kruger, Judy Lynne, Martin Moroney, Jim Murray, Greg Russell, Ian Tooth, Kay Turnbull and Peter Vizzard. Near perfect weather saw the competing balloons follow the official Coonara balloon in a Hare and Hounds race from Camden to Picton.

Antique omnibuses, motorcycles, vintage cars and trains, penny-farthing bicycles and Tiger Moth aeroplanes were available for the competitors. The Coonara Great Race was held a week after the Tiger Moth National Meet and the World Penny Farthing Championships, thus ensuring adequate numbers to supply the teams; in fact almost 25 Tiger Moths, or a quarter of the world population, competed. The stage from Albury to Wangaratta along the Hume Highway became the longest penny farthing race in the world; speeds reached on the antique cycles were only slightly less than those reached by modern Tour de France cyclists.

The week-long race proved a gruelling test of endurance, not only for the ancient vehicles, but also for its participants. A gala ball the night prior to the race start set the pace for the remainder of the week: at each stopover civic receptions or charity balls were held and the competitors wearily danced into the small hours.

At its conclusion the race became pure farce, with balloons at the Melbourne end being thwarted by the declaration of a total fire ban. Organisers hurriedly re-scheduled the finale, ironically replacing the balloons with ancient fire engines, to dash the teams from Clarkefield to the finishing line at the Henley landing on the Yarra River, where Queen Elizabeth and Prince Philip stood beside a tethered balloon to await the winners. That night those who could still summon the energy attended a reception, during which the Queen announced the results: Tony Barber and Alyce Platt (of TV's *Sale of the Century*) and their charity team were declared the overall winners, having scooped all the prize money by winning each race stage.

Most of the notable modern balloon flights in Australia carried balloon mail in the form of souvenir postal envelopes, the first being delivered after Terry McCormack's and *Teijin I*'s 23 April 1966 trial flight at Cargo. They carried two hundred specially printed and signed postcards to financially assist the Aerostat Society. Due to several postponements of the intended trans continent flight, Terry McCormack later flew 3228 articles of mail on 2 July 1966 at Canowindra, on the flight that ended with damage to runaway *Teijin I*.

The history of balloon mail carried in Australia is published in the Australian Airship and Balloon Airmail Catalogue 1965-1988, compiled by John M Smith. Suffice it to say that private companies have produced the majority of souvenir balloon envelopes conveyed in Australia and sought by collectors. Despite commissioning various stamp series depicting Australian aviation history and popular sports, it took Australia Post until 2008 (the 150th year of flight in Australia) to produce stamps featuring balloons. A multicoloured aerogramme depicting hot air balloons issued in 1984, had been the only prior recognition of the balloon's existence.

Brian Smith and *Captain Starlight* featured in a 1974/75 BBC documentary, *The Green Centre* and Tony Norton appeared with his airship on an ABC documentary, *Skyship*. In 1976 Paul Gianniotis and Rolf Harris filmed the story of an aborigine boy who stowed away on a balloon, but the closest to a box office hit was the film, *Young Einstein*, whose star Yahoo Serious used the balloon *Destiny* for transport. However, Australian balloon films have never equalled the numbers made overseas. None of these films have rivalled Sir Lawrence Olivier as Lunardi in the 1938 epic, *Conquest of the Air*, nor Peter Cook and Dudley Moore's crazy balloon car in *The Bed Sitting Room*, nor Albert Finney's *Charlie Bubbles*, David Niven in *Around the World in 80 Days* or Katherine Hepburn in *The Great Balloon Adventure*.

Whilst some Australians devoted their time and skills to achieve first flights in other countries - a reversal of the nineteenth century pattern of overseas aeronauts undertaking 'firsts' in Australia - others were more focused on making or breaking Australian and world records.

Each record flight claim requires certification by official observers registered with the ABF, which forwards a report for ratification to the governing body of all aviation sports, the Fédération Aéronautique Internationale.

I have no intention of detailing records set in Australia or elsewhere by Australians but will mention in passing a few notable hot air balloon records. I credit Dave Martinson with inspiring the push towards toppling records when he broke Australian distance, height and endurance records in a single flight in *Puff* from Horsham to Corack in August 1975.

Many balloonists favoured Northam in WA for record attempts, resulting in the setting of Australian, British and Japanese standards; over 140 world and national records have been set there, including 17 by three members of the HKBAC, Geoff Green, Ron Taaffe and Paul Gianniotis in the years 1977-82.

British airline pilot, Geoff Green was the first (22 November 1975) to fly a balloon in that colony, with Australian aeronautic engineer Ron Taaffe on board; Australian flight engineer Paul Gianniotis accompanied Geoff on 25 July 1976 to become the first to fly a balloon over Mt Fuji in Japan.

At a recorded height of 23 500' Geoff Green dropped hang glider enthusiast Bill Llewellyn from the *Cathay Pacific* balloon on 21 March 1977 at Waikerie SA; Bill missed the world standard but set an Australian one.

Paul Gianniotis, in *Sprite*, became the first Australian, on 16 August 1980, to hold a world ballooning record, when he flew 675 kms, from Northam to Wickepin. The flight gained Paul four national records, Paul's small build being ideal for such attempts. *Sprite*, essentially a one-man balloon, normally carried two fuel cylinders but, for record attempts three extra cylinders were slung outside the basket, attached to tiny parachutes for jettisoning, in accordance with FAI rules. Gren Putland also used this balloon to set national altitude records.

Ron Taaffe set national records and was the first to fly a balloon in South Korea, where he also took out the world altitude, distance and duration records for a hot air airship.

In an attempt to beat the hot air world endurance record, Geoff Green and Northam local Geoff Tetlow, lifted off on 28 September 1982. After 15 hours their flight ended prematurely on a beach at Jurien when winds threatened to send them seawards; however, they claimed the national duration record.

After 1982, interest in setting ballooning records subsided, but in May 1991 Chris Dewhirst took a parachutist up to 11 000 metres, the level of many domestic airline flights. The parachutist broke the Australian skydiving altitude record with his leap from the basket but Chris' flight, although the highest in Australian skies, was not official.

(1) It was left to Chris Dewhirst, on 26 April 1989 to complete the first crossing of Port Phillip Bay, taking off from Albert Park, landing on a 30' police launch and exchanging passengers, before completing the 2 hour 45 minute trip at Queenscliff.

(2) Coonara Great Race Ball invitation.

# Trans Australia Balloon Challenge

The Bicentenary of British settlement on Australia Day 26 January 1988, was the cause for an ecstatic celebration by many. The major focus was on Sydney Harbour where a grand flotilla of the world's sailing ships - accompanied by virtually anything that could float - sailed up the Harbour. Millions of people, including British royalty and Australian Prime Minister Bob Hawke, witnessed the colourful spectacle.

Further west, ten Australian balloonists held their own 200th birthday celebration at Parramatta Park, ascending into the sky in quick succession. The Australia Day celebration became an annual event, but on that occasion, it was a precursor to what remote area Australians would see later that year during the Great Trans Australia Bicentennial Balloon Challenge, when 73 balloons from 18 countries hovered over the outback and their retrieve crews bounced over the difficult terrain.

This epic, financed by the Australian Bicentennial Authority and other sponsors, was the brainchild of Queensland journalist cum publicity consultant Ruth Wilson. A former National Balloon Champion, Ruth had ballooned since 1976; her entry to the sport paralleling that of Judy Lynne. On assignment in New Zealand for *Cleo* magazine, Ruth interviewed an aeronaut and went for a flight. Ten weeks later, besotted with ballooning, she bought a balloon.

It took Ruth as Challenge Director, and committee members Phil Hanson and Geoff Tetlow, five years to organise the marathon event, held over 16 days in March/April and spanning 6400 kms of the continent, from Perth beside the Indian Ocean to Sydney on the Pacific coast. It was to be the ultimate test of flying skill, endurance, stamina and team spirit with ten flights scheduled for ten different sites across Australia.

Interested citizens were invited to apply to participate as ground crew and to provide 4WD vehicles for international competitors. The resulting enthusiasm almost swamped organisers; eventually from 4000 responses, 120 vehicles and 600 people were chosen. Balloon repairers, observers and communication personnel were found. A TNT semi-trailer became the command post, with telephone, telex and computer facilities and a link to Sydney Regional Met. Dr Peter French and Nurse Mary Anne Officer were deployed, and the Royal Flying Doctor Service was on standby in remote regions to deal with medical problems. Each location had to provide a suitable launch site, petrol, accommodation and meals for large numbers of competitors, crews, back-up staff and organisers.

High winds prevented the 30 March initial flight over Perth and were responsible for the cancellation of the first competition event, scheduled for the WA wheat town of Merredin.

The plan was for the ballooning entourage of 4WDs, army trucks, camper vans, buses, balloon and communications trailers and the 20 tonne gas tanker, to snake its way across the continent from west to east, with competitors taking advantage of the weather system that moved in the same direction. Unfortunately, this worked against the competitors, for the bad weather conditions they experienced in the west kept pace with them across the continent.

Consequently, after a flightless week, morale was low and frustration high as the teams gathered in Kalgoorlie, the gold capital of the west. At the dawn briefing, enthusiasm mounted as participants realised the wind was a bare ruffle; however, launching had to be curtailed until after a jet exited the airport at 0710. By takeoff time at 0800, wind was gusting at a marginal 13 knots, but pressure to fly was intense, with pilots spurred on by the knowledge that this was the last scheduled West Australian flight and by the task prize of

15 ounces of local gold. Only 40 of the field of 73 pilots chose to fly; they had to contend with thermals and fast difficult landings. Only 4 competitors managed to drop markers on the target area, with Canadian Alastair Russell declared task winner.

Quite a few teams made repairs to torn envelopes before the next event at Kimba in South Australia, two time zones and 1100 miles away across the dusty Nullarbor Plain. During the scorching drive, several teams experienced vehicle problems: tyre punctures, overheated radiators or more serious mechanical breakdowns.

Towns and citizens vied to supply the 'balloonatics' with the greatest welcome, plying them with balls and civic receptions and inadvertently keeping keen competitors from sleep; pilots took care to observe the standard rule: 'eight hours from bottle to throttle.'

The Challenge became an endurance test, with the likely winner emerging as the team with the most stamina over the sixteen days of the contest. The routine meant out of bed by 5am, fly competitively at dawn and evening and find time between to eat, study maps, make repairs to balloon or vehicle, refuel, sign autographs, answer spectators' questions, socialise at night, catch some sleep, then drive on ever eastwards across salt pans, dry plains and through grey/green scrub. Where possible, pilots were also expected to take residents and town officials on non-competitive flights as a token of their appreciation.

The arrival of over 600 people in places as tiny as Kimba (population 140) was momentous. Their efforts were rewarded on 5 April as 69 balloons graced the landscape and evening sky with their bright colours and unusual shapes. No doubt the locals clutching beer cans on hotel verandahs tightened their grasp on the railings and blinked to clear their vision as the balloons drifted dreamlike overhead. Three special shape balloons - more shimmering mirages than reality - floated past: the *Sydney Opera House*; the flying gas bottle *Elgas* and *Virgin Jumbo*: a plane passing through its own material cloud.

Unusual balloon names included *British Bacon*, *Dakota Roughriders*, *Yellow Pages*, *Vitamin E* and *Rosie O'Grady's Flying Circus* (whose pilot Joe Kittinger was a US astronaut, decorated Vietnam veteran and holder of world balloon and parachute records). Perhaps the locals felt more comfortable with balloons called *Tumbleweed* or the aboriginal *Ulinga*.

Meteorologist Wally Williams was out early next morning, with a theodolite gauging wind speed and direction at different heights. Again, conditions were marginal: individual teams had the option to fly or not. Several pilots had envelopes cave in from wind shear and all had risky landings with ground winds gusting to 25 knots. The medical team was busy placing plaster casts on Frenchman Serge Brunias' and Denmark's Suzanne Milke's broken ankles. The all-woman team flying *Canadian Airlines* had a heavy drag landing, resulting in one sprained ankle and a plethora of bruises. The usually sleepy outpost of Kimba suddenly found itself on TV and in newspaper headlines. By this stage in the competition, the current world champion American David Levin was in first place, hotly pursued by rival contenders.

The next venue, the beautiful Barossa Valley - renowned for its wineries - provided perfect flying weather at last. In a Hare and Hounds task, Alan Shore's *Carrington Bubble* as hare played with the air currents at different levels and deviously switched direction - much as a yacht tacks or a train shunts - to outwit the hound balloons before it landed. David Levin overshot the target, leaving the youngest competing pilot Mark Wilson, 20 (organiser Ruth Wilson's son) as task winner.

Just inside the Victorian border is Mildura, known for its citrus orchards and more hours of sunlight per day than anywhere else in Australia, but Mildura produced only wet, windy and unseasonably chilly conditions. Frustrated by more bad weather, the teams wearily packed yet again and drove 200 miles north, to the mining metropolis of Broken Hill in NSW. This proved to be 'the land of the long retrieve' in untracked bush country: an army truck traced one balloon and returned it to base six hours after touchdown. Another balloon disappeared, seemingly without trace, until eventually spotted from a chartered search aircraft.

High winds meant the cancellation of a further two flights. Desperate to placate despondent townsfolk, sponsors and contestants, the committee gave the green light to a voluntary task, with the plea that only experienced high wind flyers compete to pluck an $8000 silver ingot from the top of a cherry picker. Several balloons tried unsuccessfully; the crew dubbed 'the wild men from Wyoming' made two attempts from two inflations within the allotted time. Their second bid for the ingot ended with the pilot descending too low too fast; he sliced through treetops and clipped the roof of a house. This sudden impact tipped the basket and its occupants 45 degrees, causing the burner flame to ignite the envelope. The sun set as onlookers saw flames and the silhouette of the balloon as it disappeared from view; pilot Jerry Elkins landed safely and escaped with relatively minor bruises, cuts and shock. TV viewers across the nation saw vivid footage of ballooning. Those who had enthused over the earlier coverage of the majestic, charming balloons, and been lulled by their drifting gracefully over red earth or verdant pastures, now shuddered at the danger suddenly apparent in the sport.

To Australian balloonists this should have acted as a warning, or at least an omen for the future. With hindsight it is easy to see why Australians were complacent about the accidents on the Bicentennial Balloon Challenge, for hadn't they happened only to overseas pilots, who may not necessarily have been as safety conscious as Australians?

Five hundred miles further east in Dubbo, the weary contestants gathered for the final events. Burners roared life into the balloons early on the fifteenth day. The outcome of the Challenge rode on this last task, a Hesitation Waltz, for point tallies were close. Results were not immediately clear. At midday the computers churned out the results as nervous challengers waited to quaff their celebratory champagne. American David Levin and *Vitamin E* had held onto first place by just 13 points out of a possible 8000; Australian army captain Daryl Stuart was second and third was Japan's Masahiko Fujita in *Fujito-san*. Australian Rosalind Davies in *Pal* was the highest placed woman and ninth overall.

A cavalcade of contestants and crew descended on Sydney. All that was left to complete the event was the anticlimactic tether of ghostly balloons in a Sydney mist and to attend the presentation dinner at Sydney's Circular Quay, where the British had first settled two hundred years previously.

# A Series of Tragedies

If, as Marie Antoinette declared in 1783, ballooning is 'the sport of the gods' and balloons themselves suitable 'chariots of fire' for the use of such deities, then it might be concluded that the underworld and its evil associates were responsible for the tragedies that shocked Australia in 1987 and 1989, for it is inconceivable that kindly supernatural beings could have wrought such misery in 'God's own country'.

In Australia commercial ballooning was fast becoming a growth industry. Passengers were discovering the peaceful effect ballooning had on the senses and how the turmoil and strife of everyday life receded as the earth does from the balloon.

Australian ballooning had an enviable safety record. In the years 1969 to 1987 there had been 52 reported incidents (occasioning no injury or serious consequences). Of these, 33 involved manned balloons and 19 unmanned (of the latter, 13 were advertising balloons that broke their moorings, 3 were CSIRO Hibal research balloons, 2 weather balloons and 1 a model). The ABF investigated all incidents reported and where necessary, counselled or reprimanded an offending pilot; it lacked power to do more. Accidents where injury occurred or was narrowly avoided, were the responsibility of the Department of Aviation.

In early August 1987, during a balloon festival in Baton Rouge, USA, a balloon envelope collapsed, causing the basket to plummet to the ground, killing the sole occupant, the pilot. That fifteen second death plunge was every pilot's nightmare - no matter that in this case the envelope was old and porous and had been illegally patched many times. No matter that the pilot had allegedly been previously banned for reckless dangerous flying and had virtually melted the crown material by grossly over-burning. The worst scenario had eventuated, witnessed by thousands of spectators and by millions of television viewers around the world.

On 15 April 1986 a balloon accident occurred at Alice Springs involving Mike Sanby. It appears that Sanby effected an intermediate landing. While awaiting a passenger changeover a strong wind blew up, caught the balloon and dragged it towards trees. The pilot burned, in order to clear the treetops; at first the balloon responded and climbed steeply, then descended rapidly. When it hit earth, the basket bounced and Sanby was ejected, leaving the passengers in the basket as it was blown along. One passenger clambered into the pilot's section and applied heat causing them to rise. Sanby chased his runaway aircraft on foot until he was picked up by a retrieve vehicle in pursuit. The balloon landed 3½ kilometres away, leaving 10 of the 11 passengers with injuries,1 serious.

Investigators found deficiencies in the balloon operation and were concerned with overcrowding, leaving inadequate space for passengers to brace for landing. They reported that the number of passengers exceeded the number of handholds in the basket. On a separate occasion, the same pilot earned a reprimand for vacating a balloon, ostensibly to take photos of the balloon and passengers, leaving it vulnerable to becoming airborne without a pilot.

Although the *Aviation Safety Digest* published reports of accidents and results of investigations, the general public remained unaware of such happenings.

Michael Sanby "was almost born to ballooning. As a child he watched his meteorologist father release weather balloons over the plains of South Africa," wrote Walter Reisender. In Australia Sanby operated wildlife tours but opted to run balloon trips after viewing a TV documentary. On completion of his commercial pilot's training he ordered a giant, 12 passenger hot air balloon. At 240 000 cubic feet, the black and orange balloon

*A Town Like Alice*, was in 1985 the largest passenger balloon in Australia and with it Sanby ran Toddy's Balloons. For several years the flights gave visitors to Alice Springs a unique view of the surrounding desert and MacDonnell Ranges. In his article, Reisender wrote that, "His early takeoffs and landings - making up in excitement what they lacked in expertise - earned him the nickname of 'Captain Kangaroo' due to the bouncing of the hard-to-handle basket after landing." He hastened to point out that Sanby was now a more accomplished pilot but retained the nickname, with his balloon being dubbed *Big Joey*. (1)

In 1987 Mike Sanby, with 800 flying hours in his logbook, took delivery of a second 240 000 cubic feet balloon, a brilliantly coloured gold and silver one he named *Gondwana*, and a "specially reinforced basket, necessary in the rough terrain of the Centre." (2)

In Australia, as elsewhere - the ballooning fraternity occasionally experienced adversity: power line strikes; an envelope torn after inadvertently 'gift wrapping' a tree; the odd fire hastily extinguished. Nothing had prepared aeronauts for the horrific onslaught to come.

Exactly a week after the Baton Rouge tragedy, a similar event happened in Australia, claiming the lives of a 24 year old pilot and his twelve passengers and sealing for Australia an unwelcome record: the worst hot air balloon disaster in history.

It was in the 'dead heart' of Australia on Sunday the thirteenth day of August 1987, that a balloon and its thirteen occupants dropped out of a windless sky on a sparkling Alice Springs morning, after colliding in mid-air with a second balloon piloted by Mike Sanby. This sent the balloon into a death plunge in the desert, to hit the ground with such impact that all on board were killed instantly.

Holidaymakers and honeymooners had gathered at dawn 10 miles (14 kms) southeast of 'Alice', on the Santa Teresa Mission road. Within minutes of each other four balloons lifted off in perfect weather: Mike Sanby owned two of the balloons; his brother John Sanby - who ran Aussie Balloons - owned the others. All four balloons had settled into a routine flight at around 3000-4000', when passengers in John Sanby's balloons noticed *Big Joey*, piloted by Victorian Anthony Fraser rise rapidly, directly beneath Mike Sanby in *Gondwana*.

Although it is the responsibility of each pilot to be aware of his position in relation to others, a time-honoured rule is applied: aeronauts have traditionally yielded to the ascendant balloon (to avert a collision) due to the upper pilot's visual advantage.

With his view of *Gondwana* obliterated by his own spherical envelope Anthony Fraser unwittingly ascended into the upper balloon and collided. Witnesses stated that the envelope of the lower balloon struck the basket of the upper, to the extent that their basket penetrated into the other envelope. The control cords and crown ropes of the lower envelope became entangled; the rip panel and parachute vents opened and in separating tore five panels to shreds. As a great rush of air entered, the envelope deflated and elongated and, despite Anthony Fraser applying all burners in a desperate bid to maintain control, it completely collapsed 600 metres above the ground, streamered and crashed with a sickening thud. Those who rushed to the scene could do nothing to help, for all thirteen had died on impact: three were thrown out; ten were huddled and wedged at the bottom of the basket.

Killed were Anthony Fraser a commercial pilot for only six weeks, and fellow Victorians Daniel Fitzgibbon, Maurice Longden and a young honeymooning couple Veronica and Laurence Murphy who had been married just nine days earlier. Belinda Reid, her mother, Claire Taylor, Daphne Overton, Jennifer and Gary Dover were from NSW. A South Australian holidaymaker Rosemary Smith, Denmark resident Priben Onen and an unnamed Italian man also died that day. Seven of the dead were on a coach tour of Australia.

Anthony Fraser's body was returned to Melbourne. His funeral took place at his old school Xavier College, which he had left only five years previously: his coffin bore the hat and pilot wings that always accompanied him on his flights.

The Bureau of Air Safety Investigation (BASI) and the Coroner's Inquiry discovered nothing abnormal or defective in the materials, structure or manufacture of the balloons that might have contributed to the cause of the accident. They found that both pilots had erred to some extent, thus causing the collision but charged the surviving pilot with thirteen counts of manslaughter and one of committing a dangerous act. With his livelihood and reputation in tatters, Mike Sanby apparently panicked and was arrested on 16 August 1990 at Perth Airport on board a jet bound for Zimbabwe.

At his trial in the Supreme Court in Darwin, 39 year old Mike Sanby said that he believed the ill-fated balloon would pass beneath his. When asked whether he had been negligent in not carrying the mandatory instrument pack, Sanby replied, "in the rules yes, in reality no." (3)

After a week's trial Sanby was found guilty of committing a dangerous act but not guilty of manslaughter. Mr Justice Kearney in summarising, said the experienced Sanby knew of his obligation to give way to Fraser's balloon and had last seen *Big Joey* 30 seconds before the collision just 100 metres beneath him,

"You made no effort to try to keep track of Anthony's balloon after he passed out of your sight. I'm satisfied you could have done so with great ease," the judge said. "In my view, not to make any such efforts indicates a lack of proper lookout. 'The judge said the fact that Sanby had flown without required flying instruments reflected "a cocksure attitude" and a lack of adequate concern for the safety of his passengers and other balloonists." (4)

On 2 December 1992, Sanby received a two-year jail sentence with an eight months non-parole term imposed. Sanby was fortunate his sentencing was delayed as an ambiguity was realised in the jury foreman's reply to the court,

"The jury foreman was asked whether Sanby was guilty or not guilty of committing the dangerous act in aggravating circumstances. The foreman replied: 'yes.'
The judge said justice demanded the conviction be amended to delete the aggravating circumstances.
Had Sanby been convicted on the additional element of the charge of dangerous act, he would have faced a minimum of ten years jail." (5)

In 1993 Mike Sanby appealed the decision in the NT Supreme Court of Criminal Appeal and was cleared of negligence. By then the CAA was unable to take action for any breaches of civil aviation regulations, due to the twelve month limit having passed, but it did cancel Sanby's commercial Pilot's Licence.

The balloon fatalities spread waves of disbelief and horror in Australians generally and the ballooning community in particular. Balloonists no longer boasted that theirs was the safest form of aviation. Instead they painfully realised the truism that, "aviation in itself is not inherently dangerous but...it is terribly unforgiving of any carelessness, incapacity or neglect." (6)

Commercial ballooning collapsed in Australia as soon as news of the tragedy swept around the world. However, commercial ballooning had more suffering to endure, for it was to be dealt further devastating blows. A windy spring morning on 7 October 1989 created havoc at Bullengarook, northwest of Melbourne. After half hour flights and stand up landings, groups of passengers were exchanged and pilots Ray Smith and Danish-born Asbjorn Damhus took off in separate balloons on further flights. It was 7 am and surface wind speed was minimal with winds expected to increase mid-morning. Within five minutes the weather front arrived early and with it, strong winds. Small paddocks, forests, hills, powerlines, turbulence and a settlement prevented the balloons landing for another forty minutes. Ray Smith touched down heavily and fast but dragged safely to a stop.

Asbjorn Damhus was not as lucky; his balloon landed heavily, with the basket and occupants dragged for ninety metres up a slope, before hitting a corner fence post which knocked out the pilot. Eventually the balloon smashed into trees and the passengers were flung out, resulting in all five being injured. One woman broke a shoulder and suffered a severe hip injury and the pilot later required plastic surgery to extensive facial injuries.

Within four days another accident occurred. Balloonists who knew Ross Spicer, aged 45, regarded him as a lovable rogue with an effervescent personality; as an eccentric free spirit who passionately loved flying. In 1983 Ross took his first flight with Ruth Wilson; like many others he was smitten at first sight. He quickly gained his private pilot's licence then his commercial. Ross moved from Sydney to his Mudgee farm where he based his commercial balloon operation, using his *Hilux* balloon.

A capable and experienced pilot, Ross twice attempted, in 1988 and 1989, to cross the Blue Mountains, not as famous explorers, Gregory Blaxland, William Lawson and William Wentworth had on foot in 1813, but by balloon and in reverse, from west to east. Anne Blaxland, a descendant of one of the explorers, accompanied him on both occasions. Difficulty lay in the height to be attained on the eighty-kilometre voyage, in order to clear the mountains and the turbulence they created. The first attempt ended with a landing short of their Penrith Plains target, due to a faster fuel consumption rate than anticipated for the 4-5 hour journey. The second attempt also failed to reach its goal when a news helicopter got too close during inflation, causing a small rip in the envelope which increased fuel consumption. Undaunted, Ross described his Blue Mountains flight as "nothing short of exhilarating, fantastic and mind-blowing! The curl-over at the top of the ridges at 3000 feet was something to experience. It carried us down sometimes over 1000 feet. We also had a refuelling stop on the side of a cliff face." (7)

Ross Spicer's zest for aerostation and life was extinguished on the morning of 11 October 1989. After an uneventful flight at Mudgee, Ross prepared to land in a large paddock but failed to see power lines on his line of approach, until he was five metres away and too late to avoid them. The balloon's suspension cables struck, and the balloon slid 30 metres along the conductors before the basket hit the ground, dragging down the power lines. When one passenger received an electric shock, the pilot ordered an evacuation: he and two others exited, leaving one passenger in the basket. From the injuries he received, it would appear that Ross reached towards the basket and pulled the metal parachute vent line, with the intention of deflating the balloon and rescuing his passenger. In that instant, he and thirty five year old Christine Cleary in the basket were electrocuted and fire enveloped the balloon.

A mere four days later, on 15 October, and the day prior to Ross Spicer's funeral, his good friend David Bowers 45, and a female passenger were killed in a powerline strike. The hour-long flight at Cessnock was calm and uneventful. An aborted landing, to prevent a horse taking fright, placed Bowers in an emergency situation with dwindling fuel and only timbered country ahead. A semi-cleared area appeared at Lovedale and David descended. Neither the ground crew, nor the pilot, saw the two high-voltage power lines ahead until late into the landing (due to ambient light conditions, the angle and background terrain, seeing power lines from above can be extremely difficult) and a wind gust carried them towards the lines.

The pilot apparently instructed the passengers to exit the balloon. One passenger did so a metre from the ground and was followed by David, with the parachute vent line wound around his forearm. The balloon began to ascend with its lightened load; a flying support wire contacted one power line which sparked and snapped. Two more passengers jumped to the ground where they saw their pilot prostrate, apparently electrocuted by a charge through the vent line, which then detached itself from David's arm and closed the vent. A fifth person exited the basket, leaving his wife Gabrielle Leslie, on board alone. The balloon became buoyant and rose. Ten metres above the ground she vacated the balloon but received fatal injuries on impact and died later in hospital. The runaway balloon continued on for two kilometres before coming to rest of its own accord.

As it was highly unusual to instruct passengers to leave a balloon while it was still airborne, perhaps David and his passengers remembered the power line deaths four days earlier and panicked. Nor was it normal practice for the pilot to wrap the vent line around his forearm.

David had flown balloons in England from 1973 until 1976 when he migrated to Australia and settled in Sydney. He helped steer Australian ballooning towards ratified sport and commercial status. He proved that ballooning was a viable proposition in tropical Cairns and flew in the more traditional regions of the Hunter Valley and Camden. An instructor and examiner, he was a popular and vastly experienced pilot.

In its report on the two NSW fatal accidents, BASI considered there to be several significant factors leading to the deaths: the type and layout of the power lines made them difficult to see and a lack of knowledge of electrical contact safety procedures contributed. The Bureau recommended the introduction of a safety education program and for balloon manufacturers to reduce the amount of exposed metal.

Seventeen deaths in three years devastated the relatively small Australian ballooning fraternity; disbelief was expressed at it happening in Australia - a world leader in licensing practices, balloon regulations and in its safety code. Balloonists who had previously sought media exposure dived for cover, as that same media thereafter sensationalised the tiniest of incidents involving balloons, labelling them as dangerous. The previous love affair the media had with ballooning ended with all that loss of life in 1989.

As one Australian aeronaut said, ballooning came abruptly of age; it was the end of innocence. Many sought a scapegoat and turned on commercial balloon enterprises as the cause of their collective misery. Grieving commercial balloon operators and pilots across Australia were dealt a triple blow: three of their members were dead; their livelihoods disappeared as thousands of pre-booked passengers cancelled flights and they faced hostility and resentment from private sport balloonists.

From the fatalities came a resolve to analyse the causes, act on the recommendations and "put in place alternatives that, in the future, may prevent or at least reduce the chances of these accidents reoccurring." Swift action followed to formulate further safety policies and to set up an ABF Operations Committee. Effective electrical and bonding properties rectified inherent balloon design deficiencies. (8)

It was a brave person indeed who continued to fly after such life destroying events, yet fly they did, sometimes in defiance, but also to show faith in their beloved aerostation, still statistically the safest of all aviation sports. Those still hesitant to fly think that pilot Rob Robertson may well have shown prophetic powers when he once joked, "ballooning is not the sport of the gods; 'balloonists' are the sport of the gods." (9)

It was not really so difficult to resume flying many said. One only had to think of Ross Spicer's poem to be enveloped anew:

*"AN EARLY MORNING ASCENT*

*Good Morning Maiden*

*The soft smooth touch of your breath*
*upon my naked neck so early in the morning*
*as I float between fantasy and reality*
*is so familiar to me.*

*I fall so gently into your embrace*
*and I succumb so readily*
*to your subtle touch.*

*I rise out of the fog to greet you*
*and to meet you for the very first time.*
*A new day"* (10)

(1)   *The Sunday Mail*, 20 March 1986.
(2)   *Aeronotes*, July/August 1987.
(3)   *Herald Sun*, 26 Nov 1992.
(4)   *The Age*, 3 Dec 1992.
(5)   Ibid.
(6)   Letter Roger Meadmore, *Aeronotes*, Sept/October 1989.
(7)   *Aeronotes* July/Aug 1988.
(8)   Ian Tooth President ABF, *Aeronotes*, Sept/Oct 1989.
(9)   *Aeronotes* Mar/June 1988.
(10) Ibid.

# Australian Balloons over Everest

21 October 1991 is a significant date in ballooning history. On that day the Australian who gave up mountaineering for ballooning, became the first person to pilot a balloon over the summit of Mt Everest. Chris Dewhirst was accompanied by cameraman Leo Dickinson and followed in a second balloon by English pilot Andy Elson and photographer Eric Jones.

Since Chris' previous attempt in 1985, two other teams had been inspired to try. A Japanese pilot had a lucky escape when he hit a Himalayan mountain ridge and fell 300 metres within the basket, sustaining a fractured femur and making for a difficult rescue. In 1990 a joint Australian/British expedition had permission from the Chinese government to fly over the peak and land in the then Autonomous Region of Tibet, but the attempt never eventuated.

During test flights in Victoria, Chris experienced regular pilot light failures on rapid ascents above 25,000', until a burner modification by Phil Kavanagh ensured a separate oxygen feed to the pilot lights. Arriving in Nepal in early September 1991, they had to await the right weather conditions: suitably cold air and a 40 knot jet stream. As for the 1985 attempt, Martin Harris provided meteorological information. He set up a portable satellite receiver and plugged into the world grid. Using a radiosonde, Harris was able to gain continuous, precise wind speed and direction information across Everest. On his previous attempt Chris had launched 100 kms from the peak; for this attempt base camp was at Gokyo just 25 kms from Everest.

Australian adventurer Dick Smith, flew his Cessna over the peak, photographing it from every angle and contacting base camp with wind measurements and possible landing positions. Days after Smith's departure, and after a nineteen-day wait, weather conditions were right for the following morning. Ground camera and crewman, Dr Glenn Singleman and his mountaineering wife Irina, made a difficult night ascent to a 20 000' peak above Gokyo, where the team had set up camera equipment.

Both 240 000 cubic feet balloons launched a few minutes apart early on 21 October from a glacier in the Everest foothills. Chris Dewhirst piloted the lead balloon, *Star Flyer I*. Immediately the VHF radios failed, isolating the balloons. Chris again discovered the atmospheric temperature to be about 15°C higher than anticipated. With a climb rate at a minimum 1000' per minute required to overfly Everest, Chris knew this would produce an envelope temperature in excess of 135°C, far greater than the recommended safety level of 125°C. That extra 10 degrees at the top of the envelope doubled the fuel consumption rate.

They had decided on a slow climb out from Gokyo to 20 000' to facilitate photography, then to increase the climb rate dramatically, to minimise time spent in the jet stream tracking south of Everest. The plan was to gain an altitude of 33 000' and level out for the final approach to the summit, thus giving a suitable safety margin. Maximum clearance was essential if they were to avoid turbulence downwind of Everest, a terrifying prospect. By the time Chris' ground speed had increased to 56 knots in the jet stream, the thermistor needle exceeded 170°C and eventually disappeared off the dial, causing real fear of envelope meltdown. Parachutes were at hand in case of emergency, but they dared not think of the consequences.

Chris described the approach, "The solid black pyramid of rock that seemed so small from Gokyo was now engulfing our little balloon...even at 29 000' it seemed that we were still looking up at Everest." (1)

Then came the sublime moment when, "Leo Dickinson and I looked directly down on the summit. We could see the footprints of the Spanish and Americans who climbed Everest 10 days earlier. It was an extraordinary feeling and the first time in the flight that I had a chance to enjoy what I was doing. We crossed over the summit of Everest with the Hillary Step on one side of the basket and the summit on the other side... It felt like we could reach out and touch it...The east face was completely white - ice fluted and elegant. The mountain had totally changed character, it was as if the dominant black pyramid that we had lived with at Base Camp for the past 20 days just ceased to exist. We had escaped from the Underworld, rowed across the River Styx and emerged into the land of the living." (2)

Chris Dewhirst had fulfilled his dream with a safety margin of 300 metres. He became the first person to pilot a balloon and undertake an unpowered flight over the world's highest peak (8848m). Leo Dickenson wrote of the sensation,

> "Everest had been just between my legs, Lhotse under my armpit. Further right was Makalu, looking ridiculously easy. Beyond, in the distance, lay Kanchenjunga, peeking up through low cloud at 22 000ft. To my left Lo La, on the border, carved a link around to Cho Oyo in Tibet where the Russians we met a few days ago were now struggling at 8000 metres. Away on the far horizon lay Shisma Pangma and to the southeast lay Annapurna and Dhaulagiri, eight of the World's 8000 metre peaks lay below us. Few people can claim to have witnessed such a spectacle, and certainly not from the open basket beneath a hot air balloon." (3)

In the *Star Flyer II* balloon Andy Elson was struggling with four separate pilot light failures and thus a slower rate of climb. Eventually, with five burners blazing, he and Eric Jones limped over Everest's South Col, to be confronted by the sinister sounds of flying wires snapping, caused by excessive heat in the mouth of the balloon. Six out of seven steel strands in one corner alone had detached; if the seventh solitary strand had given way the weight would have wrenched the wires from the adjacent corner, leaving basket and burners dangling precariously at right angles to the balloon. With the parachute vent line to the top of the envelope also burnt out, Andy was unable to dump hot air. Mercifully the flying strand held, and *Star Flyer II* executed a perfect stand up landing in Tibet's Ronxar Valley.

Chris and Leo in *Star Flyer I* were not as fortunate. Travelling at sixty knots, Chris was concerned the eight cylinders of fuel would not last. If he landed before the designated Ronxar Valley it would mean a week's walk and no possibility of equipment recovery. A further anticipated problem was the giant mountain peaks Amadirne and Nyannori, which guarded the Valley on Chris's approach.

Grappling with hypoxia, Chris checked his estimates every few minutes. Not until he had flown sixty of the eighty-minute flight, was he certain he had the fuel to overfly Amadirne and attain the Valley beyond. Just above the valley floor, he was greeted by car-sized glacial moraine and by a 15-knot ground wind, generated from hours of intense sun on the peaks. Landing was horrendous: they dragged and bounced then were flung from the basket; Leo smashed into a boulder that crushed a rib and lay in a snowstorm of duck feathers from his exploded jacket. Chris, with a torn finger ligament went in pursuit of the runaway, finally jumping in and deflating the balloon after a two-mile chase. As Leo Dickinson later wrote, "the Gods of the Mountains had let us off lightly." (4)

With the inflated envelope of *Star Flyer II* acting as a beacon, the retrieve ground crew quickly reached the men and returned all four to the Tibetan base camp within twelve hours. By the time they had celebrated with fried chips and eggs washed down by beer, the world already knew of their mighty achievement - the first ever traverse of Everest by balloon.

Two international awards recognised their outstanding achievement; the Green Salver - once the property of pioneer English aeronaut Charles Green - was jointly awarded to Chris Dewhirst and Andy Elson by the British Balloon and Airship Club. The Royal Aeronautical Club in London and Prince Andrew presented all four men with the Salaman trophy. Governor General Bill Hayden awarded Chris the Oswald Watt medal, Australia's most prestigious aviation award, previously granted to Sir Charles Kingsford Smith, Bert Hinkler and Dick Smith.

With such a variety of challenges available to man over the centuries, few have engrossed him as totally as the sky. Although the days of the scientific balloons are all but over, and the showmanship balloon is gone forever, the sports balloon lives on and thrives.

The majority of aeronauts prefer a more relaxed approach to their beloved sport and passion. To them all, I can offer no better blessing than that expressed in the Balloonist's Prayer,

*"May the winds welcome you with softness,*
*May the sun bless you with warm hands*
*May you fly so high and so well that God joins*
*you in laughter and sets you gently back into*
*the loving arms of Mother Earth."*
Unknown.

(1) Chris Dewhirst, Everest, *Aeronotes*, Mar 1992.
(2) Ibid.
(3) Leo Dickinson, Balloon over Everest, *Sport Parachutist*, Feb 1992.
(4) Ibid.

# APPENDIX

## Australian National Records

Class A refers to free balloons.

Subclass AX means the balloon obtains buoyancy solely from heating of air.

4,5,6 etc refers to the cubic capacity viz:

| AX- classifications | Capacity |
|---|---|
| AX-4 | 31,000 cubic feet |
| AX-5 | 41,000 cubic feet |
| AX-6 | 56,000 cubic feet |
| AX-8 | 84,000 cubic feet |
| AX-9 | 140,000 cubic feet |
| AX-10/15 | More than 141,258 cubic feet. |

| Sub Class | Altitude | Distance | Duration |
|---|---|---|---|
| AX-4 | G J Putland, 10,094.5ft; Cameron 18/8/80 | P Gianniotis, 154.68km, Cameron, 16/8/80 | P Gianniotis, 4hr 08min, Cameron, 16/8/80 |
| AX-5 | G J Putland, 10,094.5ft; Cameron, 18/8/80 | P Gianniotis, 154.68km, 16/8/80 | P Gianniotis, 4hr 08min, Cameron, 16/8/80 |
| AX-6 | R W Taaffe, 30,634ft; Cameron, 10/10/78 | R W Taaffe, 354.87km, Cameron, 8/8/80 | R W Taaffe, 4hr 19min, Cameron 8/8/80 |
| AX-7 | R W Taaffe, 30,634ft; Cameron, 10/10/78 | R W Taaffe, 354.87km, Cameron, 8/8/80 | L Springett, 6hr 21min, Cameron 1/8/92 |
| AX-8 | R W Taaffe, 30,634ft; Cameron, 10/10/78 | R W Taaffe, 354.87km Cameron, 8/8/80 | L Springett, 6hr 21min, Cameron, 1/8/92 |
| AX-9 | R W Taaffe, 30,634ft; Cameron, 10/10/78 | R W Taaffe, 354.87km, Cameron, 8/8/80 | L Springett, 6hr 21min, Cameron, 1/8/92 |
| AX-10 | R W Taaffe, 30,634ft; Cameron, 10/10/78 | R W Taaffe, 354.87km, Cameron, 8/8/80 | L Springett, 6hr 21min, Cameron, 1/8/92 |
| AX-11 | R W Taaffe, 30,634ft; Cameron, 10/10/78 | R W Taaffe, 354.87km, Cameron, 8/8/80 | L Springett, 6hr 21min, Cameron, 1/8/92 |
| AX-12 to AX-15 | R W Taaffe, 30,634ft, Cameron, 10/10/78 | R W Taaffe, 354.87km, Cameron, 8/8/80 | G J Tetlow, 15hr 03min, Cameron, 27/9/82 |

# Australian National Hot Air Balloon Championships

| 1978 | Belconnen ACT | Bill Watson |
| 1979 | Greenthorpe NSW | Ruth Wilson |
| 1981 | Northam WA | Bob Dickson |
| 1982 | Seppeltsfield SA | Peter Vizzard |
| 1984 | Northam WA | Judy Lynne |
| 1986 | Seppeltsfield SA | Peter Vizzard |
| 1988 | Canowindra NSW | John Wallington |
| 1990 | Benalla Vic | Phil Kavanagh |
| 1992 | Leeton NSW | John Wallington |

# Australian World Hot Air Balloon Champions

1983    Nantes, France

*Lovely! Lady* balloon

Crew:  Peter Vizzard (pilot)

Roger Meadmore (navigator)

Judy Lynne

Mike Conran

# Australian Airship Records

(all set in Northam, WA)

Ron Taaffe (Australian)

Aug. 1982         24 World, 24 Australian Records - BX - 3

Altitude Record 10250ft

Distance Record 47km

Duration Record 1hr 29min

Capt. Geoff Green (British)

Aug. 1982         24 British Records - BX - 3

Altitude Record 5200ft

Distance Record 26.6km

Duration Record 1hr 23min

# ACKNOWLEDGEMENTS

I would like to thank those who guided me to sources and those who gave me information. My main debt is to Charles Henry Brown who chronicled past and contemporary ballooning history so superbly. His living descendant, Paul Brown, was exceptionally generous in trusting me with his ancestor's scrapbook and memorabilia for the years it took me to research and write this history.

No less generous were Jenny Lefebvre, who typed every word of this manuscript gratis, in her valuable spare time whilst bringing up two small children and Norma Tovey who so diligently and meticulously proofread and edited the book and who rescued me when I was becoming overwhelmed with the complexities of the project.

My own children, Rachel, Keiran and Daniel I wish to thank for being so patient with a mother who was often busy writing when they would have preferred a playmate or companion. To them I dedicate this book.

The following people gave me information, photos or undertook research for me, guided me to sourcesor helped in myriad other ways:

Dale Allen, John Abell, 'Spider' Anderson, Samuel Burns, Trevor Burns (DOA), Mimi Callaghan, Ron Campbell (CSIRO), Lindsay Colenso, Frank Cusack, John de Figueiredo, Joanne Delesantro, Fred de Silva (CSIRO), Chris Dewhirst, Carole Dusting (RMIT Melbourne), Bridget Everett, Susan Ferguson-Brown, John Frew, Ian Galbally, Mike Galvin, Gary Geier, Paul Gianniotis, Marie Goldsworthy, Bill Grey (MCC Museum) Rex Harcourt (MCC Museum librarian), Lesley Head, Keith Isaacs, Joan Lang, Linton Lethlean (Director, Royal Exhibition Building, Melbourne), Dr J Lill, Judy Lynne, Cherry McCormack, Robert McLaren, Roger McLeod (DOA), Keith Meggs and Fred Morton (Aviation Historical Society Victoria), Frank Mines, Marion Mitchell, Marjorie Morgan, Felicity Murray, Tony Norton, Gren Putland, Rob Robertson, Dave Robson, Kiff Saunders, Barbara J Savill, Michael Small, Brian Smith, John Smith, Mike Tonks (DOA), Tiit Tonuri (Australian Balloon Federation), Kay Turnbull, Betty Van Heyst, Angela Wallace, John Wallington and Kathy Wickham.

A special thank you to the members and staff of the many organisations who helped me: Australian Balloon Federation, Genealogical Society of Victoria, Australian National Library, Balloon Association of Victoria, Battye Library Western Australia, Exhibition Trustees, State Library of Victoria, State Library of Queensland, Melbourne General Cemetery, Mitchell Library, Sydney and the Richmond Historical Society Victoria.

# PHOTO CREDITS

## Archives and Museums

Australian War Memorial, Museums Victoria, National Library of Australia, State Library of NSW, State Library of Victoria, Trove.

## Companies

Award Advertising & Ad Agency (now Campaign Pacific).
Global Ballooning

## Individuals

Andrew Chapman, John and Peter Casamento, Chris Dewhirst, CD and Leo Dickinson, Terrence Fitz-Simon, Gary Geier, Jenny Houghton, Keith Isaacs, Eric Jones, Thomas Laird, Bob Lye, Judy Lynne, Cherry McCormack, Tony Norton, Jan Reynolds, Glenn and Irina Singleman, Michael Small, Brian Smith, Dick and Pip Smith, John Smith, Shane Smith (Coonara), Kiff Saunders, Kay Turnbull, Peter Vizzard, David Whillas (CSIRO).

# ACRONYMS AND ABBREVIATIONS

| | |
|---|---|
| 4WD | Four Wheel Drive |
| ABF | Australian Balloon Federation |
| AEC | Atomic Energy Commission (USA) |
| AWM | Australian War Memorial |
| AWS | Automatic Weather Station |
| BASI | Bureau of Air Safety Investigation |
| BAV | Balloon Association of Victoria |
| BLS | Balloon Launching Station |
| CAA | Civil Aviation Authority |
| CSIRO | The Commonwealth Scientific and Industrial Research Organisation |
| DCA | Department of Civil Aviation |
| DOA | Department of Aviation |
| FAI | Fédération Aéronautique Internationale |
| FL | Flight Lieutenant |
| FO | Flight Officer |
| FRS | Fellow of the Royal Society |
| GSV | Genealogical Society of Victoria |
| HKBAC | Hong Kong Balloon and Airship Club |
| LTA | Lighter than Air |
| MCC | Melbourne Cricket Club |
| MCG | Melbourne Cricket Ground |
| Met | Bureau of Meteorology |
| NADACS | National Air Defence and Air Space System |
| RAAF | Royal Australian Air Force |
| RMIT | Royal Melbourne Institute of Technology |
| SABAC | South Australian Balloon & Airship Club |
| VIC | Victoria |
| WA | Western Australia |
| WABAC | Western Australian Balloon & Airship Club |

# BIBLIOGRAPHY

## Unpublished Material

Brown, Charles Henry - Aeronautica - Correspondence of C H Brown and other aeronauts - State Library of Victoria.

Brown, Charles Henry - Notebook, scrapbook held by descendants.

Taylor, George, The Challenge of Aviation 1968 (in the Mitchell Library Sydney).

## Official Sources

*Aviation Safety Digest.*

*Registry of Births, Deaths and Marriages (Public Record Office Victoria).*

*Coroners Inquest (Public Record Office Victoria) 24 January 1870.*

*Commonwealth Government, Historical Records of Australia.*

*Passenger List of Simla from 1856 to 1857 (Public Record Office Victoria).*

*Parliamentary Debates, Queensland 1890.*

# Newspapers

The following newspapers were consulted for various events throughout this history.

*The Age*

*Argus*

*Australasian Sketcher*

*Ballarat Courier*

*Ballarat Star*

*Barrier Miner*

*Bathurst Times*

*Bell's Life in Sydney*

*Bell's Life in Victoria*

*Bendigo Advertiser*

*Bendigo Mercury*

*Bulletin*

*Canberra Times*

*Castlemaine Mail*

*Chambers' Book of Days*

*Courier de L'Europe*

*Courier Mail (Brisbane)*

*Daily Telegraph (Sydney)*

*Daily Mirror (Sydney)*

*Era (Sydney)*

*Empire*

*Evening News (Sydney)*

*Geelong Advertiser*

*Geraldton Express*

*Gympie Times*

*Harpers' Weekly*

*Illustrated Melbourne News*

*Illustrated Sydney News*

*Kapunda Herald*

*Journal of Australasia*

*Launceston Examiner*

*Le Globe (Paris)*

*Lloyds Newspaper*

*Manchester Examiner*

*Melbourne Daily News*

*Melbourne Herald*

*Memphis Avalanche*

*My Note Book*

*New Orleans Crescent*

*New York Herald*

*New York Tribune*

*Northern Argus*

*Northern Territory News*

*North West Times*

*Rockhampton Argus*

*Sacramento Union*

*Seattle Post Intelligencer*

*South Australian Chronicle*

*Standard of Freedom (London)*

*Sun Herald (Sydney)*

*Sunday Telegraph*

*Sydney Evening News*

*Sydney Morning Herald*

*Sydney News*

*The Adelaide Observer*

*The Australian*

*The Australian Teacher*

*The Australasian*

*The Chambers' Journal*

*The Evening Star*

*The Illustrated Australian*

*The Illustrated Journal of Australasia*

*The Illustrated Sydney News*

*The Leeds Express*

*The Leeds Mercury.*

*The Melbourne Daily News*

*The Morning Advertiser*

*The People*

*The Queenslander*

*The South Australian Advertiser*

*The Sun (Melbourne)*

*The Sun-News Pictorial*

*The Weekly Times (Melbourne)*

*The West Australian*

*Watertown Reformer Extra*

# Articles in Newspapers and Periodicals

*Aircraft* 1925, 1931, 1971, 1983.

Antarctica *Reader's Digest* Sydney 1985.

*Department of Civil Aviation News* Vol 2 No 1 1969.

*Flight* Jan 1913.

Historical Papers Vol III. Historical Press Cuttings Vol V Held at the State Librtary of Victoria.

*Illustrated Journal of Australasia* Vol IV No XXI 1858.

The Invention of the Balloon and the Birth of Modern Chemistry *Scientific American* Jan 1984.

Adam-Smith Patsy, Maldon - A Museum Piece *Walkabout* Vol 35.

Bacon Rev JM, Scientific Ballooning *Contemporary Review* Vol LXXIV Isbister & Co. London 1898.

Barnes FW, Dirigibles may have role in Australia's Defences *Pacific Defence Reporter* Vol 12 No 8 1986.

Belgrave Dr, Exploration and Signalling by Captive Balloon *Geographical Society of Australia* Vol 2 Sydney 1885.

Davis John, Escape to the Air *Walkabout* Sydney 1972.

Galvin Mike, Professor Wilfred Burns Early Aeronaut and Smoke Balloonist *Balloon Life* US 1987.

Isaacs Keith, Letter *Navy and Army Illustrated Magazine* Vol IX 1989.

Isaacs Keith, Australia and the Military Balloon *Defence Force Journal* No 43 1983.

Kurasawa Susan, *Geo* Vol 3 No 1. 1981.

Martinson David, Puff Too *Australian Airsport Magazine* 1980.

McLaren Ian, Australian Aviation: A Bibliographical Survey *Victorian Historical Magazine* Vol 28 Melbourne 1858.

Roach-Pierson Capt. P, The Use of the Kite Balloon in the *Navy Sea Land and Air* Vol II UK 1919.

Skelton RW, Ballooning in the Antarctic, *The South Polar Times* Vol I Antarctica 1907.

Wilson Mr, poem *Universal Magazine* November 1784.

Yost Ed, Silver Fox: Longest Manned Balloon Flgith 2 *National Geographic* February 1977.

# Published Material - Early Sources

Aero Club of America, *Navigating the Air* Doubleday, Page New York 1907.

Alexander John, *The Conquest of the Air: The Romance of Aerial Navigation* London SW Partridge 1902.

Abbott JHM, *Tommy Cornstalk* Longman, Green London 1902.

Australian War Memorial, *Australians At War* 1882-1972.

Battye Dr JS (Ed), *Cyclopaedia of Western Australia* Hussey and Gillingham Adelaide 1912-1913.

Battye Dr JS, *The History of the North West of Australia* Perth VK Jones 1915.

Battye Dr JS, *Western Australia: A History from its Discovery to the Inauguration of the Commonwealth* Clarendon Oxford 1924.

Bean CEW, *The Official History of Australia in the War of 1914-1918* Vols I and II Angus and Robertson Sydney 1915.

Burbidge WF, *From Balloon to Bomber* John Crowther London 1946.

Cobby AH, *High Adventure* Robertson and Mullens Melbourne 1942.

Coxwell Henry, *The Balloon, or Aerostatic Magazine* H Steill London 1845.

Coxwell Henry, *Exploration of Australia by Balloon* Mechanics Institute London 1859.

Coxwell Henry, *My Life and Balloon Experiences* WH Allen London 1887.

Davy MJB, *Lighter-Than-Air Craft* Science Museum London 1934.

de Fonvielle Wilfrid, *Adventures in the Air* Stanford London 1877.

de la Bretonne Restif, *La Découverte Australe Par Un Homme-Volant* Paris 1781.

Garran Andrew (Ed), *Picturesque Atlas of Australasia* Vols 1,2,3 The Picturesque Atlas Publishing Co Sydney 1868-88.

Garryowen, *The Chronicles of Early Melbourne 1835-1852* Fergusson and Mitchell Melbourne 1888.

Glaisher James (Ed), *Encyclopaedia Britannica* 1878.

Great Britain War Office (Ed), *Manual of Military Ballooning* War Pamphlets Vol 76 No 5 London 1905.

Harding William, *War in South Africa* Dominion Chicago 1899.

Hatton Turnor Christopher, *Astra Castra: Experiments and Adventures in the Atmosphere* Lion, Chapman and Hall London 1865.

Heaton JA, *Australian Dictionary of Dates and Men of the Time* SW Silver Sydney 1879.

Hodgson JE, *The History of Aeronautics in Great Britain* Oxford University Press London 1924.

Houdini H, *A Magician Among Spirits* Harper and Brothers New York 1924.

Jose AW, *Official History of Australia in the War of 1914-18* Vol IX Angus and Robertson Sydney 1928.

Jose AW, *The Illustrated Australian Encyclopaedia* Angus and Robertson Sydney 1925-26.

Kellock Harold, *Houdini: His Life Story* Heinemann London 1928.

Leavitt, TW, *The Jubilee History of Tasmania* Vol I Melbourne 1887.

Leavitt TW, Lillburn WD, *History of Victoria and Melbourne* Vol II Duffus Melbourne 1888.

Le Cornu J, *La Navigation Aérienne* Nony Paris 1903.

Lynch Col. Arthur, *My Life Story* John Long London 1924.

Marion F, *Wonderful Balloon Ascents* (translated from French) Charles Scribner New York 1870.

Mason WG, *Australian Picture Pleasure Book* JR Clarke Sydney 1857.

Mason Monck, *Aeronautic; or, Sketches Illustrative of the Theory and Practice of Aerostation* Westley London 1838.

Millbank Jeremiah Jnr, *The First Century of Flight in America* Princeton University Press Princeton 1943.

McDonald Donald, *How we kept the Flag Flying* Ward Lock Melbourne1900.

Selby Isaac, *The Old Pioneers Memorial History of Melbourne* Old Pioneers Memorial Fund Melbourne 1924.

Smith JB (comp), Eastwood JJ (Comp), *Historical Studies, Australia and New Zealand* Department of History, University of Melbourne 1937.

Strange LA, *Recollections of an Airman* Hamilton London 1935.

South Kensington Science Museum, *Lighter-Than-Air Craft* London 1934.

Tolmer Alex, *Reminiscences of an Adventurous and Chequered Career in the Antipodes* Sampson Low, Marston, Searle, and Rivington London 1882.

Wells Rufus G, *The Boys Own Paper* 1888-1889 England.

White Leo, *Wingspread: The Pioneering of Aviation in New Zealand* Unity Press Auckland 1941.

Whitworth Robert, *Official Handbook and Guide to Victoria* Bailliere Melbourne 1880.

Wise John, *Through the Air: A Narrative of Forty Years Experience as an Aeronaut* To-day Publishing Philadelphia 1873.

Wise John, *The End of an Era* Houghton Boston 1902.


# Published Material - Contemporary Sources

*The Encyclopedia of Aviation* Cassell Stanmore NSW 1977.

*The Story of The Camera in Action: The Balloon Photography of Melvin Vaniman.*

Anderson EW, *Man the Aviator* Priory Press London 1975.

Bagot Alec, *Coppin the Great* Melbourne University Press 1965.

Barr Pat, S*imla: A Hill Station in British India* Scolar Press London 1978.

Blainey Geoffrey, *A Land Half-Won* Macmillan Melbourne 1980.

Bartlett Norman (Ed), *Australia at Arms* Australian War Memorial Canberra 1955.

Bennett Arthur L, *The Glittering Years* St. George Books Perth 1981.

Blackman Grant, Larkin John, *Australia's First Notable Town, Maldon* Hodder and Stoughton Sydney 1978.

Brogden Stanley, *Exploring the Air* Longmans London 1961.

Brown Robin, *Collins Milestones in Australian History 1788 - Present* Collins Sydney 1986.

Carroll Brian, *Australian Aviators: An Illustrated History* Cassell North Ryde New South Wales 1980.

Colls K, Whitaker R, *The Australian Weather Book* Child Frenchs Forest 1990.

Copley Greg, *Australians in the Air 1964* Rigby Adelaide 1976.

Crouch Tom, *The Eagle Aloft: Two Centuries of The Balloon in America* Smithsonian Institution Washington DC 1983.

Deeson AFL, *An Illustrated History of Airships* Spurbook Bourne End 1934.

Dollfus Charles, *The Orion Book of Balloons* Orion NewYork 1961.

Dunstan Keith, *The Paddock That Grew: The Story of The Melbourne Cricket Club* Cassell North Melbourne 1974.

Dwiggins Don, *The Complete Book of Airships: Dirigibles, Blimps and Hot Air Balloons* Tab Books Blue Ridge Summit PA1980.

Ege Lennart, *Balloons and Airships 1783-1973* Blandford London 1973.

Ewing Ross, Macpherson Ross, *The History of New Zealand Aviation* Heinemann Auckland 1986.

Fergusson Sir James, *Balloon Tytler* Faber London 1972.

Gardiner Leslie, *Man in The Clouds* Chambers Edinburgh 1963.

Garrison Paul, *The Encyclopaedia of Hot Air Balloons* Sterling New York 1979.

Gibson Ron J, *Australia and Australians in Civil Aviation* Qantas Airways Sydney 1971.

Giles JM, *Some Chapters in The Life of George Augustus Taylor: A biography* Building Publishing Sydney 1957.

Griffith Kenneth, *Thank God we Kept the Flag Flying* Hutchinson London 1974.

Gordon Arthur *The American Heritage History of Flight*, American Heritage New York1962.

Gunston Bill, *Janes Aerospace Dictionary* Janes Publishing London 1980.

Gwyn-Jones Terry, *Aviation's Magnificent Gamblers* Lansdowne Sydney 1981.

Haining Peter, *The Dream Machines* New English Library London 1972.

Hart Clive, *The Dream of Flight: aeronautics from classical times to the Renaissance* Faber London 1972.

Hodges Goderic, *Memoirs of an Old Balloonatic* Kimber London 1972.

Holmes Richard, *Falling Upwards* Pantheon Books New York 2013.

Iggulden David, *Hot Air Ballooning* Mosman Pierson Sydney 1991.

Inglis KS, *The Rehearsal: Australians at War in the Sudan 1885* Rigby Adelaide 1985.

Isaacs Jennifer, *Australian Dreaming: 40,000 Years of Aboriginal History* Lansdowne Sydney 1980.

Isaacs Keith, *Military Aircraft of Australia 1909 - 1918* Australian War Memorial Canberra 1971.

Jackson Donald Dale, *The Aeronauts* Time-Life Books Alexandria VA 1980.

Jensen Paul (Ed), *The Flying Omnibus* Cassell London 1953.

Johnson WW, *Ripcord Australia* self-published 1984.

Joy William, *The Aviators* Shakespeare Head Sydney 1965.

Kamenka Eugene (Ed), *Utopias* Oxford University Press Australia 1987.

Kearns RHB, *Broken Hill* Vol I 1883-1893: *Discovery and Development* Vol II 1894-1913: *The Uncertain Years* Broken Hill Historical Society Broken Hill 1973-74.

Kelly William, *Life in Victoria* Vol 1 1853 Vol II, 1858 Lowden Publishing Kilmore Vic 1977.

Kirschner Edwin J, *Aerospace Balloons: From Montgolfiere to Space* Aero Fallbrook CA 1985.

Laiwanne E, *The Romance of Ballooning: The Story of Early Aeronauts* Patrick Stephens Ltd 1971.

Lewis Miles, *The Essential Maldon* Greenhouse Richmond Melbourne 1983.

Madgwick Sir Robert Bowden, *Immigration into Eastern Australia 1788-1858* Sydney University Press Sydney 1970.

McKernan Michael (Cont), Australian War Memorial *The Australians at War 1885-1972* Collins Sydney 1984.

Mason Francis, *Air Facts and Feats: A Record of Aerospace Achievements* Guinness Superlatives London 1970.

Morris Alan, *The Balloonatics* Jarrolds London 1970.

Moult Allan, *Australian Adventures in Leisure* Reed Books Frenchs Forest NSW 1984.

Norgaard Erik, *The Book of Balloons* Crown Publishers New York 1971.

Noye RK, *Clare: A District History* District Council of Clare Clare 1986.

Oppel Frank (Ed), *Early Flight: From Balloons to Biplanes* Secaucus New Jersey 1987.

Parnell Neville, *Fly Past* Australia Government Publishing Services Canberra 1987.

Pollard Jack, *Ampol's Sporting Records* Pollard Sydney 1971.

Rechs Robert J, *Who's Who of Ballooning* Rechs Indianola LA 1983.

Rolt LTC, *The Aeronauts* Alan Sutton London 1985.

Scamehorn Howard L, *Balloons to Jets* Henry Regney Chicago 1957.

Serle Geoffrey, *The Golden Age: A History of The Colony of Victoria 1851-1861* Melbourne University Press Melbourne 1963.

Shavelson Melville, *The Great Houdinis: A Vaudeville* WH Allen London 1977.

Shepherd Dolly, *When the 'Chute Went Up: The Adventures of an Edwardian Lady Parachutist* Robert Hale London 1984.

Sinclair Kevin, *Over China* Angus and Robertson North Ryde 1988.

Smith Anthony, *Ballooning: The Dangerous Sort* Allen and Unwin London 1970.

Spate OHK, *The Pacific: Home of Utopias* Annual Symposium of the Australian Academy of the Humanities (Ed Eugene Kamenka) Oxford University Press Melbourne 1987.

Stehling Kurt R, Beller William, *Skyhooks* Doubleday Garden City New York 1962.

Swan RA, *Australia in the Antarctic* Melbourne University Press Melbourne 1961.

Swinglehurst Edmund, *Cooks Tours: The Story of Popular Travel* Blandford Poole Dorset 1982.

Voisin (jnr) Gabriel, *Men and Women and 10,000 Kites* Putnam London 1963.

Weickhardt FC, *Information from Clunes 1839-1872* Clunes 1972.

Weidenhoffe Margaret (Ed), *Garryowen's Melbourne: a Selection from the Chronicles of Early Melbourne 1835-1850* Nelson Sydney 1967.

Wirth Dick, Young Jerry, *Ballooning: The Complete Guide to Riding the Winds* Random House New York 1980.

Wolters Richard, *The World of Silent Flight* McGraw-Hill London 1982.

Woodman Jim, *Nazca: The Flight of Condor I* John Murray London 1980.

Yeatman Jonathan, *Daffodil and Golden Eagle: the saga of two balloons crossing the Sahara* Aidan Ellis Henley-on-Thames 1972.

# Pamphlets

Brown CH, *A Letter to a Friend Descriptive of Two Excursions with Mr Coxwell's Balloon Which Ascended from the Leeds Royal Gardens* 1856.

Back to Clunes Committee (Ed), *Back to Clunes Celebrations* 1920.

*Hibal Balloon Launching Station Mildura* Balloon Launching Station Mildura 1974.

Moon Jonathon, *Tarrangower, Past and Present: A History of Maldon from 1853* Howlinson Tate Maldon 1864.

Weickhard FC, *Clunes 1839-1972* Clunes Shire Council 1972.

# INDEX